NO LONGER PROPER... ...OF
KING COUNTY LIBRA... ...M

D0952731

NOV   2018

THE FORGOTTEN AMERICANS

ISABEL SAWHILL

The Forgotten Americans

AN ECONOMIC AGENDA FOR A DIVIDED NATION

Yale

UNIVERSITY PRESS

NEW HAVEN & LONDON

Published with assistance from the foundation established in memory of
Amasa Stone Mather of the Class of 1907, Yale College.

Copyright © 2018 by Isabel Sawhill. All rights reserved. This book
may not be reproduced, in whole or in part, including illustrations, in
any form (beyond that copying permitted by Sections 107 and 108 of the
U.S. Copyright Law and except by reviewers for the public press), without
written permission from the publishers.

Yale University Press books may be purchased in quantity for
educational, business, or promotional use. For information, please email
sales.press@yale.edu (U.S. office) or sales@yaleup.co.uk (U.K. office).

Set in Scala type by Westchester Publishing Services.
Printed in the United States of America.

Library of Congress Control Number: 2018942605
ISBN 978-0-300-23036-9 (hardcover : alk. paper)

A catalogue record for this book is available from the British Library.

This paper meets the requirements of ANSI/NISO Z39.48-1992
(Permanence of Paper).

10 9 8 7 6 5 4 3 2 1

CONTENTS

PREFACE

LIKE MANY PEOPLE, I WAS DUMBFOUNDED by the 2016 election. I began working on this book before the election and then had to rethink it afterward.
Who was it that voted for Trump? What is it about their lives that caused
them to vote for him? And, most importantly, what should an economic
policy look like in the post-Trump era? I began to question old assumptions
about what might be both effective and politically feasible in this new era,
which required that I reexamine almost everything I thought I knew. Can we
boost the rate of long-term economic growth enough to make a lot of people
better off, or is that a pipe dream? Are unprecedented levels of inequality
here to stay, or can we redistribute whatever level of prosperity we have more
broadly? How do we achieve a broader version of prosperity in today's toxic
political environment? What might work best, given the country's attitudes
and existing institutions?

This book wrestles with these questions. It argues for policies that are
better aligned with American values and responsive to people's actual day-
to-day needs. It focuses on the value of work and the importance of jobs
and wages. Work is a unifying concept, something everyone understands
and supports. But we need a more honest accounting of what does and
does not improve people's job prospects. That means getting beyond simple
"trickle-down" and "trickle-up" theories and political rhetoric about their
importance. In late 2017, Congress enacted a giant tax bill sold to the public in
trickle-down clothes. On the left, there was talk of the need for a universal

basic income where income would almost magically trickle up to literally everyone. Those are, for the most part, fake remedies. Instead, we need to better prepare people for the jobs that exist and use the tax system and a more inclusive form of private-sector–led capitalism to boost the job opportunities and wages of the bottom half.

Although I am a solutions-oriented economist, I like to ask basic questions, review evidence on what we know about them, and guide the nonacademic reader through the underbrush and the data to a set of hopefully reasonable conclusions. In the process, I learn a lot. My hope is that readers with a serious interest in such topics as growth, inequality, and the labor market will benefit from this review. Whether one agrees with my ideas or not, their foundations should be transparent—the basis for a healthy dialogue.

On a more personal note, I have long believed that life is unpredictable and often unfair. For this reason, much of my career has been devoted to studying poverty and inequality. More often than not that leads to a focus on the poorest Americans. But just above them is a group that believes it is playing by the rules and not getting ahead. Of course, the poor deserve compassion but they have gotten plenty of scholarly attention. The working and middle classes have received less. All of them are part of a group I call "the forgotten Americans."

I have also focused a lot of my work on opportunity—on what scholars call "intergenerational social mobility." Together with my colleague Ron Haskins, I wrote a book on *Creating an Opportunity Society*. We developed and have jointly written about "the success sequence"—the idea that if you get an education, work fulltime, and wait to have children until you are married or in a committed relationship, you will have a good chance of escaping poverty and joining the middle class. In my most recent book, *Generation Unbound: Drifting into Sex and Parenthood without Marriage,* I tackled the family piece of the success sequence, calling for a shift in norms and for greater use of long-acting forms of contraception to produce more responsible parenting and family formation. In this book, I focus on work. If I stick to the "success sequence" frame, my next book will have to be about education!

I have the good fortune to have had a long career as a scholar at the Brookings Institution. I work with some of the smartest and best-informed people imaginable—a rare privilege. As an economist who has served in government, and been on the firing line for making difficult decisions in President Clinton's Office of Management and Budget, I take a pragmatic approach to most problems. I am no fan of President Trump but still hope that Republicans will reach out to that broader slice of America they seem to have forgotten of late, despite the president's rhetoric. Their messaging is fine; their policies are wanting. As for Democrats, I admire their fighting spirit and their compassion but believe there is a risk that they will overplay their hand, pleasing their base but neglecting the moderate but quiet middle that wants stability, pragmatism, and dignity in public life, not a new swerve to the left.

I have many people to thank for help with this book. First and foremost is Eleanor Krause. She was my research assistant at Brookings through this period. I have marveled at her patience, her work ethic, her ability to see long before I did the many flaws in the book (some of which, I'm sure, remain), and her willingness to tackle almost any subject and master it in short order. In her spare time, she climbs cliffs and rides a bike in zero-degree weather. Nothing is too hard for her.

Richard Reeves, Alice Rivlin, and Robert Reischauer all gave especially generously of their time to help me see ways to improve the manuscript. Richard proved that it's possible to teach an aging scholar how to write or think more clearly. Other colleagues to whom I am grateful for advice on the book include Henry Aaron, Martin Baily, Ben Bernanke, Emily Bowden, Elaine Kamarck, Gary Burtless, Bill Galston, Ted Gayer, Carol Graham, Josh Gotbaum, Ron Haskins, Delaney Parrish, Jonathan Rauch, Molly Reynolds, Martha Ross, and David Wessel.

Outside of Brookings, I received valuable comments from Dominic Barton, Harry Holzer, Elisabeth Jacobs, Tamar Jacoby, Robert Solow, Steven Pearlstein, Christopher Schroeder, Ben Veghte, and the "Gang of 10," my favorite group of business economists.

Many family members and friends have also read or suffered through interminable discussions of very early drafts of this book. Among this group, I especially want to thank David Adoff, Sarah and Win Brown, Monroe and Fred Hodder, Bob and Jane Stein, Sally and Ed Supplee, Hildy Teegen, and Jamie and Evelyn Sawhill.

Finally, I want to thank Seth Ditchik at Yale University Press for giving me the right advice when I needed it most, and Adriana Cloud, Ann-Marie Imbornoni, and Debbie Masi for careful attention to the copyediting and production of the manuscript.

My goal for this book is very simple: to catalyze a new discussion about how to create a jobs-based prosperity and a less-divided nation in the coming decades. Although I offer some specific ideas as fodder for that discussion, if these ideas do no more than catalyze a richer debate, and some still better ideas, I will be pleased.

THE FORGOTTEN AMERICANS

Introduction

WHEN RONALD REAGAN WAS CAMPAIGNING for the presidency in the 1970s, he regularly referred to a Chicago welfare recipient who, Reagan said, had bilked the government of $150,000. "She has 80 names, 30 addresses, 12 Social Security cards and is collecting veterans' benefits on four nonexist-ing deceased husbands," he said.[1] Although fact-checking showed that Rea-gan was exaggerating, the story resonated with the public, so he repeated it over and over again. Thus was born the idea of a "welfare queen."

Bill Clinton, although far more sympathetic to the poor than Ronald Rea-gan, campaigned on "ending welfare as we know it." He wanted welfare to be a way station and not a way of life. His stance was so popular that when I joined his administration in 1993, my top assignment was to help craft a plan to reform welfare. It became a bipartisan issue, and in 1996, Con-gress voted to turn the old unconditional cash welfare program into a new and temporary program that required recipients to work.

But welfare is not just for the poor. The rich get welfare as well. When someone dies and gives a large bequest to his or her children, the inheri-tance is a windfall, an often large and unearned gift for the recipient. The tax bill enacted in 2017 only taxes such bequests if an individual decedent has more than $11 million and a couple has more than $22 million.[2] That bill ballooned the nation's debt and provided most of its benefits to corpo-rations. Some commentators looked at the new law and labeled it a reward for wealthy donors and special interest groups.

There is nothing new about corporate welfare. Oil companies and ethanol producers receive large and mostly unwarranted subsidies.[3] Big Wall Street banks were rescued while equity in people's homes was wiped out during the financial crisis. Corporate tax reductions fatten profits earned from past, not future, investments. Rising rates of concentration are limiting competition and increasing control over prices in many industries, leading to supernormal profits.[4]

Government welfare, in whatever form, and whoever the recipients are, makes a lot of people mad.

Hand-Ups, Not Handouts

The problem with welfare, whether for the rich or the poor, is that it is incompatible with the principle that individuals should *earn* their money. Americans do not like freeloading. They expect to work unless they are disabled or elderly. And they don't want their taxes going to pay for those getting something for nothing—whether they are welfare recipients or corporations that avoid taxation by exploiting various loopholes. The Clinton-era welfare reform may have saved some money, but it was a pittance compared to what we gave up when we stopped taxing all but a tiny number of estates and a large portion of business profits. And because these tax cuts were put on the national credit card, it is the middle class that will ultimately have to pay for them.

This book is about returning to a system in which work is rewarded over welfare, hand-ups over handouts, wages over windfall profits. It is about improving the lives of those who are neither rich nor poor but somewhere in the middle. And it is about policies linked to mainstream values such as family, education, and work.

A Focus on Middle- and Working-Class Families

In recent decades, experts, advocates, and elected officials have paid a lot of attention to relatively narrow groups, whether rich or poor. They have neglected the middle and working classes—a very large group. Many in this group have been affected by the economic disruptions caused by changes in trade and technology, and are struggling with a lack of jobs and stagnant earnings. Economists have long argued that trade and technology create winners and losers, with net benefits for society as a whole, but unless the political system creates mechanisms for sharing the benefits more widely, there is bound to be pushback or alienation on the part of the losers.

Throughout this book, I focus on these forgotten Americans. There is no precise definition that captures exactly who they are, but to set some broad parameters, I assume they are working-age adults (twenty-five to sixty-four) without four-year college degrees whose family incomes put them in the bottom half of the income distribution. Defined this way, they have annual family incomes below about $70,000 and they represent 38 percent of the working-age population.

Not all of this group is in trouble, but many need help—a hand-up if not a handout. It would be relatively simple to devise an agenda that addresses their needs, but there are two big constraints: the country is more divided than ever, and trust in government is at a low ebb.

A Divided Country

The country is not just divided economically, it is divided culturally and politically as well. Income inequality, to be sure, is at an all-time high. But the population is also sorting itself into communities of like-minded people. About half of partisan Democrats and Republicans don't want their children to marry someone who supports the opposite party.[5] We live in information bubbles that shield us from understanding other people and other points of view. Many people don't trust the mainstream media and are increasingly turning to family, friends, and self-selected media to create their own versions of reality. In my concluding chapter I liken us to the boys who were stranded on an island in the novel *Lord of the Flies*. They broke into warring tribes, began to believe in illusory beasts, abandoned civilized norms, and eventually turned violent. Granted, we are not at that stage but it's a cautionary tale.

Lack of Trust in Government

Not only are we divided but trust in government is at rock-bottom levels. Many people believe that government doesn't work, that it is spending their tax dollars unwisely, and that elected officials are self-interested if not corrupt. Because government hasn't addressed the problems they see every day—a lack of jobs, crumbling infrastructure, inadequate schools, an opioid epidemic—they have lost faith in it. Congress and the president have rarely been less popular.

The social contract is based on the idea that government can deliver what people need to succeed, to have a fair shot at the American dream. When trust evaporates, we lose the ability to manage economic and social changes that require a collective response. It becomes a vicious circle. The less-responsive government is to people's real concerns, the more their trust in it wanes. And without that trust, nothing much can be done. Paralysis or a symbolic or rhetorical politics that doesn't effectively address the problems people care about takes over. The federal government is especially mistrusted. For the foreseeable future, we may need to rely more heavily on other institutions, such as state or local governments, civic and religious organizations, families, schools, and employers. To be sure, social insurance programs, such as Social Security and Medicare, remain popular. Who can forget the guy at a town meeting in 2009 who told Representative Bob Inglis to "keep your government hands off my Medicare"? This suggests these programs may have roles to play as well, given their popularity and the fact that their benefits are earned.

Right now, it's hard to be optimistic that the federal government is going to function in normal mode anytime soon. This is not an argument that dispersed responsibilities are always ideal as much as it is an argument about what's feasible and consistent with pluralism and diversity in a very large and divided country. Perhaps we can rebuild a new foundation for jobs-based prosperity and a healthier democracy through pragmatic and grounded experimentation.

The Importance of Values, Especially Work

To address these divisions and this distrust, our first task must be to honor and uplift certain widely shared values, such as work, education, and family. Of the three, I give the greatest attention to work—to people's aspirations for decent-paying jobs. In an American context, people are expected to work—and want to work—but government is expected to make it possible for them to do so. A recommitment to these values and to policies that actually (as opposed to rhetorically) embed them could help to bridge some of our divides.

Not only are these core values in American society, but they are also the key determinants of success. In chapter 3, I show that if you graduate from high school, work fulltime, and wait to have children until you are married and ready to be a parent, your chances of achieving the American dream are high. Among American households that follow these three rules, about 70 percent will achieve middle-class incomes or better.[6] The policies I recommend in this book are all based on the importance of these three values, especially the value of work. The social contract I'm proposing is that if you get an education, work fulltime, and form a stable family, you should be able to achieve the American dream.

If we take these values seriously, then policy should not be formulated as if values didn't matter. Conservatives have talked about personal responsibility for a long time. Liberals are losing their connection with voters by not emphasizing it enough. Personal responsibility means acquiring the skills you need to support yourself, working hard, and not having children until you are in a stable relationship such as marriage. That's not too complicated. If conservatives have been good about endorsing these mainstream values, their follow-through on policy has been weak, often counterproductive. Many have compromised their own principles to remain in power. Liberals have the opposite problem—dozens of good policy ideas but a values framework that is sometimes out of step with the country's or is overly focused on narrow issues and specific subgroups. Republicans who once championed limited but effective government now seem intent on simply "starving the beast" by cutting taxes, thereby forcing indiscriminate spending cuts in response to rising debt. Democrats want to raise taxes but too often in ways that seem out of step with core American values. There should be a middle ground here that involves knitting together the right values with policies that embed them and, in the process, finding common ground and an agenda that most of the public can get behind. There's no sense pretending it will be easy. We have reached a point where a vicious circle may have narrowed our options. As government becomes more removed from people's everyday concerns, their faith in it continues to shrink.

A Possible Way Forward

With these constraints in mind, I focus on policies consistent with mainstream values, especially the value of work, and policies that rely as much as possible on still-trusted institutions. I reject both far right and far left ideas in favor of a radical centrist approach. *Radical* combined with *centrist* may sound like an oxymoron. But it doesn't need to be. Several of my proposals are bold and new. In any case, ricocheting between the extremes is a recipe for political civil war. It's also a recipe for making America small again.

As General Stanley McChrystal put it, "Our politics lurches from one bitter breakdown to the next, consumed with petty partisan controversies. Meanwhile, massive issues that affect our national prosperity and security languish unaddressed."[7] These are my sentiments as well. I focus on a set of ideas derived not from some Platonic ideal but from what seems like a feasible way to rebuild trust in the dysfunctional political culture and divided nation we currently inhabit. My goal is not just to help those left behind; it's also to bring us together by emphasizing values that most people support. Of course, common ground will be hard to find in today's toxic environment. But we should try.

I propose four approaches to helping those who have been left behind in today's economy. First, more vocational education and adjustment assistance for workers adversely affected by new developments in technology and trade, including a chance to retrain or relocate. Second, a broad-based tax credit that bumps up wages for those who are currently working hard but at inadequate wages. Third, a new role for the private sector in training and rewarding workers. And finally, a social insurance system refocused on lifelong education and family care in addition to retirement. Each of these remedies is sharply focused on *earned* benefits, not handouts, and on the expectation and dignity of work.

I argue that the policy conversation needs to be less about economic growth or inequality and more about jobs. Work is a unifying theme, an objective we can agree on. Growth is helpful, but it is not the Holy Grail that many people, conservatives in particular, assume. It can't be counted on to solve the jobs problem. Rising productivity or automation may be good for the economy in the long run, but it displaces individual workers and destroys communities in the short run. Redistributing income, a favorite remedy on the left, could help—and it is something I personally favor—but most people don't want handouts; they want jobs.

A middle way that bridges our political and cultural divides requires balancing government's responsibilities with those of individuals. The social contract is about rights but also about duties. Conservatives have talked a lot about personal responsibility, including the importance of education, working hard, and forming stable families. Some say these are old-fashioned values to be rejected because they are "bourgeois," but, as I will show, they are central to individual mobility. Elites are not doing any favors for the forgotten Americans when they advocate for a permissive culture—a culture that most of them reject in their own lives and those of their children. Legalizing drugs or normalizing teen sex may be fine, but how many of the elite approve of either where their own children are concerned?

In an era when government is mistrusted, the private sector may need to play a stronger role in ensuring that prosperity is more broadly based. That means reviving and expanding a form of inclusive capitalism that looks to the long term and treats all stakeholders, including workers, as partners in the process of producing goods and services and rewards them accordingly. It means more profit sharing, more employee ownership, and more work-based training. We have an unprecedented amount of inequality in our society, driven in large measure by runaway incomes at the top. CEOs are earning huge amounts while wages for the average worker have stagnated. At the end of 2017, Congress handed corporations a gift that may make them more competitive in international markets but did nothing to shore up our democracy at home. That needs to be amended, and what I have discovered in the process of researching this book is that it can be corrected without sacrificing productivity or profits. Some of my fellow economists have led us to believe that the welfare of workers and of their employers are at odds, and I understand their logic. But it turns out that in practice this is much less true than many assume.

One implication of a focus on the importance of work is the need to rethink how we allocate working time over the life cycle. The goal should be more work when we are older but still healthy and less work when we are young but need time for learning new skills and raising children. I tackle how we might achieve this goal in the context of an updated social insurance system. Social Security saves us from our shortsighted and myopic selves by forcing us to put a little money aside for retirement in every paycheck. We need to extend this principle to cover other things we might want to save for but don't—such as staying home to care for a new baby or taking a course at the local community college to update our skills. Aren't those needs just as important as a comfortable retirement?

The remedies I propose in this book are only a start on addressing the problems we face. And our political institutions may not be up to the challenge. For these reasons, a bit of humility is in order. If this book does no more than catalyze a debate about the remedies, it will have achieved my goal.

In the pages that follow, I will explain how a significant number of Americans found themselves so disillusioned with the ability of their country's leaders to address their problems that they elected a real-estate mogul and reality television celebrity to the highest office in the land (chapter 2).

I'll look at how these and other "forgotten Americans" have been left behind, and at the ever-increasing inequality that fuels their resentment (chapter 3). I'll explain why the standard prescriptions offered by politicians on how to solve these problems—growth from those on the right, redistribution from those on the left—are not sufficient to deal with the challenges we face (chapters 4 and 5). Instead we need an emphasis on jobs and wages.

In subsequent chapters, I argue that rebuilding skills through vocational training and repairing the culture through national service is needed (chapter 6), that any new income-boosting assistance should be tied to a willingness to work (chapter 7), and that business knows better than government how to get things done (chapter 8).

Finally, there are still a few large government programs—such as Social Security and Medicare—that are broadly popular with the public. We can build on their success to address some new needs such as more time for family care and for lifelong learning (chapter 9).

Each of these ideas finds common ground between the values of compassion on the left and personal responsibility on the right, and calls for cooperation between the public and private sectors. Each of them recognizes the importance of families and education but puts the value of work at its core.

In the final chapter (chapter 10), I reprise this entire agenda and why I think something like it is needed to strengthen not just our economy but also our democracy—even our right to call America great again. This is the agenda the forgotten Americans want—and deserve.

2

The Forgotten Americans

IT'S DECEMBER 2016, just before the Christmas holidays. I'm on my way from Washington, D.C., to Palm Springs, California. My flight from Phoenix to Palm Springs is canceled. Faced with a night in a motel in Phoenix and missing holiday time with my family, I am feeling a bit desperate. I overhear a young man from my flight talking to a friend on his cell phone. He says he plans to drive to Palm Springs. I sidle up to him and ask if I can go along. That's how I began my brief but unusual friendship with Streeter (not his real name). What did we have in common? He had just turned thirty; I am old enough to be his grandmother. He was a high school grad; I have a PhD. He had a blue-collar job in rural Texas; I have a white-collar job in Washington, D.C. He liked Trump; I supported Hillary. What we had in common was that we were both Americans. And we were both mad as hell at United Airlines. With that beginning we spent the five hours driving across the night-time Arizona desert learning about each other's families, likes and dislikes, experiences in school and at work, favorite movies (I can never remember mine; he was more articulate). At rest stops he smoked cigarettes and I ate junk food from McDonald's. After polite offers to share, I passed on the cigarettes and he passed on the junk food. He knew the way and did all the driving very skillfully; I was totally clueless about where we were or where we were going but tried to make up for it by contributing more than my share of the costs. It was a successful partnership. At the end of the trip, we parted company as friends. I can't say we've stayed in touch, and that's probably too bad, because closing the kind of divides I address in this book may begin and end with us all getting to know each other better.

The election of Donald Trump in 2016 stunned the country. The polls had predicted strongly that Hillary Clinton was going to win. But that was not to be. We know that, for four decades now, economic growth has not been broadly shared. Were the people who voted for Trump those who have been left behind by slow and uneven growth, or was something else going on?

My aim here is not to wade deeply into these political waters. Rather, it is to delve into public aspirations as manifested in their electoral behavior and the lives of a group of Americans who appear to be frustrated and angry and who voted for change. This will set the stage for a longer discussion of how we might address their problems and those of others who have been left behind in today's economy. Although I begin this chapter with a focus on a subgroup of the forgotten Americans, the white working class—because they are a large and politically salient group—the rest of the book is about all the forgotten Americans, defined as those with less than a bachelor's de-gree (BA) whose incomes put them in the bottom half of the distribution.

I conclude with some observations about our politics that I believe have serious implications for the policy choices we make in the future. Most important is the declining confidence in government itself. How do we move forward to address people's real grievances when the mechanism for doing so is broken, when the social contract is unraveling, when inspiring leaders are in short supply? What happens when our discourse is fueled by emotion rather than facts, and by information bubbles and tribal sorting? These developments leave us—not hopelessly, but sharply—divided. They mean we are going to have to think out of the box to find policies that can command enough support to become law—to move beyond talking points, political games, and impassioned rhetoric from each side of the divide.

The 2016 Election and What It Means

One group that voted overwhelmingly for Trump was the white working class, usually defined as those without a college degree. Nearly two-thirds of them voted for Trump, and by a margin of 30 percentage points over Clinton, according to data from the American National Election Study.[1]

Let's use the phrase that President Trump used at the Republican National Convention and call them the "forgotten Americans." Here is what Trump said: "My message is that things have to change—and they have to change right now. Every day I wake up determined to deliver a better life for the people all across this nation that have been neglected, ignored, and abandoned. I have visited the laid-off factory workers, and the communities crushed by our horrible and unfair trade deals. *These are the forgotten men and women of our country and they are forgotten but they're not going to be forgotten long*" (italics added).[2]

What he promised this group was to bring back manufacturing jobs, erect barriers to trade, build a wall on the border with Mexico, ban Muslims, focus on law and order, repeal and replace Obamacare, cut taxes and regulation, and drain the swamp in the nation's capital.

Trump voters had many concerns, but the candidates' stances on specific policy questions didn't seem to play a major role. What mattered more was the desire for change and a disgust with career politicians in Washington. As Guy Molyneux argues, there are two kinds of populism. There is Bernie Sanders's economic populism and there is Donald Trump's political populism. The first is anti–Wall Street and corporate greed, while the second is anti-Washington and political greed. Molyneux argues very persuasively that it was the latter that put Trump in the White House, aided by a do-nothing Congress through most of the Obama years and a perception that elected officials are self-interested if not corrupt.[3]

In the aftermath of the 2016 election, pollsters and other experts have tried hard to make sense of Trump's victory. People had many reasons to support him: a desire for change, a dislike of Clinton, a fatigue with political correctness and broken campaign promises, and just plain party loyalty. In fact, the strong influence of partisan leanings on the outcome of the election deserves special emphasis; 87 percent of self-identified Democrats voted for Clinton, and 86 percent of Republicans voted for Trump.[4] Among those who found Trump not just a disturbing figure but unqualified to be president, this pattern raises challenging questions. As Lynn Vavreck, a political science professor at UCLA put it, "Has the party label become an efficient shortcut for voters, helping them decide which candidate best meets their priorities and goals? Or is support for a party more like support for a favorite sports team, devoid of any content other than entertainment, drama and identity?"[5]

Democratic strategists have been consumed with analyzing the implications of Trump's victory for their party's agenda going forward. They understand that the white working class can't be ignored. Although this group is a diminishing slice of the electorate, not only did they overwhelmingly support Trump but they also constituted 45 percent of all voters in 2016. The Center for American Progress, an influential progressive think tank, believes the response needs to be a bigger and bolder set of policies that address the genuine economic concerns of the working class. As Stanley Greenberg puts it, Democrats need "dramatically bolder economic policies" that work for average Americans and not just for "the rich, big corporations, and the cultural elites."[6] Still others advise that the party must modify its stance on trade and immigration in ways that acknowledge the anxieties these have created and that move in a protectionist or "secure-the-border" direction.[7] And although few have explicitly called for the party to abandon its commitment to racial or gender equality, there are hints of the need to soften the edges of that commitment by reaching out to all groups, including too-often-forgotten white males.[8] Many are suggesting less talk about bathrooms and a stronger focus on jobs.

In polls where they are given a choice between a statement calling for a more active versus less-active government, phrased in many different ways, the white working class overwhelmingly favors a smaller government (by a ratio of about two to one). It is the collapse of trust in government that dominates their perceptions. While 61 percent of white working class voters view corporations unfavorably, 93 percent have an unfavorable view of politicians.[9] This creates a dilemma for Democrats; any activist agenda risks driving even more of the working class into the Republican camp, especially if that agenda relies on Washington-led policy making and new taxes. At the same time, there is an opening for Democrats to point out that sending a billionaire businessman to Washington does nothing to curb political favoritism and special interests. In fact, Trump himself could be painted as the ultimate self-interested politician.

If this diagnosis is right, both parties should want to restore trust in government. The alternative is, if not anarchy, then at least a rejection of the idea that we can govern ourselves. Jack Goldsmith, a senior fellow at the Hoover Institution who served in the Justice Department in the George W. Bush administration, argued in the *Atlantic* magazine that our formal institutions, such as the courts and Congress, have checked Trump's worst instincts reasonably well, but that his norm violations will be harder to reverse. In particular, trust in mainstream institutions—already badly eroded before Trump took office—is likely to suffer an even steeper decline. As Goldsmith wrote, "this is perhaps the worst news of all for our democracy."[10]

How far should any political party go in order to curry favor with a particular voting bloc? The white working class is declining in numbers, and their views clash with other important elements in the Democratic Party's base, such as minorities, millennials, and the college educated. Efforts to court white working class voters have left some Democrats worrying about whether, in the process of focusing on this group, they have turned their backs on "the truly forgotten," such as minorities and the poor. My way of reconciling the two is to remind people that the electoral power of the white working class, perhaps even more than their objective circumstances, requires some focus on this group. For this reason, I give special attention to this group in this chapter. But I should make clear that the rest of the book focuses on all those who have been left behind in today's economy, especially those without a college education and those in the bottom half of the income distribution.

If Democrats are rethinking their strategy, Republicans should be doing so as well. Their single-minded focus on tax cuts as the best way to create growth and jobs has one big advantage: simplicity. But it is also wrong for the reasons I describe in chapter 4. And President Trump's embrace of restrictions on trade and immigration is misguided as well. Republicans' focus on the family and on the importance of work and personal responsibility could provide the foundation for a robust policy agenda, connecting them to the concerns of ordinary citizens, and countering the perception that they are the party of the rich and powerful. There is a group of conservative intellectuals worrying about such issues but hitting a wall when it comes to getting anything enacted.

Beyond these first-order partisan reasons, much of the broader intellectual debate has been about whether it was economics or culture that motivated Trump voters. It's worth remembering, of course, that although he won the Electoral College, he did not win it overwhelmingly and he lost the popular vote by a wide margin. It could simply have been a black swan election—a race won by a slim margin and possibly influenced by last-minute events such as Comey's announcement that the Clinton email investigation was being reopened or the WikiLeaks revelations about DNC emails or Russia's attempt to influence the outcome. In short, we shouldn't overinterpret the data or the commentary on why he won. Moreover, Trump voters were diverse, to say the least.[11] Yes, they were primarily less-educated, older, and male, but they included many soccer moms and establishment Republicans.

Political analysts have plumbed these and other data in an attempt to extract some lessons from the election. After reading a number of those studies, I think it's fair to conclude the following:

First, the biggest gap between Republican and Democratic voters is around cultural issues. As the authors of one study put it, "the primary conflict structuring the two parties involves questions of national identity, race, and morality, while the traditional conflict over economics, though still important, is less divisive now than it used to be."[12] Other studies have also found that the best predictor of whether a person identifies as conservative or liberal is his or her position on moral issues. Disagreements about economic issues are smaller.[13]

Second, on the economic front, more detailed analysis shows that both Trump and Clinton voters felt left behind. Differences between the two groups were smaller on this topic than on many others.

Third, another common view in both parties is that the political system is "rigged." The loss of trust in political institutions is huge. This is bad news for Republicans and Democrats alike, but especially for Democrats.

Fourth, there are exceptions to this dislike of government programs. A higher minimum wage and paid family leave are well regarded, for example. Social Security and Medicare are even more popular.

Finally, both Republicans and Democrats believe that the lack of well-paying jobs is the critical issue facing the country.

More broadly, it would seem that if they want to expand their bases, Republicans need to move left on economic issues and Democrats need to move right on cultural issues. Despite our divisions, there is a middle ground that might command wider support. As Ross Douthat notes, "The Republican Party as an institution, or at least its congressional incarnation, has long been well to the right of its own voters on economics."[14]

Democrats are losing the culturally conservative but economically liberal portion of the electorate. This was the group that supported Trump and that is now up for grabs, depending on how each party responds to the splits within their own ranks. Republicans seem hell-bent on sticking to a very conservative economic policy while Democrats seem equally intent on championing the rights of minority groups, immigrants, pro-choice supporters, and the LGBTQ community. That may be a recipe for continuing division and political stalemate and an electorate that throws the reigning party out of office at each opportunity because voters remain frustrated and angry. But to the extent that there is an opening for a more centrist or sustainable agenda to take root, it is around economics and not around culture. Whatever cultural divides currently exist, they should narrow as the more socially liberal younger generation matures, but focusing on them right now is not going to help in the search for common ground. My conclusion: *If there is a set of concerns that transcends party, it is the fact that too many Americans feel they have been left behind by an economy undergoing rapid change. And the lack of well-paid jobs is at the heart of that problem.*

Trump's rise was made possible by the Republican Party and it is now warping their agenda. Norm Ornstein argues, persuasively in my view, that the Republican Party created fertile soil for a Trump to rise by its oppositional stance throughout the Obama years and its far-right antigovernment positions (best represented by the Freedom Caucus in the House). That opposition deepened public skepticism of government as an institution because it meant the government couldn't get anything done. It may be that no establishment politician can get elected in this environment—only an outsider who runs against now-discredited mainstream candidates—whether Republican or Democratic.[15] Trump didn't just prevail over Hillary Clinton; he prevailed over all the Republican mainstream candidates in the presidential primaries leading up to the 2016 election. Republicans could have used his election to update their agenda. Instead, their party platform and their early actions on taxes and regulation have, if anything, moved the party further to the right.

Democrats face their own political challenges. If many of Trump's supporters are motivated as much by cultural as by economic distress, Democrats can only tap into this distress by abandoning their deepest values, such as respect for tolerance and inclusion. That is something they are unlikely to do—although this does not mean they couldn't put less weight on identity politics and lifting up specific subgroups and put more weight on the common economic concerns of all those who are struggling to get ahead, including minorities and the poor.

The White Working Class

In this section, I focus on the white working class, for several reasons. First, they are a very large group. Second, they are in trouble. Their grievances, as we shall see, are real. Third, to the extent that they continue to support populists like Donald Trump, they will, intentionally or not, inflict grave damage on all Americans, especially on racial minorities, women, and the poor. From the perspective of these other groups, the Republican Party's unholy alliance with Trump has produced some of the most egregious policies imaginable—decimating the safety net, banning immigrants, undermining civil rights, reducing women's reproductive rights, and moving the country backward on environmental issues—all while cutting taxes on the rich and greatly exacerbating inequality. Unless white working-class Americans can be brought more into the fold, the entire population will remain vulnerable to more Trumpism in one form or another.

So, who is part of the white working class? In what follows, I define them as whites between the ages of twenty-five and sixty-four without a bachelor's degree. I will call their same-aged non-Hispanic white counterparts with a BA or better the educated "elites" for short.[16]

Defined in this way, the white working class includes roughly 63 million adults. They are a little older and more than twice as likely to live in rural areas as white elites. Although they lack a BA degree, many of the white

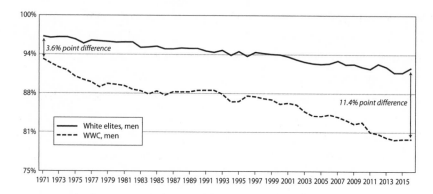

Fig. 2.1. Labor force participation rates have fallen rapidly
for white working-class men

Source: Author's analysis of BLS Current Population Survey, March ASEC supplements

working class (48 percent) have at least attended college, and some have obtained an AA degree, with women being a little better educated than men.[17]

Perhaps the most striking difference between the white working class and the elites is a growing gap in male labor force participation rates. In 1971, non-Hispanic white working-class men had a labor force participation rate of 93 percent, compared to 97 percent for white male elites. Since then, the participation rate for white working-class men has fallen 13 percentage points, to 80 percent (fig. 2.1). Working-class women have gone to work in greater numbers over this period, filling some of the gap, but it is still the case, ironically, that the elites are much more likely to be working than the so-called working class.

A lack of well-paid jobs for this group has made them more pessimistic than other Americans about their ability to get ahead. Fewer than four in ten think it's still possible. As a man who participated in a study conducted by PRRI and the *Atlantic* said, "The middle class can't survive in today's economy because there really isn't a middle class anymore. You've got poverty level, and you've got your one, two percent. You don't have a middle class anymore like you had in the '70s and '80s. My dad started at Cinco making a buck ten an hour. When he retired he was making $45 an hour. It took him 40 years, but he did it. You can't find that today; there's no job that exists like that today."[18]

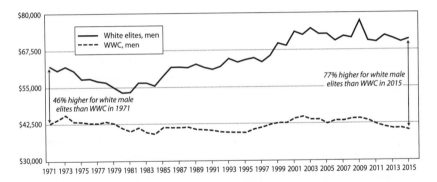

Fig. 2.2. Wage and salary incomes haven't kept up for white working-class men
Source: Author's analysis of BLS Current Population Survey, March ASEC supplements
Note: Wage and salary income adjusted for inflation using CPI-U-RS to 2015 dollars.
Population includes white men ages 25–64 who are in the labor force and employed.

As this quote suggests, there is also a growing gap in wage and salary incomes for employed workers, with elite white men earning 77 percent more than working-class men, as contrasted with only 46 percent more in 1971 (fig. 2.2).

Among employed women, the income gap is also large (83 percent) but it hasn't changed as much over time. Underlying these data is the fact that decent-paying jobs are disappearing as the result of advances in trade, technology, and deindustrialization. With a scarcity of good jobs, many people—men in particular—have become discouraged. Some have chosen not to work at all rather than accept very low-paid jobs. Although there is now a robust literature on the declining labor force participation of working-age men, exactly how they are supporting themselves without jobs remains a bit of a mystery. Some have turned to disability or other government programs for support, and some are living off the earnings of spouses or other family members, but neither can explain more than a modest proportion of the drop in work among this group.[19]

The economic story must be understood not just as a problem of too few jobs or too little income. It needs to be viewed in the context of expectations, of how one is doing *relative* to one's friends or relatives or to historical patterns in one's community.

This relative lens helps to explain why it is that whites, and especially white males, seem to be the most unhappy and the least optimistic about the future. This is a surprising but well-documented finding from my colleague Carol Graham.[20] She finds that blacks are far more optimistic than whites and somewhat more optimistic than Hispanics, even after adjusting for various sociodemographic differences between the groups. In terms of absolute conditions, the white working class is still far better off than African Americans or Latinos. In fact, the white working class was as likely to be employed as those who voted for Hillary Clinton.[21] Their problem is a lack of hope about the future, which seems to be largely conditioned by historical experience. Mobility rates for younger generations have declined sharply relative to the past, and members of the white working class feel like they are not participating in whatever economic growth the country has experienced. (As I show in the next chapter, their perceptions are all too real.)

Family formation is another important element in this story. The white working class would be better off if more of them were married, since having two earners is one way to boost family income. Back in 1971, marriage rates among the white working class were 3 percentage points higher than those among white elites. But marriage rates have plummeted. That decline has been sharpest for the less educated, driven not by higher divorce rates, as many assume, but by people never marrying in the first place, even when there are children involved. By 2016, a 9.4 percentage point gap had emerged between the white working class and white elites (fig. 2.3).

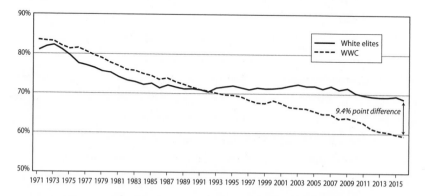

Fig. 2.3. Once higher, the portion of the white working class who are married is now much lower than for the college-educated

Source: Author's analysis of BLS Current Population Survey, March ASEC supplements

Still another ingredient in this cauldron of falling prospects among the white working class is a rise in early deaths. Anne Case and Angus Deaton, two Princeton scholars, have found that midlife mortality rates actually *increased* for white men and women between 1999 and 2013—but only for those with less than a college degree.[22] Midlife mortality rates among blacks, Hispanics, and better-educated whites have fallen. The increase among the white working class was caused primarily by drugs and alcohol, suicide, chronic liver diseases, and cirrhosis. The authors call these "deaths of despair." Their analysis does not attempt to identify the specific causes of these trends, but they hypothesize a plausible story in which progressively worsening labor market opportunities for less-educated whites produce additional problems not just in the job market but with family life and personal health as well.

White working-class Americans are twice as likely as the white college educated to say someone in their family has struggled with substance abuse and 50 percent more likely to say they or someone in their family has experienced depression. Within the group, these rates are also highest among those experiencing financial distress.[23] It's impossible to sort out how much of this correlation is because financial distress causes addiction and suicide, and how much substance abuse and depression due to other factors (for example, the overprescribing of opioids) constrain the ability to get and keep a job. For whatever reason, there was a high correlation between premature mortality in a county and whether it voted for Donald Trump in 2016.[24] Perhaps the same kind of desperation or feelings of helplessness that leads to addiction and suicide also led people to vote for a strongman who promised to solve their problems—to make America great again.

The white working class and white elites not only differ by the standard markers of "success"—family formation, educational attainment, and work. They also differ in their political views and attitudes. The white working class tends to be less supportive of affirmative action, free trade agreements, gay marriage, the Affordable Care Act, and government action on climate change or gun control. A majority of both groups, on the other hand, are supportive of providing paid leave for new parents and raising the minimum wage. Less than half of both groups want the government to reduce income inequality (fig. 2.4).

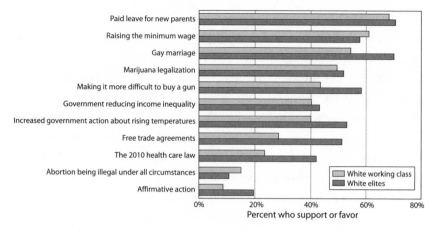

Fig. 2.4. The white working class is generally supportive of paid leave,
raising the minimum wage; less supportive of gun control, free trade
Source: Author's analysis of the American National Election Survey 2016 Time Series

One of the biggest differences between the two groups is in attitudes toward immigration. This is perhaps unsurprising, as Donald Trump ran a campaign that was fiercely critical of immigrants, suggesting that many Mexican immigrants are "criminals, drug dealers [and] rapists." His most consistent campaign promises involved building a wall on the United States–Mexico border, banning Muslim refugees, and eliminating federal funding for sanctuary cities. These promises apparently spoke to a large portion of the electorate, and data from the American National Election Study confirm that many in the white working class share similar attitudes toward immigrants. Nearly half support building a wall with Mexico, and only 13 percent support allowing Syrian refugees into the United States. They are nearly twice as likely as white elites to agree that immigrants increase crime rates, and half as likely to agree that immigrants are good for the economy (fig. 2.5).

More generally, the white working class appears more reluctant to accept social and cultural change than white elites. If Trump won because of support from these voters, his message to make America great again spoke as much to their wariness toward cultural change as it did to their economic vulnerability. The white working class is 12 percentage points more likely than white elites to agree that we should place more emphasis

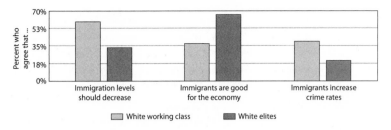

Fig. 2.5. White working class more wary toward immigrants
Source: Author's analysis of the American National Election Survey 2016 Time Series

on traditional family values (65 versus 53 percent of white elites). They are more likely to support traditional gender roles, agreeing that it is better if the man works while the woman stays at home (39 versus 27 percent). They are 15 percentage points more likely to agree that "newer lifestyles are breaking down society" (53 versus 38 percent). Over two thirds agree that "blacks should work their way up without special favors," compared to less than one-half of white elites (fig. 2.6). The white working class is also more likely than other Americans to have an authoritarian orientation and to prefer a strong leader to get the country back on track, with these views being strongest among older and more religious members of the group.[25] In short, they see the country losing its distinctive culture and identity.

Despite these differences in political views, the white working class and white elites express similar attitudes toward spending on at least some government programs and policies. According to data from the General Social Survey, a majority of both groups believe that we spend *too little* on social security, the environment, health, child care, and education. The white working class is particularly skeptical of welfare and spending that directly relate to improving the conditions of black Americans. They think the economic system is unfair, and, along with other Americans, nearly six in ten support raising taxes on those with incomes over $250,000 a year.[26] A majority would like to see increases in spending on infrastructure and education, and they favor paying for these new initiatives by raising taxes on the wealthy and on businesses. Republicans don't seem to have gotten this message.

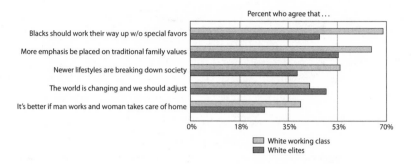

Fig. 2.6. White working class has more traditional views than elites
Source: Author's analysis of the American National Election Survey 2016 Time Series

The Culture of the White Working Class

Trump's bigoted comments, his refusal to be deterred by elite opinion, his success in business, and his outsider status all appealed to small-town and rural white Americans of modest means. They were more alienated than poor. As Arthur Brooks has put it, they had lost dignity, not just income.[27]

Evidence for this cultural argument is strong, as noted earlier. And it is not entirely new. Thomas Frank argued in 2004 in *What's the Matter with Kansas?* that the white working class is so concerned with guns, gays, and abortion that they vote Republican despite its very negative implications for their own economic prospects. (Frank has a new book called *Listen, Liberal* arguing strongly that the fault lies with Democrats for not paying enough attention to this group.)[28]

More recently, several new books and articles have elaborated on the theme. The two most important, I think, are *Hillbilly Elegy* by J. D. Vance and *Strangers in Their Own Land* by Arlie Hochschild.[29] Both are closeup portraits of two white working-class communities, one in Appalachia and one in southwest Louisiana. They portray a group of people in rural or small-town America with middling jobs and a host of problems from broken families to drug addiction, but also with a fierce loyalty to family, community, and church. They resent upwardly mobile minorities, immigrants, and liberal elites. And even the women in these communities believe that women should not compete with men. They dislike government in almost all of its manifestations, even though they are often dependent on it themselves. They are especially critical of bureaucrats or white-collar professionals who have "cushy jobs" and of people who rely on "handouts" from the government.

J. D. Vance's book became a best seller because it provided a firsthand account of someone who grew up in Appalachia but managed to escape and achieve mainstream success, despite a troubled childhood. Vance's book describes how many people in Appalachia believe that the media lies, that mainstream institutions like universities are "rigged," and that there are too many people fraudulently collecting government benefits. He raises the question of how much of this culture is created by economic despair versus a kind of fatalism or "learned helplessness" born of having too little control over one's life. That fatalism is partially responsible for a variety of behaviors, from drug addiction to violence, that cause further social decay. He is sympathetic but doesn't flinch from concluding that many of the wounds of the white working class are self-inflicted. He notes, "The wealthy and powerful aren't just wealthy and powerful; they follow a different set of norms and mores."[30]

The white working class, he says, doesn't trust the institutions of society, including the mainstream press, the education system, or politicians. He writes, "To many of us, the free press—that bulwark of American democracy—is simply full of shit . . . We can't trust the evening news. We can't trust our politicians. Our universities, the gateway to a better life, are rigged against us. We can't get jobs."[31]

Vance sees families and education and jobs as critical. "The most important lesson of my life is not that society failed to provide me with opportunities . . . the real problem . . . is what happens (or doesn't happen) in the home."[32] Vance quotes a teacher from his old high school telling him, "They want us to be shepherds to these kids. But no one wants to talk about the fact that many of them are raised by wolves."[33]

He also cites the concentration of the poor in the same neighborhoods where the schools are lacking and boys associate doing well in school with femininity. He writes, "Boys who got good grades were 'sissies' or 'faggots.'"[34]

Hochschild's masterful book makes clear that the conservative politics she finds in Lake Charles, Louisiana, has no rational basis. It appears to be delusional and self-defeating. As in Frank's Kansas, people are clearly voting against their own self-interest. The terrible human and natural devastation wrought by toxic chemicals in the area goes hand in hand with hatred of the EPA and a ready acceptance of wrongdoing by corporate polluters (although the latter do at least provide jobs). She calls this "the great paradox." There is a direct correlation at the county level between exposure to pollution and conservative political views. What she finds is an *emotional and irrational* attachment to a set of conservative views, driven by Fox News and its equivalents, by resentment of elites, and by the fact that everyone else holds the same antigovernment attitudes. These conservative beliefs are a comforting tribal imperative reinforced by friends, family, and neighbors. It's almost as if the beliefs themselves are a source of succor because they provide emotionally satisfying ties that bind within these communities. They are what you believe if you want to belong. And feeling as if you belong, that you are part of a group in similar circumstances, is one of the few gratifications available when your ability to move ahead seems blocked.

Hochschild develops a deeper explanation for "the great paradox." She creates a metaphor of people waiting in line to climb a hill to achieve the American dream, which is just over the brow of the hill. They have worked hard, done all the right things, but still feel stuck. Not only stuck, but resentful of those who they believe are cutting in line and moving ahead of them: blacks, women, immigrants, and refugees. Obama and other liberals are seen as being on the side of these groups. It's not that members of the white working class dislike such groups, and don't sometimes sympathize with them. It's more that the line cutters are violating the basic rules of fairness. Those in the white working class have had a tough life themselves but aren't complaining about it. There is, in such communities, a kind of "sympathy fatigue."[35]

The economic part of the story is also important. These resentments exist against a backdrop of no progress. The line isn't moving. Automation, outsourcing, the loss of jobs that pay around $60,000, and the indignity of having to work at jobs paying half as much, especially if you are an older white male, have left deep scars. You believe in self-sufficiency and don't like all the government aid you believe is going to the line cutters. The government seems to be providing welfare, but not the kind of job training programs that could help people like you prosper in the workplace.

At the same time, you see yourself portrayed in the media (in programs like *Duck Dynasty* and *Here Comes Honey Boo Boo*) as "white trash" or "all raggedy" with "two missing front teeth." You hear Hillary Clinton say that half of you belong in a "basket of deplorables" and you cringe. Hochschild sums it up: "You are a stranger in your own land. You do not recognize yourself in how others see you. It is a struggle to feel seen and honored. And to feel honored you have to feel—and feel seen as—moving forward. But through no fault of your own, and in ways that are hidden, you are slipping backward."[36]

These were the feelings and circumstances that Hochschild believes motivated people to turn conservative and join the Tea Party. Although *Strangers in Their Own Land* was written well before the 2016 campaign, Hochschild's portrait perfectly captures the feelings that Donald Trump tapped into.

Hochschild tries out her metaphor about standing in line to achieve the American dream on her new friends and acquaintances in Louisiana to see if it resonates. It does, but several people add to it. One interviewee says, "You have it right, but you've left out the fact that the people being cut in on are *paying taxes* that *go to* the people cutting in line!" Another says, "That's it, but the American Dream is more than having money. It's feeling proud to be an American, and to say 'under God' when you salute the flag, and feel *good* about that. And it's about living in a society that believes in clean, normal family life."[37]

Behind this story, according to Hochschild, is not just resentments of minorities and women but of anyone getting a "handout" in the form of welfare, food stamps, or a disability check. It's worth noting, in this context, that whites without a college degree are, in fact, heavily dependent on government safety-net programs. According to a Center on Budget and Policy Priorities analysis, 6.2 million white individuals without a college degree ages 18 to 64 were lifted above the poverty line in 2014 by the safety net, compared to 2.8 million blacks and 2.4 million Hispanics lacking a college degree.[38] Despite this, the people Hochschild spoke to see the market as good and the government as bad. They have adopted the language of "makers" and "takers." She writes, "The free market was the unwavering ally of the good citizens waiting in line for the American Dream. The federal government was on the side of those unjustly 'cutting in.'"[39] Above all, they believe that one should work for a living. Work provides honor, self-reliance, and discipline. As one of her interviewees says, "If there aren't jobs around, well, get people working on the highways, using wheelbarrows and shovels instead of all those dump trucks . . . When people got home at night, they'd be tired and wouldn't be out drinking or doing drugs."[40]

So, culture, and a perception (true or not) that one is being treated unfairly, are important parts of this story. The good news is that the working class is very committed to hard work, honesty, and helping others, and they believe they are "doing the right thing." They simply feel it doesn't pay off, and that the social contract has been broken. They have lost faith in mainstream institutions, and, in light of this, believe self-reliance is the best defense.[41]

This theme of personal responsibility is very strong among the working class. In their paper, "Walking the Line: The White Working Class and the Economic Consequences of Morality," sociologist Monica Prasad and her colleagues cite the reaction of a woman they interviewed to hearing then-candidate Mitt Romney on TV. Romney talked about the need to do three things to be successful: graduate from high school, work full-time, and marry before having children. The woman exclaims, "Wow, I haven't heard anybody say that in a long time."[42] I ran across this quote quite by accident when I was researching this book but was taken aback since Romney's use of this phrase was based on my own research in collaboration with my colleague Ron Haskins. What seemed to resonate for the woman was the need to "walk the line"—to be responsible, especially about spending too much and going into debt, because economic pressures require such responsibility. And the values of education, work, and family clearly resonate with this group of less-educated Americans. The irony is that it is the elites who have most successfully incorporated these values into their actual behavior, but it is the working class who cling to their importance despite difficulties in walking the line.

Unlike elites, this group does not hesitate to judge people as either moral or immoral, responsible or irresponsible, based on their behavior. They do not give excuses for bad behavior such as a lousy childhood, the easy availability of guns, the lack of jobs, or the other "root causes" that liberals like to cite.[43]

After her conversations with less-educated residents in twenty-seven mostly rural communities in the Midwest, Katherine Cramer, a political science professor at the University of Wisconsin, writes, "What I found was resentment of an intensity and specificity that surprised me."[44] These resentments stem, once again, from people's feeling that they are not getting their fair share of respect, of government programs, of the good life that they believe is their due. They especially resent government employees and those in cushy desk jobs, such as college professors or teachers. These jobs have higher wages and benefits than what they earn, and they see their own blue-collar jobs as much harder. As one of Cramer's respondents put it, "they shower before work, not afterwards."[45] What she heard over and over again is that these rural residents were working very hard, couldn't afford even the basics, and were paying taxes that were going to support a less deserving group.[46] Interestingly, when she asked her rural sample where they got their news, the answer was mostly from each other. Because Cramer has been doing this work for almost a decade, we cannot attribute the views she discovered to a Trump-induced flowering of such resentments. As with most of the other studies I have reviewed above, these resentments predate his arrival on the scene. Trump didn't create them, but he played them like a fiddle and he may have exacerbated them in the process.

Joan Williams, a professor at the University of California, observes that "the professional class seeks social honor by embracing the edgy; the white working class seeks honor by embracing the traditional." She goes on to note that "the focus on character, on morality, and family values is a key expression of class disadvantage; we all choose baskets we can fill."[47] She believes there is a message for Democrats here. They need to understand four things. First, the working class is not the same as the poor. The working class is, for example, not interested in taking minimum-wage jobs even if they pay $15. Second, the working class resents the poor, believing that they get too many benefits. Third, class divisions are more place-based than ever. Many of the working class, whatever their individual financial situation, live in poor communities. Finally, and importantly, economic concerns, especially the need for middle-class jobs, remain central.[48]

Williams cautions against writing off blue-collar resentment as racism. In her words, that's just "intellectual comfort food."[49] How liberal groups deal with this advice is unclear. Some of the values of the white working class are simply out of step with the values of progressives everywhere. Progressives are unlikely to abandon their advocacy on behalf of women, minorities, the LGBTQ community, and immigrants, but they may want to trim some cultural sails while strengthening the economic hull of the ship.

Distressed Communities

People are increasingly sorting themselves by community, a trend documented by the journalist Bill Bishop.[50] Those who remain in rural or small-town America have not fared well. Smaller counties' share of job and new business growth has been shrinking, while larger communities and urban areas are booming. As my colleague Mark Muro says, "America faces a small-county crisis of dire proportions."[51]

The trend away from smaller communities is long-standing but has accelerated sharply in the last decade or so, driven by developments in technology and where businesses can find the most educated workers and the robust supply chains needed for success. The trend is exacerbated by the tendency of educated, more cosmopolitan, and more liberal Americans to want to live in places with like-minded people and with the cultural amenities they have come to value.

One reason that Clinton won the popular vote but lost the electoral vote in 2016 is because her voters were overwhelmingly urban (and cities are where most people live), while Trump's were mainly from small towns and rural areas (which are disproportionately represented in the Electoral College). As the reporter Annie Lowrey put it, "It is these geographic inequalities that help to explain why the recovery left so many voters enraged, and the peculiar structure of the American electoral system explains why that rage proved so politically potent."[52] The 14 percent of the population that lives outside of metropolitan America remains largely white, is older, and is declining in size—factors that may limit its future political clout.[53]

The decline in work among men is especially pronounced in distressed areas, particularly in Appalachia, parts of the South, and the Rust Belt. About half of working-age men are jobless in parts of West Virginia and eastern Kentucky, for example.[54] (This statistic makes Trump's contention during the campaign that the unemployment rate was 42 percent seem less ridiculous, though it is still wildly inaccurate.) These areas are, of course, the ones that have been losing jobs due to the decline of jobs in manufacturing and mining.

Some people will conclude that economic policies are needed to revive these "forgotten communities." While we can't save every community in America, we could do more to provide them with the infrastructure and information they need to secure new ways of earning a living.

A lack of infrastructure, from broadband to highways and public transit, limits many rural areas' capacity to engage with their regional or national economies, limiting employment prospects, geographic mobility, and economic opportunity. As the former general counsel to the Federal Communications Commission (FCC) Jonathan Sallet notes, the demographic characteristics of Americans without broadband largely mirror those who voted for Trump— both were disproportionately rural, middle income, and less educated.[55] Expanding broadband access would not only help connect isolated communities with larger population centers and economies, it could also enable a larger number of residents to work remotely, providing job opportunities that aren't contingent upon bringing back manufacturing or reviving the dying coal industry.

A CLOSEUP LOOK AT ONE COMMUNITY: BEATTYVILLE

Beattyville, Kentucky, exemplifies many of the divides discussed above. This town of about 1,500 in the eastern part of the state is less than one hundred miles from Inez, another small Kentucky town where President Lyndon Johnson famously declared his "war on poverty" in 1964. Beattyville was heralded by the *Guardian* as "America's poorest white town"; such designations are, not surprisingly, met with bitterness from local residents.[56]

Beattyville illustrates what happens when entire communities get "left behind." While Beattyville was never a bustling metropolis, it did have a sewing factory, a prison, and a handful of other employers that have since left. Less than one-tenth of the town has a college degree, but it wasn't required for most of the decent-paying jobs in the area.

Thanks to one of my colleagues, Eleanor Krause, who grew up rock climbing in the Red River Gorge just a few miles north of Beattyville, I have gotten a slightly better understanding of the perspectives of some of the area's residents.[57] On one of her many visits, she spoke with some of the residents in the surrounding area about the changes they've witnessed in the local economy and community. All those she spoke with have been living in either Beattyville or the surrounding counties for several years, if not their entire lives. It would be impossible to capture the full richness of her interviews, but here are the major themes distilled from her reporting:

There is strong reluctance to rely on "government handouts." The public assistance programs associated with the "war on poverty," initially waged just next door, are largely met with resentment and shame, despite the fact that a huge portion of the community benefits from these programs. People would rather receive a paycheck than a handout, but given the lack of employment prospects, many are faced with little alternative but to swallow their pride and accept public assistance.

One man who had been living in Beattyville his entire life remembered when the "poverty" of his friends and their families was broadcast on the evening news. They had never thought of themselves as poor and hate the idea of becoming dependent on public assistance. But now, a large share of the community takes advantage of government programs, although many do so reluctantly. This same resident said, "I can remember when people wouldn't take food stamps. They was ashamed. And now it's just like, it's an entitlement . . . What in the heck has happened to people? Everybody's a victim." Another man explained how he was finally forced to go on food stamps when he went broke, but he would drive an hour away to Richmond to buy his groceries for fear of someone seeing him swiping his food stamps card. He reflected, "I'll never forget. The shame . . . I remember sitting right at the table eating the first meal. And I couldn't swallow. It made a knot in my throat."

Dwindling job opportunities are taking a toll on the economy and the community. A local business owner said that "the best way to get people off of welfare is to get them jobs." But jobs are scarce. One sixty-five-year-old man who has been living in the area for thirty-four years said that after the tobacco companies left, there was "nothing to do for these young people." Without the decent-paying jobs of the past, many turned to drugs or alcohol. "They're bored. There's no work. Boredom is the worst evil around. When you become bored you become spoiled, you become lazy." In discussing the region's economic prospects, everyone noted the lack of jobs. One man said, "I don't want your damn money. I want a job." When asked what could be done to improve the local economy, a cashier at the gas station in the center of Beattyville responded, "jobs . . . plain and simple. We need jobs." When asked what people do to get by, another resident said, "They either travel or work minimum wage jobs or live off welfare . . . There's just not decent paying jobs. You're either gonna work at the gas station or at the Dairy Queen." Others noted that there actually are job opportunities in nursing and teaching, but they require additional training and are not particularly attractive to men who have traditionally made a living in male-dominated professions that require hard physical labor. But even those decent jobs are hard to come by; one young woman said that "it would be downright impossible" to find work in the area, even with a bachelor's degree.

Desperation isn't inevitable, but change is. While most residents were quick to note the dwindling job opportunities in the area and the toll that it has taken, many people seemed genuinely optimistic about the future. An owner of a small Beattyville shop noted that "for this area in particular, I think tourism really is a big thing. I think if we focused more on tourism instead of what we used to have on coal, timber, and other resources, I think we'd do a lot more good." Many interviewees placed a big emphasis on bolstering the tourism industry, which is the fastest-growing industry in the area.[58]

One previously laid off manufacturing worker talked about his own path to reemployment, noting how important it is to get the right kind of education. He suggested a stronger emphasis on vocational schools, noting that "people just don't know how to change a flat tire. We've got people who just don't know how to do nothing now."

But many people noted that the local labor market will never offer enough jobs. Some people are just going to have to move. With that said, many residents were wary of the idea of relocating, even if it would improve their economic prospects. Instead, many hope that more emphasis will be placed on attracting local investors and expanding broadband access, so that more individuals could work remotely. As one young woman noted, improved broadband would enable more individuals to telecommute.

She said, "People here are very smart and they want to learn things but they also don't want to leave their home."

In general, residents were skeptical that the federal government could do much on its own to help these small local economies. Instead, they see a role for local entrepreneurship, art, creativity, and the area's inherent natural beauty to attract investment. Of course, many of these investments are funded by the federal government, whether individuals are aware of it or not. There is an underlying tension between a yearning for local control and self-sufficiency and the reality that many of the needed investments (infrastructure, education, workforce training, etc.) may require state or federal dollars. The challenges voiced by the residents of this eastern Kentucky region mirror those noted throughout this chapter. What's needed is an agenda that addresses the lack of good jobs in many parts of the country but delivered in a way that preserves the dignity and values of those involved.

What about Minorities and the Poor?

While the white working class is experiencing rising mortality rates, high levels of pessimism about the future, and an economic and cultural malaise that delivered Trump his biggest margins, I do not want to leave the impression that the black or Hispanic working class, and indeed the entire poverty population, should no longer be an important policy priority. The reason why it would be a mistake to neglect the white working class is because they are a large portion of the population, and if they continue to gravitate toward candidates like Trump, the consequences for the poor and for minorities would be devastating. Everything from the future of Medicaid and other safety-net programs to voting and reproductive rights are now threatened. Liberals may not like it, but, of necessity, this may be a time for defending existing programs and policies rather than securing new victories in the struggle to reduce poverty and racial inequities. They may rally around a liberal populist with very bold ideas in reaction to the 2016 election but should ask themselves whether this will translate into a win at the polls. A very large fraction of the electorate is not on their side and needs to be coaxed toward the center. The Republican Party has become more conservative, leaving space in the middle for a more moderate political leader.

To be sure, minorities are worse off on just about every indicator we could consider. Black Americans in particular are more likely to be jobless, have less education, have higher rates of incarceration, and experience lower rates of upward mobility than whites.[59] On the other hand, their plight and that of the poor will only worsen if the far right continues to gain power in the White House, in Congress, and in the courts.

With this as background, the remainder of this book focuses on all "the forgotten Americans"—whatever their race or ethnicity. They are a large group. If we were to define them as all working-age adults (ages twenty-five to sixty-four) without a four-year college degree, they are about 64 percent of the population. If we additionally restrict the definition to those in the bottom half of the income distribution, they are about 38 percent of the working-age population.[60] The challenge is daunting and likely to require major changes in our institutions and attitudes, not just a few more government programs. Can we pull that off when confidence in government is so low and our divides so great?

Confidence in Institutions

We now come to a troubling catch-22. The major vehicle for improving the lives of the forgotten Americans is public policy. But if the public has lost trust in the ability of government to address their problems, then what are those in public office to do? Elected officials are now held in very low esteem, especially at the federal level. As someone who has known many competent and dedicated public servants, I am always amazed at the very negative reaction outside the Beltway to what goes on within it. But that may be because I am a swamp dweller myself, a member of the now-distrusted "elite." The fact remains that however competent or dedicated our public officials may be as individuals, they have not been able to get much done.

Public trust in government has reached near historic lows. The proportion of adults who say they trust the government to do what's right always or most of the time is about 20 percent.[61] For the past two decades, about

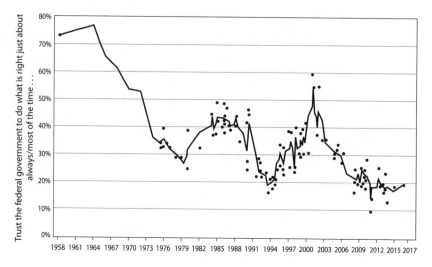

Fig. 2.7. "Public trust in government remains near historic lows"
Source: Pew Research Center

four-fifths of the public has been telling survey takers that they are either frustrated or angry at the federal government. The only exception was in 2001, a short-lived response to the 9/11 terrorist attack on the homeland (fig. 2.7).[62]

Equally important, a majority of Americans do not have consistently liberal or conservative views. What they yearn for is elected officials willing to compromise with one another to solve the nation's problems. Because this "messy middle" center of the country is relatively inactive in politics compared to the tails of the ideological distribution, their voices have not been heard. They have been drowned out by an ideologically oriented or activist political class whose views they seldom share.[63]

It is not just the federal government that is in trouble with the public. Confidence in a wide array of other institutions has reached near record lows, according to Gallup polling data. People voice the greatest confidence in the military, small businesses, and the police, while Congress and the executive branch receive much lower marks. No entity is perceived more negatively than the Congress of the United States. But confidence in organized religion, banks, and the news media has also waned significantly over the past decade, while confidence in the military has remained consistently high (about 73 percent report a great deal or quite a lot of confidence in the military).[64]

This waning confidence toward various institutions suggests that any new agenda should be sensitive to such views. A large new federal program emanating from Washington might not appeal, even assuming it could be enacted. By contrast, tapping into the respect accorded to the military and, to a lesser extent, businesses might be a better alternative. For example, using the military as a model and a vehicle for a broader program of national or community service or to provide training and apprenticeships might appeal, as I argue in a later chapter. Similarly, the resentment toward elite colleges contrasts with a recognition that almost everyone needs more than a high school degree. If fourteen years of education is the new twelve in terms of years of schooling needed to get a decent job, community colleges are the obvious path to the new fourteen. The 1,462 community colleges in the United States are, for the most part, nonselective, provide practical skills, and can be found in every state. Seventy percent of their students are the children of parents without four-year degrees.[65] These facts make them natural candidates for meeting the needs of a working class that is falling behind economically. They may need to be improved and given additional resources, but they are the right locus for educating and training the forgotten Americans.

We can also contrast the popularity of spending on Social Security and education with that of spending on, say, welfare or foreign aid. The continuing support for universal social insurance programs, including both Social Security and Medicare, contrasts sharply with the support for programs that are viewed as providing assistance to specific groups or areas of the country. As noted earlier, the general attitude among the white working class is that the federal government provides too many handouts.

Yuval Levin, in his book *The Fractured Republic*, argues that in light of the kinds of divisions described in this and later chapters, the right way to rebuild or revitalize our society is by relying more on "the middle layers of society, where people see each other face to face" and by "putting power, authority, and significance as close to the level of the interpersonal community as reasonably possible."[66] I think he is right. For this reason, in coming chapters, I suggest an agenda that relies where possible on state or local governments and the private sector to achieve more inclusive growth. Where it is not possible, I will argue for using the still-popular social insurance programs to deliver some new benefits to the forgotten Americans.

Devolution of responsibility has the potential to rebuild trust in government and in democratic institutions that have all but lost their legitimacy. And a contributory social insurance system to which everyone contributes and from which everyone benefits and that avoids the annual appropriations battles in Congress has merit as well. Finally, any new agenda needs to be built around the three places where people actually spend their time, forge relationships, and find meaning in their lives. Those three places are families, schools, and workplaces. One thing that a majority of the public seems to support is the need for personal responsibility in each of these domains.

We shouldn't leave this story about a lack of trust without addressing how people come to believe what they believe. If all news is fake news and there is no agreement on the facts and no authoritative voices, how does a democracy survive? We like to think that most people are capable of *independently* assessing a situation, learning at least the basic facts, and then making political or other decisions based on an assessment of the situation in the context of their personal values.

This model of how a democracy works may be naïve. In their book, *Phishing for Phools: The Economics of Manipulation and Deception,* George Akerlof and Robert Shiller argue that we are all far more vulnerable to being misled or manipulated than we would like to believe. A phool is someone who has been successfully phished or manipulated. Advertisers play on our emotional attachments, identities, and insecurities to get us to buy products we don't need: mouthwash to prevent bad breath, shampoo to shine up our hair, and soft drinks that make us feel "cool."[67] Advertisers know that this manipulation works or they wouldn't spend billions of dollars on it. But politicians and their allies in some parts of the media have learned how to do this as well. Thanks to the work of behavioral economists, we now understand far better than in the past how this process works.

Not only are we vulnerable to emotional appeals, but, in addition, no one can know everything they need to know to make decisions about what to buy or whom to vote for. We have limited time and cognitive bandwidth and must rely instead on shortcuts, including party labels or the opinion of others. Those shortcuts often take the form of habits or opinions formed early in life (brand X or political party Y are a "trusted brand" in our household), what our friends think (are they mostly liberal or conservatives?), and our media consumption (Fox News vs. MSNBC). As one report put it, "Voters today are not so much shaped by news as the news is shaped for them. In cafeteria-style format, we consume news from a personalized menu that, in addition to informing us, satisfies our appetite for reinforcing our individual beliefs, friendships and politics. As a result, liberal, moderate and conservative voters virtually live in alternative realities depending on their personal point of view and preferred news sources."[68]

Social media and cable TV have proliferated the diversity of sources and the tendency of people to form self-perpetuating bubbles of opinion on various issues. We tend to favor sources that confirm what we already believe, and even when exposed to counter facts or arguments, we may not be swayed to change our minds. However, there is an asymmetry here. Conservatives are more likely than liberals to rely on a single news source, such as Fox News or talk radio. Liberals have their own favorites (such as CNN or the *New York Times*) but tend to have more diverse tastes.[69] Democrats are more likely to follow fact-checking organizations and neutral media than are Republicans, and less likely to favor partisan shows, even those that cater to them (such as MSNBC).[70]

A striking study by several scholars, reported in the prestigious *American Economic Review* and using a clever methodology to distinguish causation from correlation, found that Fox News viewership increased the Republican Party's share of the vote by 6 percentage points in 2008. The authors of the study admit there is some uncertainty around their estimate, but even if it is considerably smaller, it's easily large enough to swing an election. And once again, Fox News has, according to the evidence, had far more influence than, say, MSNBC, and has also had growing influence over time.[71] Should big money or rising concentration in cable programming further enhance this influence, control of the media could become the determining factor in electoral outcomes. And given the asymmetrical effects of conservative- versus liberal-leaning media on voting behavior, this could give Republicans a strong advantage.

Even more concerning is the fact that political campaigns are learning how to profile people's beliefs and attitudes so that they can test and then target specific messages to those most likely to be swayed to vote in favor of a particular candidate or issue, without the individuals involved even knowing what is happening to them.[72] Attempts by Russia to influence our election are an extremely troubling case in point. Both the education system and especially the mainstream media try to lean against these forms of manipulation. But efforts by President Trump and his allies to discredit the media are taking their toll and making the job harder, even if it is more important than ever. As the *Atlantic* reporter Jack Goldsmith put it, "Trump's extremes require the mainstream press to choose between appearing oppositional or, if it tones things down, 'normalizing' his presidency. Either way, Trump in some sense wins."[73]

Ongoing efforts to both discredit and defund institutions such as the Congressional Budget Office and the Census Bureau are also a direct attack on the factual underpinnings of democratic discourse.

One interpretation of the education gap in the 2016 vote is that better-educated voters rely on a variety of information sources and tend to more critically assess that information. They are more likely to regularly read newspapers and magazines than the less educated and more likely to regularly watch the news on television compared to the general public. It also matters what they read or watch. For example, a majority of the readers of the *New Yorker,* the *Atlantic,* the *Economist,* the *Wall Street Journal,* and the *New York Times* are college graduates. By comparison, only about a quarter of those who watch Fox or MSNBC are college graduates.[74] This then shows up in what people know. When Pew asked the public four simple questions measuring knowledge of politics and current events, only 14 percent got all four questions right. The questions were pretty simple: Which party controls the House of Representatives, the current unemployment rate, the nation that Angela Merkel leads, and which presidential candidate favored taxing higher-income Americans? Those who scored the highest on this test were readers of the *New Yorker,* the *Wall Street Journal,* the *New York Times,* and the *Economist,* and those who watched or listened to Rachel Maddow, NPR, *The Daily Show,* and *Hardball.* Interestingly, few of those who were regular viewers of more conservative shows scored nearly as well, although

The O'Reilly Factor and *Hannity* watchers had respectable scores. Fox News, the network evening news, CNN, and *USA Today* consumers were much less informed, according to this particular test.[75]

As Bill Bishop says, "We now live in a giant feedback loop, hearing our own thoughts about what's right and wrong bounced back to us by the television shows we watch, the newspapers and books we read, the blogs we visit online, the sermons we hear and the neighborhoods we live in."[76]

There has been a lot of griping about President Trump's tweets, but no one can complain that they don't know exactly what he's thinking most of the time. Tweeting may not be presidential, but at least it's transparent.

Conclusion

Trump won the election primarily because he was a Republican, and 2016 voters were a traditionally partisan group. Trump's biggest supporters were whites without a four-year college degree. The better educated are moving into the Democratic column.

Within this group of less-educated white voters, the key factors that seem to have predicted Trump's win were anti-immigrant sentiments and a sense of being left behind and feeling helpless about it. The economic prospects of this group have indeed declined, compared to the prospects of the college educated. These less-educated white voters are also more socially and culturally conservative. They tend to live in small towns and rural areas, and they are resentful of both the elites and those whom they see as less deserving of government support than themselves.

There is little question in my mind that the white working class is voting against their own self-interest, but there are different ways of understanding that fact. One explanation is that they are misinformed and are being duped or misled by rhetoric that is superficially appealing but will, in the long run, simply cause them more pain. Certainly, there is plenty of objective evidence that voters are poorly informed. Part of the problem is that it is not rational for the typical citizen to spend a lot of time learning about the issues. They correctly perceive that their vote is unlikely to sway an election.[77] In this context, politics is a lot like sports. It is much easier to simply decide which team to support (the Democrats or the Republicans) and to then vote accordingly. Selecting a team may depend very heavily on one's history, on how other people in one's social group vote, and on just a few emotion-laden issues. If one views government as providing help to people who are undeserving (e.g., immigrants), or as an impediment to job-creation in one's local community due to some badly designed or un-needed regulation that is gumming up the works, then an agenda of lower taxes and smaller government has substantial appeal. If, on the other hand, one views current policies as redistributing income from the poor to the rich, as neglecting the environment, or as unsupportive of traditionally disadvantaged groups (e.g., women or minorities), then one may favor a more active government role in correcting such imbalances. But once an individual—or the group with which that person has close ties—has se-lected a "team" to support, he or she can usually find evidence and arguments to support that choice. Put differently, people look for confirmation of their existing biases, which are often emotionally charged and based on a very partial view of what government does.

Partisanship has always been part of our politics but it has gotten worse.[78] Consider the fact that 50 percent of partisans surveyed in 2010 said they would be unhappy if their child married someone from the other party, up from 5 percent in 1960.[79] This kind of tribal politics can have serious con-sequences by making it difficult to get anything done. Government makes many decisions that profoundly affect human welfare—whether to go to war, how to support allies and sanction enemies, how to protect the envi-ronment, whether to provide health care or education to everyone or just to those who can afford it, and who should pay the costs of whatever govern-ment does. We cannot return to a world in which individuals can safely ignore what is happening beyond their own homes or their own borders. We now have an economy and a globe that are far more interconnected than in the past. Individual welfare is thus far more dependent on good governance. Unless we can learn to manage ourselves and the world around us, we may become—if not an endangered species—a group of warring tribes. Walter Scheidel, a Stanford historian, believes it will take a war, a revolution, a pandemic, or a natural disaster to bring us together.[80] A crisis of this sort would underscore how small-minded and parochial our current political divisions have become. Hopefully it won't come to that, but the prospect should focus our attention.

The question is what, if anything, can be done to restore a better-functioning democracy—one in which pluralism or toleration of different ways of life and different views can coexist peacefully and compromises can still be found.

The current lack of confidence in government, especially the federal government, and the kind of tribalism that has emerged, lead me to suggest that, as we think about policies that might gain some traction in the future, we focus first on widely shared values, especially the value of work, and second on institutions that retain some broad-based popularity. Those institutions include local governments, community colleges, the military, religious groups, civic society (NGOs), and businesses.

I believe it may take many years to rebuild the kind of trust in representative government that is so badly needed. Although this book is primarily about economic policy, I no longer believe one can separate economics from politics or politics from culture. For this reason, in later chapters, I emphasize policies that operate where people live or work—that is, in local communities and workplaces. This is primarily a bottom-up approach, an attempt to rebuild the foundations of not just a better-functioning economy, but also a better-functioning society.

One advantage of local communities and employers as the best places to address the cultural divide is that they enable the kind of face-to-face interactions that are likely to help break down misunderstandings and tribal imperatives, including demonizing various out-groups. Social psychologists have documented that when people come into contact and get to know individual members of an out-group or another tribe, perceptions of the out-group become far more positive.[81] Community colleges, places of employment, and national service, I will later argue, have the potential to mix up the tribes.

But first we need to address the economic issues that have left so many behind. These include both slower growth and rising inequality. That story is the focus of chapter 3.

3

What Went Wrong?

THE FORGOTTEN AMERICANS ARE LOSING GROUND. That fact, as we saw in the last chapter, has had political consequences. But what exactly has gone wrong? This chapter takes a deeper dive into the economic story that seems to lie behind the political discontent.[1]

The first lesson emerging from this chapter is that economic growth has slowed, but *even should growth recover, that won't improve the economic prospects of the typical American family very much unless there is a broader distribution of its benefits.*

The second lesson is that much of the increase in inequality and its associated discontents is because *new technology and trade have eliminated many jobs* that used to provide the forgotten Americans with a decent living.

The third message is that *what young people know and can do hasn't kept pace with what today's jobs require. The education system is partly to blame.*

The fourth and final message is that *it would be a mistake to put all the blame on the schools.* They are dealing with a breakdown of the American family and other cultural developments that make their task more difficult.

The facts I review in this chapter can only take us so far. At a deeper level, what's at issue is the value propositions that divide liberals and conservatives. To what extent are the problems discussed in this chapter due to the failures of individuals versus the failures of our institutions? Like many people, I think it's some of both, and that the answer varies from case to case, making generalizations impossible. Life is way too complicated. But to find some kind of common ground, conservatives need to stop blaming the victim. Just as importantly, liberals need to stop blaming the system. Moral agency is a concept that many of the forgotten Americans take very seriously. Liberal elites make a mistake ignoring it.

If we want to overcome the great political and cultural divides in the United States and not just the economic ones, we have to come to some agreement on this point. This is a theme I will continue to stress. But first, a look at the evidence.

Whatever Happened to the American Dream?

I am part of the generation that grew up in the decades during and following World War II. I can still remember my family's backyard "victory garden" during the war, and I remember saving the aluminum foil from packages of Life Savers to recycle in support of the war effort. After I married in the late 1950s, my husband and I ate a lot of tuna casseroles (one can of tuna mixed with one can of mushroom soup, plus noodles). We drove a secondhand Ford, and borrowed money from our parents when we were unable to pay the rent on an apartment in Brooklyn. I worked at a clerical job that paid just slightly more than the minimum wage, and my husband earned just a bit more in those early years. But we went to graduate school at night, managed to save money (which was miraculous, in retrospect), and eventually bought a house and moved up the ladder at a rapid and accelerating rate through the 1960s and 1970s. By the time we were middle-aged, we were better off than our own parents.

Our story was not atypical (although we were better educated than most). Those decades enabled most people to achieve greater prosperity than what they had experienced as children. We know this because of the important work of Stanford professor Raj Chetty and his colleagues. They have combined census data and data from individual tax records to look at how different generations have fared relative to their parents. Among children born in 1940 (roughly my generation), 90 percent ended up with higher incomes (adjusted for inflation) by age thirty than their parents had at that same age.[2] Virtually everyone was getting ahead, moving up, and achieving the dream. This is the generation that experienced the golden years of not

Fig. 3.1. Rates of upward mobility are declining over time
Source: Chetty et al., "Fading American Dream"

only higher growth rates but also broadly shared growth. You might have been driving a secondhand car or eating tuna casseroles as a young adult, but you knew that there was a new car, a house, and maybe even some lobster thermidor in your future. When children came along, you saved for their college, but tuitions were much lower back then.[3] Moreover, almost everyone was married, so if budgets got tight, you could supplement the family income by sending a second earner into the job market.[4]

Fast-forward to the generation born around 1980, or today's soon-to-be forty-year-olds. Only about half of them are doing better than their parents. More generally, the Chetty team finds that this kind of upward mobility (what researchers call "absolute intergenerational mobility") has declined pretty steadily over the years since 1940, as shown in fig. 3.1.[5]

So, the up escalator has slowed down a lot. In line with this, the public is increasingly pessimistic about their children's life chances. In 2014, only 21 percent of respondents to an NBC News/*Wall Street Journal* poll thought their children's generation would be better off than their own. Back in 1990, that figure was nearly 50 percent.[6] These public views are perfectly consistent with the evidence. Some of that slowing is due to lower growth, but even more of it is because whatever growth we've had has gone overwhelmingly to the top. Specifically, the Chetty team finds that about

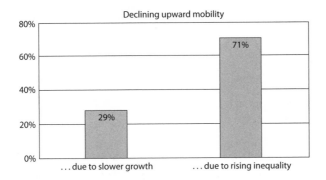

Fig. 3.2.
Source: Chetty et al., "Fading American Dream"
Note: Decomposition based on two counterfactual simulations: one assumes the same
growth rate for both cohorts; the other, the same distribution of any growth.

70 percent of the decline in upward mobility between my generation and
the one that followed was due to rising inequality. Only 30 percent was due
to slower growth (fig. 3.2).

What this means is that faster growth alone is not the key to improving
middle-class prospects in the United States. We also have to focus on the
distribution of benefits.

Economic Growth Is Slowing Down

None of this means that economic growth is unimportant. One reason
many people fail to appreciate the power of economic growth is because
they take their current standard of living for granted. We are used to the
many comforts and amenities we enjoy, from air-conditioned offices and
cell phones to supermarkets stocked with a wide array of fresh and pack-
aged foods. We forget that we have access to health care treatments that our
grandparents would have found miraculous, and that we live far longer
and healthier lives than they did.

There is no getting around the fact that economic growth is responsible
for much higher incomes and standards of living. Take what's happened to
real per capita GDP—the usual measure of growth—from 1929, when the
government first began collecting the data, to the present day. What these
data show is that GDP per capita was less than $10,000 in 1929 and had

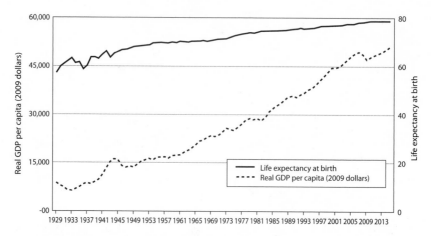

Fig. 3.3. GDP per capita and life expectancy have increased dramatically
Sources: Bureau of Economic Analysis, "National Income and Product Accounts";
Arias, "United States Life Tables, 2011"

grown to over $50,000 in 2017. The annual GDP per capita growth rate over the entire period was 2.08 percent. If the rate of growth over this period had been only 1.0 percent, then per capita GDP would have been only slightly above $20,000 in 2017.[7] At the same time, life expectancy at birth has risen from fifty-seven to nearly seventy-nine over this same period (fig. 3.3).[8]

After 1970, growth slowed. Except for a temporary burst from 1995 to 2004, which happened in conjunction with the invention of the internet and investments in computers, improvements during the most recent period have been disappointing.

Growth is helpful because it generates a surplus that can be used to compensate those who suffer the inevitable displacements due to changes in trade and technology and to shifting consumption patterns. As we saw in chapter 2, there is a large group of Americans whose incomes have risen very little, if at all, and whose economic prospects are now affecting not just their lives and their communities but also our politics.

What *actually* drives growth and whether it is likely to be slower or faster in the future are much-debated questions. On one side are some, most notably the economist Robert Gordon, who think our best days are behind us. Gordon believes that slow growth is likely to continue and might even slow further due to four headwinds: growing inequality, fewer improvements in educational attainment, demographic shifts such as the aging of the population and the peak in women's labor force participation, and the need to address the growing federal debt by raising taxes or reducing benefits and thus lowering people's disposable incomes in the future.[9]

A more optimistic view of what the future holds comes from a small group of scientists and business leaders whose ideas are best summarized in the book *The Second Machine Age* by MIT's Erik Brynjolfsson and Andrew McAfee. The authors argue that we are at an inflection point at which the seeds of faster growth are in place but need time to mature and spread. They base their optimism on three main points: the exponential growth of computing power (doubling every eighteen months, according to the latest version of Moore's Law); the digitalization of everything, creating huge databases of information; and the creative potential of an increasingly interconnected society (e.g., crowd sourcing) and the likelihood that existing innovations will be combined and spawn still greater growth. They believe the reason we have not seen any of this in the productivity statistics thus far is because of measurement error and because it takes time for these innovations to be adopted and used effectively.[10]

To be useful, these new inventions will have to be combined with the right kind of organizational and human skills before they begin to have an impact on productivity and growth. As an example, the federal government has encouraged hospitals and doctors' offices to adopt the latest technology, offering $44,000 in federal subsidies per physician for shifting to electronic health records. Uptake has been substantial, but the transition has not always gone smoothly. Workflow and personnel both need to be restructured, the right kind of computer equipment and software installed, privacy issues addressed, and the reality recognized that there will be a mixed paper–electronic system in place for a number of years.[11]

The fact is we do not know what the future holds. I believe Gordon is too pessimistic. It is hard to imagine the kinds of inventions that have yet to appear on the scene. Who in 1870 would have been able to predict that their great-grandchildren would be flying from Los Angeles to New York in half a day or motoring around Pittsburgh in a self-driving car? Those of us alive today may suffer from this same lack of imagination and ability to predict the future. But I think Gordon is right to worry about the headwinds. It is critical to create the kind of political environment in which growth and innovation can flourish by addressing the headwinds: distributional issues, investments in education, and the availability of child care and paid leave that affect women's ability to work, the growth of single-parent families, and the need for fiscal responsibility.

But whatever the future holds, what we know right now is that growth has been slower than in the past century and that it hasn't reached the bottom half. To understand why, we have to take a closer look at rising inequality.

The Gilded Age Revisited

The economists Anthony Atkinson, Thomas Piketty, and Emmanuel Saez looked at tax records going back to the early years of the twentieth century in the United States. What their studies show is a U-shaped pattern in which income inequality was very high in the early twentieth century before peaking in the late 1920s, then declined sharply during World War II, staying low through the 1950s, 1960s, and 1970s, before beginning to rise again in the 1980s.[12] It is now back to levels not seen since the late 1920s (fig. 3.4).[13]

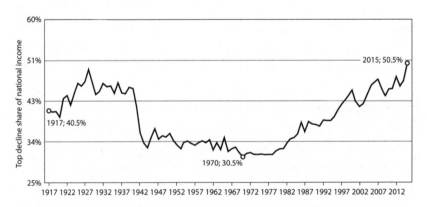

Fig. 3.4. Richest Americans receive increasing share of national income
Source: World Wealth and Income Database, "Top 10% Share," United States, http://wid.world/country/usa/

Some of the rise in income inequality has been driven by growing gaps in the earnings of workers with more and less education. The economists Claudia Goldin and Larry Katz have found that the increase in the education premium can explain about 65 percent of the growing inequality in U.S. wages between 1980 and 2005.[14] One way to close those gaps is by investing much more in education and training.

But much of the recent growth in inequality in the United States is due to the very rich pulling away from everyone else.[15] The reasons for this are disputed. One possibility is that the enhanced competition catalyzed by a larger and more integrated market for highly talented individuals has greatly boosted what they can earn. This would include corporate executives, sports and entertainment celebrities, and Wall Street financiers, although the dominant group resides in the corporate sector. In this view, they are the winners of a giant and wide-open race to find the best person for every position, and their ever-increasing compensation is commensurate with their abilities and the market demand for their services.

Another possibility is that social norms and practices surrounding pay have shifted, perhaps encouraged by much lower tax rates on top incomes and the fact that a small number of firms increasingly dominate their industries. Corporate boards have acquiesced to the excessively high salaries and bonuses expected by today's executives, whether they make sense economically or not. No board wants to pay its CEO less than the competition, and should the board demur, members will hear from compensation consultants with industry-wide surveys that *their* CEO is (horror of horrors) not in the top of the distribution. In such a world, salaries and bonuses can easily spiral out of control.

The tax data used by Piketty and colleagues are ideal for looking at top incomes, but less useful for looking at the bottom of the distribution since lower-income families often pay little or no income tax. (They do pay payroll taxes.) To get a more complete picture, we can look at data provided by the Congressional Budget Office (CBO). CBO looks at incomes by quintile, adjusted for inflation, from 1979 to 2013 (the latest year available). The bottom three quintiles (the bottom 60 percent) saw their incomes grow much more slowly than those in the top 40 percent (see fig. 3.5). At the beginning of this period, the bottom 60 percent's share of total income was about

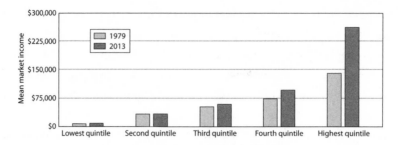

Fig. 3.5. Market income has increased very little for those in the working class,
but it has soared for those at the top

Source: Congressional Budget Office, "The Distribution of Household Income
and Federal Taxes, 2013," Supplemental data table 7 (Washington, DC: CBO, 2016),
https://www.cbo.gov/publication/51361
Note: Household quintiles are determined by market income. Market income
includes labor income, business income, capital gains, capital income
(excluding capital gains), and other income.

28 percent. By 2013 it had dropped to 22 percent. And once again, the share
going to the top grew sharply.

So far, I have focused on what CBO calls market incomes—that is, all
forms of income, whether from wages or investments, but before taxes or
the receipt of government benefits such as Social Security or unemployment insurance. When we look at after-tax income (which includes adding
in benefits as well as subtracting taxes), we see two things. First, government
plays a clear role in reducing inequality. It lowers it by about 25 percent
relative to what it would look like in the absence of government taxes and
benefits. Second, in recent decades, government taxes and benefits have
not done much to offset the rise in income inequality. Taxes have become
less equalizing (mostly because regressive payroll taxes are a rising share of
all taxes), and although government benefits have grown in size, an increasing fraction of them go to the elderly, many of whom are middle class
or even affluent, not poor.[16]

Many people look at these data and conclude that government policy (or
what government failed to do) is entirely to blame for these trends. After
all, the rise of inequality started around the time of Ronald Reagan's election and was definitely given a push by large tax cuts favoring the wealthy
under both Reagan and George W. Bush. Even Bill Clinton, a Democratic
president (in whose administration I served), proposed to "end welfare as

we know it" and succeeded with the help of Republicans and Democrats in Congress to do just that. The problem with blaming these trends entirely on government policies is that they are not unique to the United States. Inequality has risen in seventeen of the twenty-two Organisation for Economic Co-operation and Development (OECD) countries for which data are available.[17] However, with one or two exceptions, no other country has experienced as sharp a rise as the United States. This suggests there may indeed be something inherent in a capitalist system that leads to this result, as well as something specific to the United States that makes it the poster child for inequality.

When we broaden our lens to the entire globe, we find that, while the rich countries are experiencing growing inequality, less-developed countries are catching up to the developed world, with the result that global inequality and poverty are declining.[18] This fact is important to keep in mind. If the response to rising inequality in the United States or other advanced countries is to create barriers to trade and immigration, this will be harmful to those in the poorer parts of the world and in the long run will likely lead to greater conflict and more human suffering. We would be wise to find measures that do not inflict such harm, not only because it is more humane but also because it is linked to our own national security.

In conclusion, income inequality in the United States has been increasing for almost four decades, especially (but not entirely) at the very top. For many years, it was simply assumed that a rising tide would lift all boats. More recently, the recognition that the yachts are doing a lot better than the rowboats has grown. In fact, many of the rowboats haven't moved at all. A great many Americans have indeed been forgotten or left behind. This creates resentment among the forgotten Americans who don't live in gated communities, don't send their kids to Harvard, and certainly don't earn multimillion-dollar bonuses as Wall Street financiers. Although the very top of the distribution is where the greatest inequality lies, we shouldn't forget about the group just below the top—what my colleague Richard Reeves calls the "Dream Hoarders." They include not just the top 1 percent, but also the top 20 percent. As he shows, they are doing very well and are the beneficiaries of a variety of government tax subsidies, such as 529 education savings accounts, mortgage interest deductions, and the like.[19]

These trends are not benign and they have disturbing political implications, from the enhanced ability of the rich to determine electoral outcomes to
the dangers of a populist reaction on the part of the bottom half. One interpretation of the Trump phenomenon is that it represents a very conservative Republican elite partnering with a very effective demagogue to use
the grievances of the bottom half to enact policies that cloak a plutocratic
agenda in populist clothes.

The Loss of Jobs and the Decline in Work

Though some of the rise in inequality has come from the enormous increase in incomes at the very top of the distribution, it is also the case that
shifts in technology and trade have changed the nature of work and made
it more difficult for the less skilled to earn a decent living.

The March of Technology

The Industrial Revolution led to a wholesale exit of workers out of agriculture and into manufacturing. In 1800, three-quarters of the population
was employed in agriculture; by 2016, that figure was down to less than
2 percent.[20] More recently we have gone through an equally dramatic shift,
from a manufacturing-based economy to a high-tech, knowledge-based,
and services-oriented one. The idea that we can bring back manufacturing
jobs in large numbers is misguided. As the *New York Times* reporter Binyamin Appelbaum writes: "Forget the images of men in hard hats standing
before factory gates, of men with coal-blackened faces, of men perched
high above New York City on steel beams. The emerging face of the American working class is a Hispanic woman who has never set foot on the factory floor. That's not the kind of work much of the working class does
anymore. Instead of making things, they are more often paid to serve
people, to care for someone else's children or someone else's parents; to
clean another family's house."[21]

The automation of jobs has, of course, been underway for some time.
Most of this automation has involved machines doing what humans used
to do—the steam engine replacing manual labor, the hay baler replacing
the arduous work of raking hay into bundles, the copy machine replacing a

typist using carbon copies produced in small laborious batches. I started my career as a secretary. I spent hours preparing documents on an old-fashioned typewriter complete with pieces of thin, black carbon paper between sheets of white stationery. When I made a mistake (which was quite often), I had to erase each and every copy manually with a special eraser or Wite-Out, a correction fluid that got painted over the offending text like nail polish. The younger generation has no memory of what this was like and thus no way to fully appreciate the miracles that technology has wrought.

What is new about this most recent phase of automation is the promise and threat of artificial intelligence (AI).[22] It threatens to replace not just manual labor but knowledge-based work as well. AI involves teaching computers to learn. Instead of a programmer providing code or a set of instructions for a computer to follow, the computer is provided with masses of data and learns to recognize patterns or linkages and come to conclusions. A small, furry animal with pointed ears, whiskers, and a long tail is a cat. A specific configuration of images on an X-ray is a cancerous tumor. A particular image in front of a self-driving car triggers a warning signal and a turn to the right. When the machine is fed a very large amount of data, it can learn to recognize patterns on its own.

In recent years, such machine learning has made great progress. In a 2015 contest in which AI-enabled computers competed with humans on a task that involved correctly labeling images, the computers outperformed humans for the first time. (The computers are first trained by being exposed to a wide array of images that are correctly labeled but then tested with new, unlabeled images.) AI is already being used to improve search engines, voice recognition software, and the accuracy of medical diagnoses. It will be the miracle behind self-driving cars, delivery drones, and numerous other innovations. Consumers will benefit enormously. However, what happens to jobs is another issue. Many believe that new technology will replace not just blue-collar but also, increasingly, white-collar work. The distinction will not be the color of one's collar but whether one's job is relatively routine or so diverse that it cannot be encapsulated in a set of instructions or recognizable patterns.

When *Time* magazine interviewed a group of experts about a future with AI, almost all expressed a mixed view about what that future might look like, noting that AI could bring great benefits but also great harms.[23] Much depends on how the process is managed. As a White House report noted, "technology is not destiny."[24] The policies we adopt to deal with it will largely determine what happens to human welfare. Bill Gates told *Time* magazine that he believes that in the near future the benefits "should be positive if we manage it well."[25] But he added that as machines become much more intelligent, we need to watch out. Although humans are in charge right now, super smart machines could eventually take over, becoming our masters instead of our servants. As the physicist Stephen Hawking put it, AI could be "the last [event in our history], unless we learn how to avoid the risks."[26] The moral of the story seems to be: teach the machines some manners, and don't forget to turn them off before they start the revolution.

A number of experts believe that long before AI poses an existential threat, these developments will lead to massive job displacement and rising income inequality. Brynjolfsson and McAfee, for example, are optimistic about the massive "bounty" of AI-induced economic growth but deeply worried about how that bounty will be distributed. They believe that although technology will reallocate rather than eliminate jobs, it will also produce joblessness among those displaced and large income gaps between technology's winners and losers.[27]

Estimates of the magnitude of job loss vary widely. According to a much-cited study in 2013 by Carl Frey and Michael Osborne of Oxford University, almost half of all jobs are at "high risk" of automation over the next decade or two.[28] These jobs will primarily be low-skill and low-wage, especially in transportation and manufacturing. But they will include real estate agents, accountants, retail salespeople, and technical writers. (In contrast, jobs for clergy, dentists, and athletic trainers are more likely to survive.)

A more recent study by the McKinsey Global Institute predicts that less than 5 percent of existing positions will be entirely automated with currently demonstrated technologies, but that portions of every job will be.[29] The authors of the report suggest that perhaps half of today's job-related *tasks* could be automated by 2055, but this estimate is both uncertain and dependent on how policies and institutions for dealing with these changes evolve. In other words, rather than eliminating jobs, automation is more likely to transform the nature of work, requiring different skills than those required in today's labor market. The jobs most vulnerable to automation are physically demanding positions, primarily found in manufacturing, food service, and retail establishments.

In a first attempt to quantify the direct effects of robots, Daron Acemoglu of MIT and Pascual Restrepo of Boston University find that robots were responsible for up to 670,000 job losses in manufacturing between 1990 and 2007. Both men and women's jobs were affected, but the effect on male employment was twice as big. These effects persisted after adjusting for the effects of trade, demographics, and type of industry.[30]

A White House report released in December 2016 reviewed the literature on artificial intelligence and automation, arguing once again that automation will primarily affect low-paid, less-skilled, and less-educated workers, threatening to suppress wages at the lower end of the skill spectrum and to increase income inequality as a result.[31]

All in all, many believe that the march of technology is speeding up and that it is going to leave more and more people, especially those without the right skills, behind. So far, however, we are not seeing the effects of any acceleration in the productivity statistics, a mystery that leaves room for skepticism.

Does the march of technology mean there will be fewer jobs in the aggregate or does it just mean that whatever jobs exist will require a new set of skills? Like most economists, I think it's the latter. As old jobs are eliminated, new ones will emerge. Predictions that technology will produce too few jobs in total are not new, and they have consistently proven wrong. Not only the people writing about these issues today but many others, going back to textile workers in the early nineteenth century—the so-called Luddites—have blamed machinery for a lack of jobs. Yet, widespread joblessness resulting from innovation has not occurred.

One reason is because technology lowers costs, which increases demand. Take weaving, for instance. When it was automated in the nineteenth century, the labor required per yard of cloth fell dramatically, but the number of people employed in weaving quadrupled between 1830 and

1900 because cloth became so cheap that far more of it was purchased. Jobs in the industry may have been different (for example, tending machines instead of weaving cloth), but the sector did not suffer.[32] A more recent example is the displacement of bank tellers by ATMs. This reduced costs and led banks to open more branches, with the result that employment has increased, although in a somewhat different set of jobs, such as customer service and sales.[33]

The more basic point is that people's desire for more goods and services is unlimited, especially in an economy in which the invention and marketing of new products is ubiquitous. Of course, should income become so badly distributed that it cuts off consumption, then demand might be insufficient to employ all those who want to work. An economy without consumers is an economy that doesn't function. Lack of sufficient spending caused the Great Depression and has been an issue in more recent downturns as well. The proper recourse is not to slow the pace of innovation but to use fiscal and monetary policy to maintain overall spending and other policies to mitigate rising inequality. This view is widely held among economists but less so among politicians and the general public.

The *Economist* magazine, after reviewing all the arguments and the evidence, concludes that "AI will not cause mass unemployment, but it will speed up the existing trend of computer-related automation, disrupting labour markets just as technological change has done before, and requiring workers to learn new skills more quickly than in the past."[34]

Managing the process of change may be more important than ever. This time may be different because of the breadth and speed of the changes. The economist Tyler Cowen argues that although the Industrial Revolution may have produced mass affluence, it had many ugly side effects, from unhealthy workplaces to child labor. This new technological revolution may also produce both much greater prosperity and new challenges along the way. The needed adjustments may simply be too great, too slow, or too incomplete to keep everyone employed. They may be producing social and political consequences that we are already seeing and more that we cannot anticipate.[35] The outcome depends critically on the policies and institutions that are adopted in response to these changes. Ideally, we should get ahead of the curve, but I fear we are already lagging.

What about Trade?

Many people believe that it is not automation but trade that is destroying American jobs. Experts mostly disagree. One study suggested that trade was responsible for only 13 percent of the total job losses in manufacturing between 2000 and 2010, with the remainder resulting from productivity improvements. In fact, the authors apply 2000-level productivity to 2010-level production and estimate that 21 million workers would have been needed in 2010 to generate the same output that 12 million workers were actually able to produce.[36]

On the other hand, the economists David Autor, Daron Acemoglu, David Dorn, and a number of other scholars have written a series of papers showing that trade, especially competition from Chinese imports, has had more substantial effects on manufacturing jobs as well as on jobs overall. China's entry into the World Trade Organization (WTO) in 2001 lowered concerns among Chinese exporters about possible protectionist measures on the part of the United States and led to a spike in Chinese imports. In a recent paper, Autor and his colleagues find that the China trade shock led to a loss of up to 2.4 million jobs between 1999 and 2011. This reflects not just the direct effects of trade on the affected industries, but also the indirect effects on industries that buy or sell from them and on businesses that benefit from the incomes and purchasing power generated by the workers who were directly affected. Still, this accounts for less than half of the total job losses in manufacturing over this period (5.8 million).[37]

These trade shocks have interacted with a labor force that is less mobile than in the past. Fewer people appear willing to shift from one job to another or to relocate to another state.[38] The reasons for declining mobility remain unclear but may be related to the growth of two-earner families, an aging population, more homes financially under water in the wake of the recession, the high cost of housing in the fastest-growing cities, and a more culturally bunkered country in which people are reluctant to leave a community of like-minded friends and family.

The fierce debate about whether it has been developments in trade or technology that are destroying jobs may miss the point that technology has made it possible to outsource production and that only very cheap labor can compete with today's machines. Certainly competition from an additional 1.3 billion people in China has made a difference. But wages are rising in China and in other less-developed countries, meaning that, in time, trade may be a less important factor than it is now.

The long-term loss of jobs in manufacturing predates China's accession to the WTO in 2001. And even David Autor, whose research is both highly respected and more supportive of a substantial trade effect than many others, agrees that trade has been less important than automation. As he put it to the *New York Times,* "Some of it is globalization, but a lot of it is we require many fewer workers to do the same amount of work. Workers are basically supervisors of machines."[39]

Stagnant Wages and the Retreat from Work

One consequence of changes in trade and technology has been a decline in wages among the less educated. Education has simply not kept pace with the need for higher skills. There has been no growth in wages for those in the bottom half of the wage distribution for three decades, while wages at the top have continued to rise.[40] The result has been a precipitous decline in the relative wages of the less educated (see fig. 3.6).

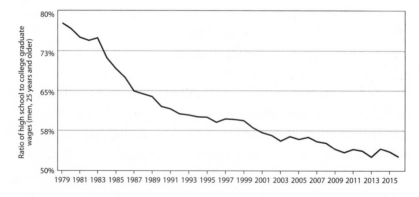

Fig. 3.6. Male high school graduates making less relative to college graduates

Source: Author's analysis of Bureau of Labor Statistics, "Weekly and Hourly Earnings Data from the Current Population Survey," https://data.bls.gov/cgi-bin/surveymost?le

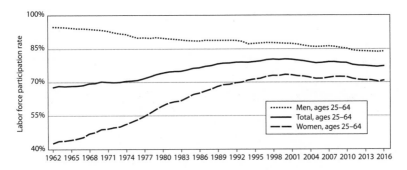

Fig. 3.7. The overall participation rate has been declining for almost two decades
Source: Author's analysis of BLS Current Population Survey, March ASEC supplements

Not only have wages declined, but so has the labor force participation rate of working-age men. Until recently, this trend was offset by women's greater participation, with the result that up until about 2000 overall participation in the labor force continued to rise. Since then, female participation rates have flattened or even dipped a little, resulting in a decline in overall participation rates among the working-age population for the first time in recent history (fig. 3.7).

The retreat from work hasn't been a universal phenomenon: it has, once again, been primarily concentrated among less-educated adults. As we saw in chapter 2 (fig. 2.1), there was only a small difference in participation rates among working-age white men with and without a bachelor's degree back in 1971. Now, there is a difference of 11 percentage points. This divergence in participation by educational attainment is not unique to white men. In fact, it has been even sharper among African-American men.

This retreat from work among adult men has led to much commentary and analysis. Other factors besides trade and technology that may have played a role include a large pool of men (especially minority men) with criminal records whom employers are reluctant to hire, and a set of government benefits that enables some to opt out of work if they can qualify as disabled or destitute. There is also less pressure on men to be breadwinners now that so many women are working.[41] As for the stalled participation rates among women, there is some evidence that the limited access to subsidized child care, paid leave, and flexible hours is taking a toll on their willingness to work.[42]

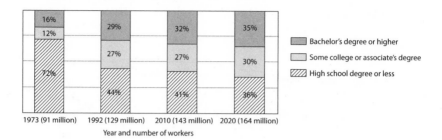

Fig. 3.8. Jobs increasingly require higher levels of educational attainment
Source: Carnevale et al., "Recovery: Job Growth and Education
Requirements through 2020," figure 4
Note: Columns may not add up to 100 percent due to rounding.

Virtually everyone agrees that the need will increase for skilled workers who can do the problem-solving and nonroutine work of the future and that education and training will be critical to the economy's success in adjusting to that need. Anthony Carnevale and his colleagues at Georgetown University project that, by 2020, about two-thirds of the 164 million jobs will require postsecondary education and training beyond high school.[43] In contrast, in 1973, nearly three-quarters of jobs required only a high school diploma or less (fig. 3.8). Many of the new jobs will not necessarily require a four-year degree. What they will require is some technical training beyond the high school level.[44]

Both technology and trade improve overall welfare. In the absence of new technologies, standards of living stagnate. Productivity growth driven primarily by technological advances is a key source of economic growth. Similarly, trade widens markets and enables countries and regions to specialize in whatever they do best, drawing on their own available human or natural resources. That keeps prices to consumers low. Imagine what would happen if every household, or every city or state, had to be totally self-sufficient, producing everything it consumed. People in New York City would have to grow corn, and people in Kansas would have to learn to be high-powered stock analysts. It is much more efficient for them to specialize and to then exchange one valuable good or service for another. Of course, if you are a corn farmer and you live in New York City, you may be out of luck. You either need to move or retrain to be a stock analyst.

The Early Determinants of Opportunity:
Families and Schools

I began working on issues of opportunity and mobility in the mid-1990s and published a little book called *Getting Ahead: Economic and Social Mobility in America* with my Urban Institute colleague Daniel P. McMurrer. We argued that "understanding what lies behind any particular distribution of income very much influences our perceptions of whether that distribution is 'good' or 'bad' and what, if anything, needs to be done about it. Those who believe that the distribution fairly reflects each person's talents and energies will have one view. Those who believe it is a deck stacked to reward those fortunate enough to have started with the right cards will have another. One cannot judge any particular distribution of incomes without knowing what produced it."[45] I still believe that this question lies behind most of our political and cultural divisions.

With this thought in mind, earlier in my career, I was motivated to understand not just where people ended up but also the process that led them there. How much meritocracy was there in the United States? Were we the land of opportunity celebrated in our history and our literature? Or were we instead a less mobile and fluid society than we thought?

Over the last two decades there has been a veritable flood of research on this question.[46] What it shows, in a nutshell, is that you need to pick your parents carefully. If you are born to parents in the poorest fifth of the income distribution, your chance of remaining stuck in that income group is around 35 to 40 percent. If you are born into a higher-income family, the chances are similarly good that you will remain there in adulthood. Substitute other indicators of family background, such as parents' education or occupation or marital status, and one finds a similar picture. Those who are born into better circumstances tend to remain where they began.

As I have long argued, when there is more inequality, when the rungs on the ladder of opportunity grow further apart, it becomes more difficult to climb the ladder. Similarly, in his book *Our Kids: The American Dream in Crisis,* Harvard professor Robert Putnam argues that there are growing gaps not just in income but also in neighborhood conditions, family structure, parenting styles, and educational opportunities.[47] Those gaps will almost inevitably lead to less social mobility in the future. Indeed, these multiple disadvantages or advantages are increasingly clustered, making it harder for children growing up in disadvantaged circumstances to achieve the dream of becoming middle class.[48]

With this as background, it seemed to me that we badly needed a better understanding of why some children move up the ladder and others don't. Family background surely plays a role, but what could we do to change the life trajectories of children, especially those who begin life at the bottom of the ladder? Put differently, what's in the black box that connects where you begin in life to where you end up?

Looking inside the Black Box: The Social Genome Model

To help answer this question, in 2010 I decided to build, with the help of colleagues, a life-cycle model of children's life trajectories. We used data from a survey of about 5,000 children, mostly born in the 1980s, who have been followed by researchers from birth to age forty.[49] Our data track children's progress through multiple life stages, with a corresponding set of success measures at the end of each. For example, children are considered successful at the end of elementary school if they have mastered basic reading and math skills and have acquired the behavioral or noncognitive competencies that have been shown to predict later success. At the end of adolescence, success is measured by whether the young person has completed high school with a GPA of 2.5 or better and has not been convicted of a crime or had a baby as a teenager. These metrics capture common-sense preconceptions about what drives success. But they are also aligned with the empirical evidence on what predicts success. Educational achievement, for example, has a strong effect on later earnings and income, and this well-known linkage is reflected in the data and the model. We cannot be sure that all such effects are causal. For example, it might be your genes that explain both your educational achievement and your later earnings. We do know that the model does a good job of predicting later outcomes.[50]

Three findings from the model stand out:

First, consistent with the broader research literature on social mobility, a child's circumstances at birth matter a lot for later success. The mother's education is particularly important. Being born black is a big handicap. Being born female doesn't hurt much during the school years when girls actually perform better than boys but does create a modest drag during one's adult years.

Second, it's clear that success is a cumulative process. According to our measures, a child who is ready for school at age five is almost twice as likely to be successful at the end of elementary school as one who is not. This doesn't mean that his or her life course is set in stone. Children who get off track at an early age frequently get back on track at a later age; it's just that their chances are not nearly as good. This seems to me to be a powerful argument for intervening early in life.

Third, we can change children's life trajectories with effective social programs. In one illustrative simulation, we chose a battery of rigorously evaluated programs where we knew the effects of the program on children's outcomes at different life stages. The interventions we examined included a parenting program, a high-quality early-education program, a reading and socio-emotional learning program in elementary school, and an effective high school reform. We then used the model to assess the possible impact on low-income children of taking these programs to scale. No single program does very much to close the gap between children from lower- and higher-income families. But the combined effects of multiple programs— that is, from intervening early and often in a child's life—has a surprisingly big cumulative impact. The gap of almost 20 percentage points in the chances of low-income and high-income children reaching the middle class shrinks to 6 percentage points. In other words, we were able to close about two-thirds of the initial gap in the life chances of these two groups of children by providing the less advantaged with a set of effective interventions from birth to age eighteen. The black-white gap narrows, too. Looking at the cumulative impact on adult incomes over a working life and comparing these lifetime income benefits to the costs of the programs, we believe that such investments would pass a cost-benefit test from the perspective of society as a whole, and even from the narrower perspective of the taxpayers who fund the programs.

As Richard Reeves and I wrote in an article for the *Milken Review* that summarized this research,

Understanding the processes that lie beneath the patterns of social mobility is critical. It is not enough to know how good the odds of escaping are for a child born into poverty. We want to know why. We can never eliminate the effects of family background on an individual's life chances. But the wide variation among countries and among cities in the U.S. suggests that we could do better—and that public policy may have an important role to play. Models like the Social Genome are intended to assist in that endeavor, in part by allowing policymakers to bench-test competing initiatives based on the statistical evidence.

America's presumed exceptionalism is rooted in part on a belief that class-based distinctions are less important than in Western Europe. From this perspective, it is distressing to learn that American children do not have exceptional opportunities to get ahead—and that the consequences of gaps in children's initial circumstances might embed themselves in the social fabric over time, leading to even less social mobility in the future.

But there is also some cause for optimism. Programs that compensate at least to some degree for disadvantages earlier in life really can close opportunity gaps and increase rates of social mobility. Moreover, by most any reasonable reckoning, the return on the public investment is high.[51]

The Success Sequence

This modeling of the process of social mobility from birth to age forty added flesh to the bones of the mobility story. It showed why some children succeed and others fail and what one might do about it. But there is an even simpler way to capture at least the main ingredients of later success. It is all about education, work, and family. It turns out that if an individual does just three things—graduates from high school (at least), works full-time, and marries before having children—that person's chance of being poor plummets from around 14 percent to around 2 percent, and his or her chances of being middle class rise to over 70 percent (see fig. 3.9).[52] My colleague Ron Haskins and I call this "the success sequence."[53]

What the country needs are policies that give people a fair chance to succeed in their roles as students, as workers, and as parents in a twenty-first–century economy. These policies should be designed to reward individual initiative and responsibility. But they must also recognize the web of disadvantages and changes in the economy that have made following the success sequence difficult for many Americans. Let's start with the family.

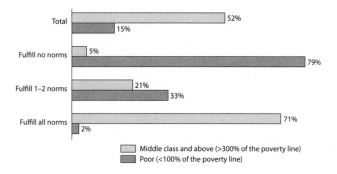

Fig. 3.9. How education, work, and marriage affect economic prospects
Source: Sawhill, "Creating Opportunity for the Forgotten Americans"
Note: Analysis of March 2013 BLS Current Population Survey data. Statistics
refer to calendar year 2012, since survey respondents are asked about income
in the previous calendar year; data only include families with heads of household,
ages 25–64, who do not report receiving disability payments.

Creating Stable Families

The first prerequisite to forging an opportunity society is establishing stable families. Too many young adults are having children before they have formed enduring ties with another adult. About 40 percent of all children in America are born outside of marriage, and almost 80 percent of those children will experience the instability associated with one or both of their parents forming new relationships and having additional children with a new partner, usually also outside of marriage.[54] The sociologists Wendy Wang and W. Bradford Wilcox show that younger generations are increasingly taking nontraditional routes into parenthood. Among baby boomers, about two-thirds of parents ages twenty-eight to thirty-four married before having children, compared to only 40 percent of millennial parents in the same age range.[55]

A large body of research shows that this instability is not good for children. Most obviously, it increasingly takes two paychecks to join the middle class; and those who have children too soon and without a committed partner frequently end up not just with less education and job experience, but also without sufficient means to support a child on their own. They end up experiencing less social mobility and more poverty as a result; their children have poorer outcomes as well; and they are often dependent on government assistance.

Most children now being born to unmarried women under the age of thirty are unplanned. These women tell us that they either did not want a baby or did not want one (or another one) so soon. If we could empower young adults to only have children when they themselves felt ready to become parents, we could reduce unplanned pregnancies and out-of-wedlock births. That alone would greatly improve the life chances of children because they would be born to more mature and experienced parents who are better educated and more committed to one another than is now the case.[56]

The solutions here are often nongovernmental and involve changing social norms around the importance of responsible parenthood, ideally within marriage. Nonprofit and faith-based organizations have a role to play. Some have called for a new generation of government-sponsored marriage programs and for reducing marriage penalties in tax and benefit programs. But these do not appear to be cost-effective ways to bring back the two-parent family. More promising are efforts to make the most effective forms of birth control (IUDs and implants) more widely available at no cost to women. IUDs and implants provide a virtually foolproof way for couples to delay parenthood until they are committed to each other for the long term and feel ready to be parents.[57] Efforts to provide women with good counseling and no-cost birth control in Colorado and a few other places have been highly successful and could be encouraged on a wider scale. A recent report from the consulting firm Bridgespan details the kinds of investments that are needed, and recommends this approach not only as highly cost-effective but also as one of the six "best bets" for improving opportunity in America.[58] We now have evidence that efforts to retrain health providers, to provide low-cost birth control to less advantaged women, and to spread the word about the most effective forms of birth control can have large effects on unplanned pregnancies and the social problems they too often cause.

The Affordable Care Act (ACA) addressed one of the barriers to responsible parenthood: the high cost of the most effective forms of contraception. The requirement to cover contraceptives proved to be one of the most controversial aspects of the ACA, and it has now been weakened. That means the cost issue still needs to be addressed. Otherwise, we will have not just more poverty and less opportunity, but also higher government costs for Medicaid and other safety net programs and much higher rates of abortion.

Improving Education

High school graduation rates for the country as a whole have improved in recent years and are now over 80 percent.[59] In the urban districts of the nation's 50 largest metropolitan areas, however, only 59 percent of students who started high school in 2005 graduated four years later.[60] Continuing to improve high school graduation rates is critical to improving opportunity, particularly for the most disadvantaged, as it is nearly impossible today to secure a decent-paying job without at least a high school diploma.

We also need to improve the quality of K-12 education to better prepare students for the realities of an evolving labor market. When the German company Siemens was recruiting for 800 positions at a plant in Charlotte, North Carolina, 10,000 people applied, but the proportion that was able to pass a basic screening test in reading, writing, and math was less than 15 percent.[61] An obvious solution is to improve K-12 education so that more students finish high school with the competencies needed for both career and college. This should be a very high priority. Right now, only about 40 percent of high school graduates are prepared for either college or a career.[62] They lack not just traditional academic skills, such as reading and math, but also computer literacy or "digital-readiness" and the kind of critical thinking and social skills needed in today's labor market. They are also woefully lacking in knowledge about the kinds of careers that are available and the skills those careers require.

Efforts to reform primary and secondary education have been underway for years with limited results. More effective efforts will take many years before they come to fruition, and a full-scale treatment of how to improve schools is beyond the scope of this book. But there are some examples of reforms that have worked. For example, Mayor Bloomberg's Small Schools of Choice in New York City, a nationwide school model called Career Academies, and an elementary school reading program called Success for All have all proven quite successful.[63]

In addition to expanding these well-evaluated efforts, another way to improve K-12 education is through disruptive innovation. That means more "no excuses" charter schools and more choice (including public school choice), more online learning, and a school financing system less dependent on the wealth of one's neighbors. Not all charter schools have been successful, but the best ones have shown that it is possible to help all children achieve success—and to close racial and socioeconomic gaps.[64] School systems in Denver, in Boston, and in Washington, D.C., have made progress by adopting new models that involve charters and the ability of families to choose among public schools.[65]

What matters more than anything, according to most education research, is what goes on in classrooms. That, in turn, depends on the quality of teachers. Differences in teacher effectiveness vary greatly even within the same school building, and these differences translate into big gains in achievement among children exposed to the right teachers. But what makes a teacher more or less effective? Countless efforts to answer this question have not identified the secret ingredient. We know a good teacher when we see one, but effective teaching isn't correlated with such things as certification, years of schooling, experience (after the first few years), or other measurable attributes.[66] It might help to pay teachers more as a way of recruiting better people into the profession, and it might also help to base payment much more on performance (as measured by what students learn) than is currently the case. It might also be a good idea to simply terminate those in the bottom ranks of performance after their first few years, in addition to rewarding the top performers more handsomely. Teachers' unions have resisted such efforts, but this is standing in the way of helping children learn.

Reform of K-12 schools is critical, but some postsecondary education is increasingly vital in today's economy. There are a number of pressing needs here. The first is more emphasis on career and technical education linked to good jobs that can enable more people to take pride in their specific skills and to launch successful careers. The second is more emphasis on student *performance* (along with need) as one basis for financial aid. American students have fallen behind students in other countries not because they spend too little time in school but because they do not learn enough in the process.[67] In most northern European countries (whose high school students routinely outscore U.S. students on international assessments), college attendance is more heavily subsidized than in the United States, but it is also more conditional on a student's academic performance. So why not base student financial assistance in the United States not just on need, but also on performance in school, creating an incentive for middle and high school students to better prepare for both college and career?[68] It would send a signal to those in high school that preparation matters. By the time a child is an adolescent, his or her own motivation and willingness to study matter. For children from advantaged homes, the motivation often comes from parents. For the less advantaged, the motivation needs to come from good counseling combined with a financial incentive to do well.

Right now the message about the importance of learning is not getting through. Eligibility for a Pell grant, the largest and most important source of financing for postsecondary education among the less affluent, is not at all dependent on performance, only on family income and the "seat time" needed to obtain a high school degree. Currently, we are spending about $30 billion a year on Pell grants.[69] Much of the money is spent on students who are ill prepared to do college-level work. They end up using much of their Pell grant funding to take remedial courses in college, often drop out, and end up in debt as well. Neither these students nor the taxpayers who fund the program are well served.

In sum, we need to not only increase educational attainment in the traditional sense (by improving high school graduation rates and postsecondary completion rates) but also improve what children actually learn. The Siemens story says it all. There will not be jobs for those who don't have the knowledge and the skills—including such soft skills as getting to work on time, taking initiative, and working well with others—that are required for success. There are many young people with a high school—or even a college—degree who are still not career ready. We need not just better schools and better teachers but also a new social contract between schools and students. The message needs to be that if you want to get ahead, you don't just need to graduate; you also need to do your homework and actually learn what you are being taught. The Defense Department estimates that 71 percent of the roughly 34 million seventeen- to twenty-four-year-olds in the United States would not be eligible to serve in the military even if they wanted to.[70] The reasons include lack of a high school diploma, obesity, mental health, drugs, and felony convictions. But it's also because about a quarter of high school graduates cannot pass the military's qualifying exam. It's not an encouraging picture of today's youth, who, according to military leaders, are less prepared than earlier generations, despite rising levels of schooling.[71]

In conclusion, children can no longer expect to do better than their parents. The days when achieving a middle-class lifestyle was an American birthright are over. For too many people, that reality has not sunk in. In addition, although government programs such as a high-quality preschool experience have a role to play, they are not a good substitute for a two-parent married family in which parenting is a choice and not an accident. This book is mainly about work, and our research on the success sequence suggests it has a powerful effect on one's chances of being middle class. But it would be a mistake to assume that we can focus on work without worrying about families and education.

4

Why Economic Growth
Is Not Enough

ALMOST EVERYONE LOOKS AT THE FACTS REVIEWED in the last chapter and says the way to improve the lives of the forgotten Americans is obvious. Conservatives call for more growth. Liberals call for less inequality. Their logic is impeccable. As we saw in the last chapter, less growth and more inequality have both contributed to less upward mobility for recent generations. But are these the best solutions? And even if they are, do we know how to achieve them?

Let's start with growth. My goal in this chapter is to convince you that it is not the panacea many assume. That's not to say it wouldn't help if we really knew how to get more of it. But we don't. The recipe for doing so remains contentious at best. And even if we did know how to create more growth, it wouldn't necessarily make most of us better off.

In the following chapter, I raise some similar questions about the merits of counting on redistribution to solve the problem.

As a reader, you may be eager to get to what I think are the "real" solutions. So why am I burdening you with these two chapters? Because the longer the political class keeps making promises on which they cannot deliver, the more disillusionment there will be. That disillusionment, in turn, is a recipe for the kind of desperation that led to the election of Donald Trump. But there could be worse to come if these issues are not better understood.

My argument is that the focus needs to be much more directly on jobs and wages—topics I will come to in the final four chapters of the book.

Economic Growth

On June 26, 2017, Ben Bernanke gave a speech at the European Central Bank Forum called "When Growth Is Not Enough." In it he mentioned four worrying trends: stagnant wages, declining mobility, social dysfunction, and political alienation. He argued that "the credibility of economists has been damaged by our insufficient attention, over the years, to the problems of economic adjustment and by our proclivity toward top-down, rather than bottom-up, policies." He concluded by saying that growth is generally a good thing, but that recent political developments have shown why it is not enough.[1]

The standard story about economic growth is not necessarily wrong—it is just very insufficient. Growth does produce higher incomes and the tax revenues needed to address various problems. Whether it produces jobs is a more complicated question. After all, in the short term, rising productivity or output per hour means fewer hours of work, not more.

Here's the heart of my argument. Boosting long-term growth is both harder than most people seem to realize and less likely to produce the outcomes they expect. First, the process of economic growth is quite mysterious, leading us to think we know more about how to improve it than we do. Second, we measure growth badly, focusing too much on GDP and not enough on whether more GDP will produce the things most people really care about, including jobs. Third, more growth will not necessarily make us happier. Finally, many of the policies pursued in the name of growth might actually make matters worse—that is, actually slow the rate of progress. Restricting immigration and trade are good examples.

Imagine that economic growth is a car. It can go fast or slow—80 mph or 50 mph. But we don't exactly know how the car's engine works. In addition, the speedometer is imperfect, making it unclear if we are actually moving as fast as we think or even moving in the right direction. Third, even if we get to our destination quickly, we may be quite disappointed when we arrive. It turns out that money doesn't buy happiness. And finally, we might be filling up the car's tank with the wrong kind of gas (for example, restricting trade)—possibly slowing it down in the process.

The Sources of Growth
(or, What's in the Engine Anyway?)

Economists have traditionally argued that long-run economic growth comes from three sources. First are increases in the size of the labor force; second are increases in the amount of physical or human capital per worker (that is, machines and knowledge); and third are increases in the efficiency with which both labor and capital are used (sometimes called "total factor productivity"). This last element is presumed to capture technological innovation, organizational effectiveness, and other improvements in the way labor and capital are used. Let's call this the Solow model after the Nobel-prize–winning economist Robert Solow, who invented it back in 1956.[2] It is a kind of recipe in which one combines labor and capital (in a ratio of about $2 of labor for $1 of capital) and mixes them in a blender with a big dose of some secret ingredients. Most people call these secret ingredients "technological change" or "innovation," but the truth is that it is all the things that we can't account for in the rest of the equation. One well-known economist called it "a measure of our ignorance."[3] When I took my PhD oral exams, one of the first questions I was asked was to describe the Solow model. When I dutifully recited its elements and then dubbed the residual "a measure of our ignorance," my examiners nodded approvingly. Of course, there have been many subsequent efforts to unpack and explain this residual (including so-called endogenous growth theory), but it still remains something of a mystery.

Although labor, capital, and technology are the major sources of *long-term* growth, over shorter periods, an economy can operate well below its potential growth trajectory. This occurs when total spending by consumers, businesses, foreigners, and government is insufficient to employ all the resources that are available. Actual GDP is often lower than potential GDP (particularly during recessions), and from 2007 to 2016 this "output gap" was large (fig. 4.1). Its total size over this period was roughly $4 trillion.[4]

The remedies for too little overall spending (demand) may be different from those that might boost supply or potential GDP. During the Great Recession, what was needed was an expansionary fiscal and monetary policy to inject more spending into the economy. But by 2017, with resources

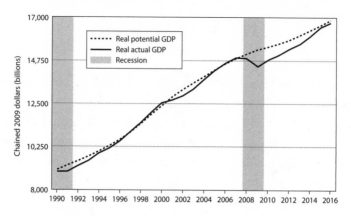

Fig. 4.1. Actual GDP can fall below potential
Source: U.S. Congressional Budget Office, Real Potential Gross Domestic Product,
FRED (Federal Reserve Bank of St. Louis), accessed August 2, 2017,
https://fred.stlouisfed.org/series/GDPPOT

more fully employed, a greater focus on expanding supply or potential GDP was, once again, more appropriate.

The story is a little more complicated than this because the demand and supply side of the economy are inextricably intertwined. There is a famous dictum learned by most economics students called Say's Law. It says "supply creates its own demand," meaning that if goods and services are produced, this will generate income for workers and capitalists that will be recirculated in the form of purchasing power for those same goods and services. But, as Harvard's Larry Summers argues, we can stand this dictum on its head by pointing out that it's also true that demand creates its own supply.[5] Without sufficient purchasing power in the economy, there is no incentive for businesses to create a supply of goods and services. They will invest less in capital equipment or in expanding their businesses; they will hire fewer workers; they might even lose their appetite for making their operations more efficient and for adopting new technologies. Let's stipulate that both versions of Say's Law are true—that supply affects demand, but that demand also affects supply. My own view is that we have given too little attention to demand. Federal Reserve Chair Janet Yellen put it well at a conference held by the Federal Reserve Bank of Boston on October 14, 2016: "If strong economic conditions can partially reverse supply-side damage after it has occurred, then policymakers may want to aim at being more accommodative during recoveries than would be called for under the traditional view that supply is largely independent of demand."[6]

Another reason why demand is important is because when labor markets are slack, it is the forgotten Americans or those at the bottom of the distribution who suffer the most—a point that I emphasize in chapter 7.

The challenge is to decide whether it is demand or supply that is dominant at a particular point in history. For the period from 2008 to 2015, for example, the problem was not too little supply; it was too little demand. As of the time when this book went to press, the unemployment rate had declined to very low levels, suggesting we may be entering a period when supply constraints are becoming more important, but also a period in which high levels of demand are coaxing out new sources of supply, thus creating more opportunities for investment and more reasons for the jobless to reenter the labor market.

What then can be done to increase the long-term growth of the economy once we have eliminated any slack with adequate demand?

The usual answers are to encourage labor force participation and to invest in plants and equipment, education, and infrastructure. However, as desirable as these may be, they provide only a temporary bump up in the *level* of GDP, not an improvement in the long-term growth *rate*. Let's say it takes a decade to boost the *level* of GDP by 1 percent—a reasonable estimate of the effects of the Republican tax bill enacted in 2017 on the economy.[7] Then the growth *rate* of GDP will be 0.1 percent higher over the decade, but once the GDP reaches its higher level, there are no further changes. Whatever investments have been undertaken as a result of the bill will have occurred and had their effect. The only way to affect the long-term growth rate is with continuing technological advances. What drives these advances, in turn, is what remains something of a mystery.

In short, economists are far less certain about which policies to pursue than our political discourse would suggest. If the key factors in the growth model are the amount of physical and human capital and a residual that is "a measure of our ignorance," what is one supposed to do? What, for example, determines private investments in research and development that then lead to innovation? How does the protection of intellectual property through patents affect innovation? How do trade and immigration affect growth by opening up an economy to new ideas and fiercer competition? What about antitrust enforcement to keep the economy competitive? All these make sense, in principle, but just how much they matter remains unclear. And how do we think about the trade-offs between the growth-enhancing benefits of trade and immigration and their possible negative effects on jobs?

Some argue that we need to reallocate resources from entitlement programs to public investments in infrastructure, education, and research, and that we need to reduce budget deficits to free up funds for private investment. The problem is that liberals don't want to slow the growth of entitlements, and conservatives don't want higher taxes. Both are necessary ingredients in a growth-enhancing deficit reduction package. The Simpson-Bowles commission tried to get an agreement on a compromise plan and failed.[8] So we are stuck.

More profoundly, how do institutions, including democratic governance itself, affect growth? The importance of political stability, lack of corruption, and the rule of law have long been recognized as key ingredients in rates of growth among emerging nations. The relevance of political institutions in more advanced countries should not be neglected. The economy of the United Kingdom in the wake of Brexit and of the United States in the wake of a populist uprising and a gridlocked U.S. Congress may suffer from self-inflicted wounds. Both a Harvard Business School report and a book entitled *The Captured Economy* by Brink Lindsey (a libertarian) and Steven Teles (a liberal) emphasize that good governance is essential to economic growth.[9] The quality of policy making and the competence of government, these authors argue, have declined. A variety of special interests have captured the process in recent years. Market concentration is increasing, corporate profits are rising, new business formation is declining, and the variation in productivity across firms is growing—all indications that the economy is less competitive and dynamic than it used to be. Although government can be a force for good, if it becomes a tool of the monied and powerful, it can lead to rent seeking (excess profits), which slows growth and redistributes income upward. Perhaps the new watchword for economic policy should be to at least "do no harm."

I am tempted to believe that in a healthy (recession-free) economy with a well-functioning democracy and education system, innovation will be the normal order of the day. Conservative orthodoxy says the way to get more growth is to reduce taxes. But Bill Gates and Mark Zuckerberg weren't worrying about their tax rates when they started down a path that has revolutionized the economy. They were simply curious as well as talented and persistent.

My main point here is that long-term growth is mysterious and that economists remain both divided and uncertain about how to increase it. We need a bit more humility on this front. We know more about how to redirect growth than we do about how to get more of it. The purposes to which growth is directed matter.

Why GDP Is a Faulty Measure
(or, Why You Shouldn't Trust the Speedometer)

Many of the benefits and costs of growth don't show up in GDP. As I emphasize throughout this book, they tell us nothing about how GDP is distributed among the population, how much time has to be spent to produce it, or the extent to which a rise in GDP creates jobs.

Economists are well aware that GDP is not an indicator of social welfare. That said, this has never stopped the media from obsessing over the latest figures or politicians from promising unrealistically high GDP growth rates and the jobs they believe more growth will create.

The United States is way ahead of countries like France on narrow economic metrics: French GDP per capita is less than two-thirds that of the United States. But when a broader metric is used, the gap is much narrower. Two economists, Charles I. Jones and Peter J. Klenow, find that the average person in France is about 92 percent as well-off as the average American, despite France's much lower GDP.[10]

But on at least three fronts, the French can claim to be leading better lives:

First, Americans work an extra hour every day. In 2015, the average employee worked around 1,470 hours in France and 1,780 hours in the United States.[11]

Second, the gap between rich and poor is much wider in the United States than in France. The share of income taken by the top 1 percent in

France increased by 7 percent between 1970 and 2012. In the United States, that share rose by 142 percent over the same period.[12]

Third, the French are much healthier than Americans. Despite the fact that the United States spends more per capita on health care than almost every other nation in the world, we lag behind countries like France in health outcomes. The French have access to universal health coverage.

For this and many other reasons, they experience higher life expectancies and lower infant mortality rates. And despite all that wine and cheese, they have lower rates of obesity than their American counterparts.[13]

While GDP leaves out a lot, it also counts some things that provide a misleading sense of progress. A prominent example is the increased market work of women and the accompanying decline in their unmeasured work at home. As women have entered the labor force, they have not only increased the size of the labor force but also substituted purchased goods and services (child care, prepared foods, commercial cleaning services, and the like) for activities that they used to perform themselves. All this gives a big boost to the GDP. Overall, new opportunities for women have been good for women and good for the productivity of the economy, but they have also masked what otherwise would have been a much slower increase in measured GDP. If you have been watching the GDP barometer in the decades since the 1970s, you can thank women for much of its rise.[14] Since about 2000, however, women's workforce participation rates have stalled, with predictable restraining effects on the growth of the economy. The next time someone tells you that we used to have higher rates of economic growth than now and that there's no reason we can't have them again, remind them that we are running out of stay-at-home wives who might be coaxed to join the paid labor force. We are also aging. Both facts further reduce increases in labor force participation, a major driver of growth.

Then there is the question of how to handle improvements in quality and variety, including goods that didn't even exist in the past. Today's TV sets are vastly superior to the boxy, small-screen versions I remember from my youth, which, in turn, were a huge improvement over my early childhood, which included no TV at all. (I had to make do with a radio, but I can attest that this had absolutely no effect on my sense of pleasure since what you don't know, you can't miss.)

Such examples are a huge headache for the statisticians, who must ad-just the GDP for price inflation, something that's dicey in a world where a product didn't exist in the past or was a very different animal.[15] They have made some limited attempts to correct for this problem, but it's fair to conclude that we have underestimated the rise in GDP for these kinds of reasons.

Finally, there is the problem of things that are free or virtually free and therefore don't get counted in GDP. The problem is becoming far more ubiquitous in our digitalized and communications-happy economy of smart phones, mobile devices, and the internet. Think of Facebook, Google Maps, Kayak, Instagram, or YouTube. Once the platform has been created, the marginal cost of adding one more consumer is close to zero. Yet the market keeps growing since what advertisers care about is eyeballs, and what users care about is a larger network and more user-generated content. So consumers may reap a surplus (more enjoyment than they have to pay for), but the GDP will fail to record any improvement.[16]

Up to this point, I have said very little about the "bads" that get included in GDP but which no one believes enhance social welfare. Damage to the environment is one prominent example.[17] Wars and natural disasters that destroy existing housing and infrastructure but require subsequent re-building are another.

In short, we need to be aware of all the things that GDP doesn't count. It doesn't count how people feel if all the gains of growth are going to the top of the distribution; it doesn't count the value of people's time when they are not at work. It doesn't count the amount of debt or deferred maintenance or environmental damage we are leaving to the next generation. It doesn't count the ways in which better health or better education enhance human capabilities, life expectancy, and self-sufficiency.

Herbert Stein, a much-respected conservative economist, once said that the problem with inequality was that "it is unlovely." So are climate change, crumbling roads, low-wage workers reporting to their jobs with the flu because they lack paid sick leave, and many other aspects of American life.

Yes, there may well be some trade-offs. We may have to accept a slightly lower rate of GDP growth to accomplish some of these other goals, such as an improvement in the environment. But I'm betting that these improvements will make us better off and that any trade-offs are small to nonexistent. I'm also arguing that we know more about how to repurpose growth than we know about how to speed it up.

So I think it's time to redirect the conversation about growth in some new directions. As Robert Kennedy said about the GDP during his 1968 presidential run, "It does not include the beauty of our poetry or the strength of our marriages, the intelligence of our public debate or the integrity of our public officials. It measures neither our wit nor our courage, neither our wisdom nor our learning, neither our compassion nor our devotion to our country, it measures everything in short, except that which makes life worthwhile. And it can tell us everything about America except why we are proud that we are Americans."[18]

Why Money Doesn't Buy Happiness
(or, What to Expect When You Think You've Arrived)

We have all heard the phrase "money doesn't buy happiness," but how many of us really believe it and live our lives accordingly?

It turns out it is half right and half wrong, based on a large number of empirical studies. What they show, in brief, is that money does buy happiness if we are talking about individuals living in a particular country at a particular point in time. In this case, the more income you have, the happier you will be. But over longer periods, as everyone's income rises and an entire society becomes more affluent, the relationship tends to go away. It's also the case that rich countries, like the United States, aren't necessarily happier than, say, moderately well-off ones, like France. This phenomenon is often called "the Easterlin paradox," after the economist who discovered it.[19]

So what explains the Easterlin paradox? Why is income related to happiness at a point in time but not over the longer run? And why doesn't the relationship hold more strongly across countries? A common explanation is that what brings contentment is being *relatively* well-off, compared to one's expectations. Those expectations are set by what others in one's own society have. Over time, as everyone's income grows, one's benchmark for evaluating well-being changes. Similarly, incomes in some other country are not as relevant a benchmark as incomes in one's own country. What matters most for happiness or well-being is how one is doing in comparison to others in one's own social circle, one's own country, and one's own time. As emphasized in chapter 2, one reason the white working class is unhappy—even less content than blacks, who are objectively worse off— is because they believe they have fallen behind where they should be, based on history and their own expectations.

The implications of this view of the world are profound. Economic growth is fine, but *if it is accompanied by growing income inequality, happiness or well-being may decline.*[20] The reason? Those in the bottom of the distribution are now *relatively* worse off even if their absolute income has grown. As we saw in chapters 2 and 3, the gaps between more- and less-advantaged Americans have grown sharply. The gain in well-being among the rich is more than offset by the decline in *relative* well-being among the not-so-rich. Why, you might ask, don't the gains and losses cancel each other, leaving the country as a whole in the same state of well-being as before? The answer is because, subjectively, people react more strongly to losses than to gains. In behavioral economics this is called "loss aversion," and it has been well documented in numerous experiments.[21]

The bottom line here should be clear. *If we want to improve well-being, more GDP accompanied by growing income inequality won't do. We need inclusive growth instead.*

Misguided Policies
(or, Driving with the Wrong Kind of Gas)

Although economic growth is mysterious, incompletely measured, and not as consistent with human welfare or human happiness as many seem to believe, that hasn't stopped our elected officials from claiming that they know how to boost growth and that more growth would be an unadulterated blessing.

The orthodox Republican view is that growth is all about tax cuts and deregulation. To this Republican orthodoxy, Trumpism has added three new ideas: bring back manufacturing jobs, restrict trade, and curb immigration.

On the plus side, Trumpism at least focuses on jobs and not just on growth. But what's the evidence that any of this will work in practice?

Supply-Side Tax Cuts and Deregulation

For decades now, ever since the election of Ronald Reagan, Republicans have been preaching tax cuts and deregulation as the way to spur the growth of the economy. Tax cuts, it is argued, will create incentives to work, to save, and to invest. This "supply-side" thinking was originally championed by economists such as Arthur Laffer, whose namesake Laffer Curve implies that lower marginal tax rates provide such large incentives to work, save, and invest that we don't need to worry that they will lose revenue and adversely affect the federal budget.[22] The Trump administration appears to have bought into this extreme version of supply-side economics, arguing that massive tax cuts will pay for themselves by producing much faster growth.

The empirical evidence on supply-side economics suggests that it is 90 percent ideology and 10 percent fact. It's not that these issues don't matter; it's that they are being blown way out of proportion to what the evidence suggests about their effects on growth, especially over the long term.[23] Lower tax rates have not generated the revenue promised, nor have they spurred significant economic growth.

President Clinton raised taxes on the wealthy in 1993, and President George W. Bush reduced them in 2001. Yet both real GDP and jobs grew much more rapidly under Clinton than under Bush.[24] Of course, these facts by themselves don't prove that tax cuts can't spur growth, but they at least shift the burden of proof to the advocates of supply-side policies.

Turning to the more rigorous evidence, my colleague William Gale, along with Dartmouth's Andrew Samwick, have reviewed much of it and found supply-side notions wanting.[25] For example, cross-country research reveals no relationship between top marginal tax rates and a country's rate of growth between 1960 and 2010.[26]

Evidence from state-level tax cuts leads to similar conclusions. The state of Kansas is the poster child for supply-side theory's flaws. Under Governor Sam Brownback, the state enacted an enormous tax cut but grew more slowly in its wake than other states. The experiment was such a disaster that the

Republican legislature finally had to raise taxes and override the governor's veto to do so.[27] Some conservatives believe tax cuts "starve the beast" and are thus the best way to shrink the government. There's some truth to this, but both the Reagan and Bush tax cuts, as well as the Kansas experience, have led not so much to smaller government as to dangerously high deficits and the need to raise taxes in response.

Gale and Samwick sum up the evidence this way:

> The argument that income tax *cuts* raise growth is repeated so often that it is sometimes taken as gospel. However, theory, evidence, and simulation studies tell a different and more complicated story. Tax cuts offer the potential to raise economic growth by improving incentives to work, save, and invest. But they also create income effects that reduce the need to engage in productive economic activity, and they may subsidize old capital, which provides windfall gains to asset holders that undermine incentives for new activity. In addition, tax cuts as a stand-alone policy (that is, not accompanied by spending cuts) will typically raise the federal budget deficit. The increase in the deficit will reduce national saving—and with it, the capital stock owned by Americans and future national income—and raise interest rates, which will negatively affect investment. The net effect of the tax cuts on growth is thus theoretically uncertain and depends on both the structure of the tax cut itself and the timing and structure of its financing.[28]

In 2017, Republicans cut the corporate tax rate from 35 to 21 percent. Some reduction in the rate made sense, given that the U.S. rate of 35 percent was high in comparison to rates in other advanced countries, but little was done to close corporate loopholes that favor one sector over another, broaden the tax base, and reduce the deficit.

This very large corporate tax cut was justified by Trump's economic advisers on the grounds that it would boost investment, create jobs, and raise wages.[29] The theory behind their contention is that corporate tax cuts increase returns to capital, lead to more saving and investment, and that more investment raises worker productivity and wages. Critics note the lack of evidence for such effects.[30] There has been no shortage of savings in recent decades; investment spending has been relatively weak, mainly because of inadequate consumer demand; and whatever productivity gains have occurred have had a limited impact on wages for the typical worker.

To be sure, there remains some uncertainty about who benefits from a corporate tax cut, but most independent analysts assume that about 75 percent goes to the owners of capital without "trickling down" to workers.[31] In short, the main effect of these tax cuts is to reward capital, not labor, and shareholders rather than workers.

As for regulations, they do need to be reviewed on a case-by-case basis, so we can see if the benefits are worth the costs. That has been the practice in all recent administrations, not just the current one. Tougher reviews may be in order. Some regulations are poorly designed or not needed. But smart regulation doesn't mean sweeping away the whole enchilada. Too little regulation can lead to financial crises or environmental damage that in the end costs far more than any immediate benefits deregulation may provide.

There is one supply-side strategy that, unlike tax cuts and canceling regulations, might really work to improve economic growth, and that is bigger and more effective investments in education and training. According to one study, simply raising the test scores of U.S. students to match those of Canadian students would—once these students entered the labor force—have a huge impact on our GDP, enough to add 20 percent to the paycheck of every worker in the United States.[32] As usual, this specific estimate has to be taken with a grain of salt, but the general value of education in a technologically sophisticated world cannot be in doubt.

Bring Back Manufacturing Jobs

Nostalgia for the days when even a high school graduate could earn a decent living working in a steel or auto plant is understandable, but those days are over. Manufacturing jobs are dwindling and are not coming back. These jobs have declined from nearly 18 million in the late 1980s to just over 12 million in 2016, a decline of 30 percent in under 30 years (see fig. 4.2).[33] Manufacturing employment accounts for just 8 percent of all jobs, and those that pay decent wages (precision welders, engineers) require more technical education and training than in the past.[34]

The major reason for this decline in employment is rising productivity. Manufacturing's output as a share of GDP has remained roughly stable over the past 50 years, despite substantial declines in employment.[35]

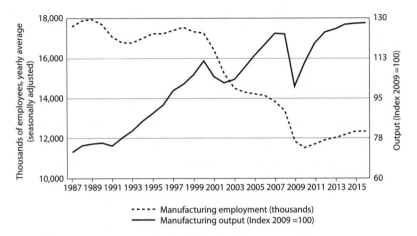

Fig. 4.2. Manufacturing output has increased as employment declines
Source: Bureau of Labor Statistics, "Databases, Tables & Calculators by Subject,"
Series ID PRS30006093 and Series ID CES3000000001

The growth of jobs is not in manufacturing. It is in health, education, social assistance, and related fields. According to Bureau of Labor Statistics (BLS) projections, six of the ten fastest-growing industries over the next decade will be in the health care and social assistance sector, while seven of the ten most rapidly declining industries will be in the manufacturing sector. BLS anticipates home health care services to add 760,000 jobs over the 2014–2024 period, a compound annual increase of 4.8 percent.[36] As Binyamin Appelbaum put it in the *New York Times*, "soon, we will be living in the United States of Home Health Aides, yet the [presidential] candidates keep talking about steelworkers."[37]

Restrict Trade

Although the public and many elected officials blame increased competition from low-wage countries like China and Mexico for the disappearance of jobs, most economists believe that automation has played a bigger role. That doesn't mean trade hasn't had some adverse effects on jobs, especially in manufacturing.

The public, in its natural concern about jobs, often overlooks the positive benefits of trade, and thus the harm that a more protectionist stance might inflict. The reason the public may be misled is because the job losses caused by trade are very concentrated and visible, while the benefits are diffuse and harder to see.

One clear benefit is lower prices to consumers. Those who have shopped at Walmart may not realize that their "everyday low prices" are linked to their ability to import much of what we buy. Imports also expand our choices; does anyone want to be denied the opportunity to buy all kinds of fresh fruit and vegetables in the winter months? Trade also provides a check on lack of competition in domestic sectors of the economy. Finally, jobs created by exports tend to pay more than those in import-competing sectors.[38]

What would happen if there was an attempt to restrict trade—by raising tariffs, for example? First, the value of the dollar would rise relative to the currencies of our trading partners as they bought more from us and we bought less from them. But that would reduce our ability to export and would adversely affect jobs in export-dependent companies, like Boeing. In addition, if these protectionist policies generated retaliatory actions by other countries, we would see less economic growth, and possibly a recession.

Even if there were no retaliation, another problem with protectionist policies is that they often boomerang on domestic producers. The simplistic view of trade is that we buy final products from other countries and that by placing a tariff on their goods we can reduce imports and save jobs. But in today's global economy the reality is that there are complex supply chains of intermediate goods that make up a large volume (about two-thirds, according to my colleague David Dollar) of trade.[39] The back of an iPhone reads "Designed by Apple in California. Assembled in China," but even this simplifies the story quite a bit. Different components might have been manufactured in Japan, Korea, or Germany, while the raw materials might come from dozens of different locations around the world. These global supply chains make it impossible to know how to target any protectionist measure such as a tariff or to predict its effects.

One reason the United States has large trade deficits has nothing to do with China, Mexico, or other low-wage countries. It is because we are consuming (via imports) more than we produce and investing more than we save (remember that budget deficits are a form of negative saving). The only way we can do this is by borrowing from (for example, by selling bonds to) other countries, especially China. This borrowing means that eventually we will have to earmark a portion of our domestic production to pay interest and dividends to foreigners. For those who don't believe our trade wounds are largely self-inflicted due to our excessive borrowing and inadequate national saving (think large federal deficits again), it is worth noting that Japan and Germany also compete with China but do not have trade deficits as a result.[40]

We need a much more robust way of helping workers hurt by all kinds of economic change, of which trade is only one component. Think of the number of clerical jobs that have been destroyed by desktop computers, the replacement of gas station attendants by self-service gas pumps, bank tellers by ATMs, and retail clerks by online shopping.

A big issue here is the speed at which change—whether automation or competition from imports—occurs. These changes have an upside—we call them "innovation" or "competition"—but if they happen very rapidly, and people do not have time to adjust, they can be very harmful to those who lose their jobs. The right response is not to restrict trade; it is to make sure it is fair and to help those who are adversely affected adjust to the shock.

Limit Immigration

Still another misguided solution to the decline in work and wages among the less skilled is to cut off the flow of immigrants into the United States. The most extreme version, of course, is President Trump's desire to build a wall.

Since 2009, the number of undocumented immigrants has remained stable at around 11 million people, with the number entering the country being roughly equal to those leaving. The net flow could increase again as the U.S. economy strengthens. Whether a wall or tougher border enforcement can significantly stem that flow is uncertain.

But do immigrants take the jobs or reduce the wages of native-born workers, or impose other costs on the nation? According to a comprehensive study by the National Academies of Sciences, Engineering, and Medicine, any impacts on wages and employment are small and concentrated among prior immigrants or native-born workers with less than a high school degree. Immigration, according to the study, has a positive impact on long-run economic growth. Skilled immigrants have been a source of new ideas, entrepreneurship, and higher productivity. Less-skilled immigrants have lowered consumer prices in areas such as child care, food preparation, house cleaning, and construction.[41]

From a fiscal perspective, educating the children of immigrants does balloon state and local budgets, although these children will typically grow up to contribute positively to the economy and to the federal budget as they begin to pay taxes. Their parents contribute more (in taxes) than they cost the government, primarily because they arrive in their prime working years but are still younger than the native-born population and thus less dependent on Social Security and Medicare.[42]

Immigration policy clearly needs reform, and linking entry into the United States to skills as well as to existing family relationships would help the economy, especially the forgotten Americans, as the number of immigrants competing with lower-wage workers would fall, possibly boosting wages among the less skilled.

Still, as two of the National Academies study researchers concluded, "The panel's comprehensive examination of the data on this contentious subject revealed many important benefits of immigration—including on economic growth, innovation, and entrepreneurship."[43] Will some native workers be adversely affected and some local governments experience new fiscal burdens? Will cultural anxieties rise? Yes, but we should be clear that the overall effects of immigration on the U.S. economy are positive.

Conclusion

We know less about how to create growth than we think, and many of the supply-side proposals on offer could actually make matters worse by ballooning the national debt. That doesn't mean more growth wouldn't help. In particular, we need greater investment in education, training, infrastructure, and research. These are the building blocks of long-term growth that only government can provide. Just as important to restoring growth is a better-functioning democracy dedicated to improving the lives of all Americans. What we have gotten instead is rhetorically camouflaged policies that deliver new benefits to the most fortunate at the expense of middle- and working-class Americans, all in the name of growth. Such policies are doubly bad. They don't solve any real problems, and they increase cynicism about government itself.

Restoring a government that is seen as caring about the broad middle class couldn't be more important. In his interesting book *The Wealth of Humans,* Ryan Avent argues that the digital revolution will create enormous tensions.[44] One tension will be between winners and losers within a society. Another will be between societies that manage the process well and those that don't. Managing the process well means figuring out how to share the wealth more adequately and how to attract the talent that exists in a global economy with seven billion people. That's a huge pool from which to draw. Talented workers will want to migrate to countries with the right kind of governance and institutions. Countries that don't manage the process well will lose out. Good governance means building the kinds of institutions that will both create prosperity and enable most people to benefit. The social democratic model that evolved in response to the Industrial Revolution, for example, created institutions such as social insurance, public education, unions, and safety nets. These institutions created the skills needed at the time but also softened the hard edges of market capitalism. What is needed now is a similarly farsighted effort to begin to adapt our social institutions and public policies to the digital revolution, an aging population, changes in the family, and unprecedented inequality.

5

The Limits of Redistribution

IF CURRENT EFFORTS TO PROMOTE OVERALL growth are misguided, what about simply trying to make sure whatever growth we have is more equitably distributed? That goal is a worthy one. We need more broadly shared prosperity for three reasons. First, an economy in which all the gains go to the top is unlikely to provide the purchasing power needed for its own sustainability. It may be no accident that both the 1930s Depression and the Great Recession of 2008–2011 were both preceded by peak levels of inequality.[1] Second, the failure of most people to experience upward mobility (as shown in chapter 3) breeds alienation and lack of trust in government, undermining its legitimacy. Finally, the moral case for reducing inequality is strong. The lottery of birth plays a major role in who wins and who loses in a market economy. Yes, hard work and talent should be rewarded, but not everyone is fortunate enough to have begun the race at the same starting line, ready to compete from day one.

Progressives have advanced a number of proposals to achieve a broader-based prosperity. In this chapter I feature two examples: a universal basic income and a children's allowance. One problem with these or related proposals is that they tend to be very expensive. Another problem is that they are inconsistent with the expectation that people should support themselves and their families through work. The sheer magnitude of the inequality challenge, in combination with Americans' dislike of taxes and anything that looks like welfare, limits what can be accomplished. So does basic human psychology, in which the losses (from higher taxes) are weighted more heavily than any promised gains and people remain overly optimistic about their own chances of becoming rich.

A Universal Basic Income?

The most radical of these new proposals would provide every American with a basic income. This idea has gotten a boost from the fact that several business and union leaders have made a strong case for it. They argue that technology is going to raise productivity to unprecedented levels but leave many without jobs in the process. The solution, they argue, is to use that enhanced prosperity to provide a basic income to those whose jobs may no longer be needed. Andrew Stern, former president of the Service Employees International Union (SEIU), believes that, as important as unions were to worker welfare in the twentieth century, they won't work as well in the twenty-first. Instead, he argues for an unconditional stipend that would go to every American as technology replaces jobs—jobs that used to enable people to earn a middle-class income. He says, "If capital trumps labor, the people who own will keep getting wealthier and the people who supply labor will become less necessary. And this is exactly what AI and robotics and software are now doing: substituting capital for labor."[2]

Some localities are experimenting with different renditions of a universal basic income, or UBI. An experiment in Oakland, California, sponsored by Sam Altman, the president of the Silicon Valley firm Y Combinator, is providing cash grants ranging from $1,000 to $2,000 a month to one hundred families. Other experiments are underway or planned in Finland, in Canada, in the Netherlands, and in Kenya.[3] In June of 2016, the Swiss voted on a plan to provide about $2,500 to every adult and $650 to every child under eighteen. The plan was rejected by 77 percent of the voters.[4]

Advocates of a UBI include scholars such as Charles Murray on the right and Anthony Atkinson on the left.[5] This surprising alliance alone makes it an interesting idea. However, Murray sees it as a replacement for Social Security and Medicare, whereas most progressives would reject such a plan.

Advocates believe a UBI will not only substitute for jobs that aren't coming back but also enhance the bargaining power of low-wage workers, relieve people from having to take dead-end jobs, eliminate the complexity and stigma associated with current social welfare programs, free people to pursue their real interests, and reduce the chances of a populist uprising.

The biggest problem, of course, is that if it were universal and provided a meaningful amount of money, a UBI would also require a huge tax increase or cuts in existing spending. If every adult American received $10,000 a year, the cost would be $2.5 trillion a year. In addition, the idea of giving people something for nothing does not mesh well with an American work ethic that remains strong.

Finally, a UBI would reallocate support up the income scale. By diverting whatever revenue we are able to raise to all Americans instead of only to those in need, we might do more harm than good.[6]

To deal with the cost concern, one option is to provide unconditional payments along the lines of a UBI, but to phase it out as income rises. This idea, originally advocated by Milton Friedman, is often called a negative income tax. Libertarians like this approach since it gets rid of bureaucracies and leaves the poor free to spend their cash grants on whatever they choose, rather than providing specific funds for particular needs. Liberals fear that such unconditional assistance would be unpopular and would be an easy target for elimination in the face of budget pressures. Right now, most of our social programs are conditional. With the exception of programs to support the aged and the disabled, assistance is tied to work or to the consumption of necessities such as food, housing, or medical care. Our two largest antipoverty programs are the Supplemental Nutrition Assistance Program (SNAP) and the Earned Income Tax Credit (EITC). The first is earmarked for food and the second is conditional on work.

A little paternalism in social policy may not be such a bad thing. In my view, progressives and libertarians alike are loath to admit that many of the poor and jobless are lacking more than just cash. They tend to be poorly educated, lack critical skills, suffer from mental health issues or addiction, have criminal records, or simply have difficulty functioning in a complex society. Money may be needed, but money by itself does not cure such ills.

A humane and wealthy society should provide the disadvantaged with adequate services and support. But there is nothing wrong, in my view, with making assistance conditional on individuals fulfilling some obligation—whether it is work, training, getting treatment, or living in a supportive but supervised environment. The idea is to provide a compassionate hand-up, not a handout.

In the end, the two biggest problems with a universal basic income are its costs and its inconsistency with the American expectation that able-bodied adults should work.

A Children's Allowance?

Another major proposal from the left is a universal children's allowance. It would provide a cash benefit to all families with children, regardless of income or other conditions. One recent proposal would provide a yearly allowance of $2,500 per child for all children (up to age eighteen) at an additional cost of about $190 billion per year. Such a program could reduce the child poverty rate by over 30 percent.[7] It recognizes that children may be the innocent victims of their parents' inability to find work or earn an adequate income. Most wealthy countries provide some form of children's allowance, and even Republicans such as Senator Marco Rubio have shown interest in defraying the costs of raising the next generation by giving generous tax credits to their parents. His support for the concept helped to ensure that the current child tax credit was made more generous in the 2017 tax law and made partially refundable—that is, available to lower-income families without sufficient tax liability to benefit from the credit otherwise. The political appeal of helping children and the potential for bipartisan support make a children's allowance or an expanded child tax credit far more feasible than a universal basic income. At the same time, most parents would prefer to support their children with their own earned income, and some may view supporting other people's children as another form of welfare. It is, once again, unconditional cash assistance. It only helps families with young children, not the much larger group who are ineligible because their children are grown or because they are childless. Finally, like a UBI and many other progressive ideas, a children's allowance carries a big price tag. How would we pay for it?

Why Redistributing Income Is So Hard

As noted earlier, our progressive tax and transfer system has not held back the tides of growing inequality. In fact, it has tended to make matters worse. As the pretax incomes of the wealthy have soared, taxes have moved in the opposite direction, reinforcing rather than offsetting growing inequality in incomes. The 2017 tax law further exacerbated this problem.

I believe that the amount of money going to those at the top is grossly excessive. As someone who has a high income and pays a lot of taxes, I would vote to pay even more. I once made a voluntary contribution to the U.S. Treasury. I was working on budget issues at the time and wanted to both do my little bit toward reducing the deficit and find out whether the Treasury really accepted voluntary contributions (they do). But without an agreement, enacted into law, that we all do our part, voluntary contributions obviously won't get the job done.

Just because policy has been headed in the wrong direction in recent decades doesn't mean it couldn't be reversed, politics willing. That said, there are three reasons why it will be hard. First, American attitudes are relatively conservative. Second, the wealthy's political power and reluctance to give up the tax preferences they have already won is a big barrier to overcome. Third, the revenue costs of using redistribution alone to restore broad-based prosperity are very high.

Conservative Attitudes

U.S. public attitudes are more conservative than they are in other advanced countries. Americans believe that they live in a society in which there is a lot of opportunity and where anyone can make it if they work hard enough.[8] A large number of Americans believe they are already in the top ranks or soon will be. For example, polls have shown that about 40 percent believe that they either are, or will become, part of the wealthiest 1 percent. These data help to show why class warfare hasn't taken root in American soil.[9]

The fact is that the public cares much more about opportunity than it does about either poverty or inequality (see fig. 5.1). They want everyone to have a shot at the American dream, but compassion comes with strings at-

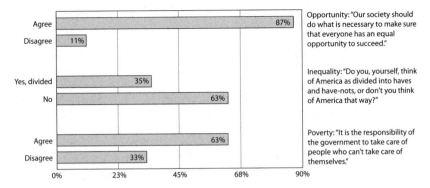

Fig. 5.1. Public cares most about equal opportunity
Source: Pew Research Center for the People and the Press, "Trends in
Political Values and Care Attitudes: 1987–2009," Pew, May 21, 2009,
http://www.people-press.org/files/legacy-pdf/517.pdf

tached.[10] The public wants to help those who help themselves, to provide a
hand-up and not a handout. As noted in chapter 2, the white working class
is especially opposed to welfare programs and believes that many of their
fellow Americans are getting benefits they don't deserve. They support instead the idea of the "success sequence," in which, at a minimum, people
are expected to get an education, work fulltime, and form stable families.
Those who follow the success sequence are unlikely to be poor, and they
have a much better shot at the American dream, as I discussed in chapter 3.

The truth is that most of us who do well in life benefited from the luck of
the draw. We were born into a rich rather than a poor country, to the right
kind of family, with good health, and good genes. These advantages have
nothing to do with merit or our own behavior. Of course, we need to play
whatever cards we were dealt with skill and energy, but the cards we begin
with matter a lot. Yet, as a number of studies have shown, the American
public believes that merit is more important than luck in explaining a high
income.[11] And even if it's good fortune that leads to a high income, people
in the United States think one should be rewarded anyway.[12]

In a nationally representative survey in which Americans were asked
what they thought the top marginal tax rate on incomes should be, the bulk
of the responses were between 20 and 40 percent, with an average (mean)
of 33 percent. These suggestions are well below the rate of 39.6 percent that

existed at the time the survey was conducted. One possible reason for this finding is a lack of information about how much money people at the top actually have. Yet, when one group of individuals was supplied with data on the high degree of inequality in today's economy and another group was not, the responses of the more informed group changed only a little. They favored a top marginal rate that was just one percentage point higher than before they received the extra information. This research was done by two academics, Kenneth Scheve from Stanford and David Stasavage from NYU.[13] They have studied the history of taxation and believe that unless there is a crisis (such as a war) or unless people believe that the government has treated the rich "unfairly," they are not likely to favor higher top rates. Note that the word "unfairly" in the last sentence has nothing to do with rising inequality. In the public mind, it is related to living in "a rigged system"—for example, being able to take advantage of complex rules and get away with manipulating or avoiding them entirely. An example might be the extensive deductions and exclusions in the tax system and the arguably preferential treatment of income from capital. But that's a very different rationale than arguing that the rich should pay a higher rate just because they have a lot of money.

To put this a little differently, in the public eye, fairness may be more about playing by the rules than it is about sharing one's good fortune with others. Is there a level playing field or do some people get special treatment? Even monkeys care about the latter. They will perform a task for an experimenter if rewarded with a cucumber, but once they see another monkey getting a grape instead, they become incensed and throw the cucumber back at the experimenter in disgust. Similarly, instances of "air rage" are much higher when passengers have to walk through a first-class cabin to get to their seats. After reporting on such experiments, Nicholas Kristof concludes, "we humans are social creatures, so that society becomes dysfunctional when we see some receiving grapes and others cucumbers."[14]

Even though laboratory experiments and studies of human development show that people have a preference for a relatively equal distribution of goods, when asked about the kind of society they prefer, they reject a more equal distribution of resources.[15] The reason seems to be because they assume that the market allocates wealth according to what people deserve, and for this reason it is fair. Thus, any attempt to redistribute income may need to be based on demonstrating that the current distribution is not just unequal but also unfair—that is, not based on what people deserve.

With all that said, it is possible that Americans are increasingly seeing the current system as unfair or rigged. More Americans would rather raise tax rates on corporations and high-income households than lower them, according to Pew.[16] Over half wanted to raise tax rates on large businesses and corporations even before the 2017 tax law cut them dramatically. That law, introduced to Congress as the Tax Cuts and Jobs Act, was relatively new as this book went to press but so far it is not very popular with the American public.[17] It is larded with special benefits for various favored groups and without further action will eventually raise taxes on the forgotten Americans.

It's worth remembering that tax cuts are much easier to enact than tax increases. Once a certain distribution of income is in place, changing it requires creating clear winners and losers. The losers will feel their pain much more acutely than the winners will appreciate their gains. Behavioral scientists call this "loss aversion." It is real. Experiments have shown that the psychological effect of a loss is about twice the benefit of an equivalent gain—an irrational, albeit widespread, phenomenon first unveiled by Daniel Kahneman and Amos Tversky.[18] Of course, if the losers have incomes in the stratosphere, it is hard to feel sorry for whatever psychological pain they may feel. If we had raised the top marginal rate by four percentage points in 2017, from 39.6 percent to 43.6 percent, it would have reduced the average net income (after taxes and transfers) of the small group that paid the top marginal tax rate from $962,600 to $933,850.[19] Can anyone possibly have difficulty living on $933,850 per year?[20]

While it is hard to worry about this group's "loss," their own focus is not on the income that's left after paying their taxes but on how much they are required to hand over to the government. If they had never seen the money in the first place, they probably wouldn't miss it.

Power of the Affluent

Even more problematic than loss aversion is the political power of the most affluent. Few people doubt that the wealthy had an inordinate influence on the Tax Cuts and Jobs Act of 2017. According to the Tax Policy Center, that law will provide 83 percent of its benefits to the top 1 percent by 2027.[21] Because most of the initial cuts for middle-class families are temporary, the majority of Americans will end up paying higher taxes than before the law's enactment, with virtually all the money then going to support a more permanent tax cut for corporations.

Much has been written about the power of the superrich to influence elections and protect their interests. In her book *Dark Money,* Jane Mayer describes the great success of the Koch brothers and their allies in swaying elections at all levels, influencing academics, think tanks, and media outlets, and outspending even the Republican National Committee. Although they were not initially supporters of Donald Trump, by the time he was elected their influence could be seen in his appointments and his support for an antitax, antiregulation regime.[22]

The *New York Times* commentator Tom Edsall called the Tax Cuts and Jobs Act of 2017 "a $1.4 trillion package of benefits for key donors and lobbyists, the richest members of Congress, President Trump, his family and other families like his." He went on to write, "How could nearly every Republican representative—and all 52 Republican senators—support the tax bill? The best answer may be the most cynical: because it benefits key leaders, their friends, their heirs and their donors."[23]

In his book *Billionaires: Reflections on the Upper Crust,* my colleague Darrell West reviews the literature on how the concentration of wealth is affecting our politics. What he shows is that, in comparison to ordinary voters, the wealthy are more politically active, tend to favor Republicans, have more conservative views, and have more impact on policy outcomes.[24]

But billionaire donors are not the only culprits. The elites, the top 20 percent, can be part of the problem as well. In his book *Dream Hoarders,* my colleague Richard Reeves tells the story of what happened when Obama tried to eliminate so-called 529 plans that enable people to save money tax-free to pay for their children's college tuition. There was such an uproar, including among Democrats, that the president had to backtrack on his plan. As if that wasn't bad enough, the Tax Cuts and Jobs Act extended the use of tax-favored 529s to cover private K-12 school tuition—another gift to the wealthy.

Some people think that an electoral outcome that puts Democrats back in charge would change everything. But consider the following: Obama's efforts to curtail the many tax deductions or exclusions used by those with incomes exceeding $250,000 a year were of no avail. His proposal never got a serious hearing in Congress, even when it was in Democratic hands.[25] It was the right thing to do but couldn't be enacted.

The High Costs of Redistribution

Restoring the level of inequality that existed back in the 1970s through redistribution alone would require massive new revenues—roughly $1 trillion a year by my reckoning.

Jason Furman, President Obama's chief economist, calculated that if we could restore the degree of income inequality that existed in 1979, the median income would have been more than $10,000, or 19 percent, higher than it was in 2015. That's a big deal.[26]

Could we accomplish what Furman suggests by taxing the wealthy and redistributing the money to the forgotten Americans in the bottom half? In principle, yes, but it would be prohibitively expensive as well as politically infeasible.

Here are my rough calculations. Reducing the share of market income received by the top 20 percent back to the level of 1979 (from 58.7 percent to 49.6 percent), as Furman suggests, would require nearly $1 trillion that would have to be redistributed to the less affluent. One way to raise at least some revenue would be to increase marginal tax rates for those in the top income tax brackets. My analysis suggests that even before the enactment of the regressive tax law of 2017, a 10 percentage point increase in the two top rates (that is, from 35 to 45 percent and from 39.6 to 49.6 percent) would have produced under $100 billion per year, far less than what is needed.[27]

My analysis is reinforced by a more detailed analysis done earlier by my colleagues William Gale, Melissa Kearney, and Peter Orszag using the Tax Policy Center's model. They explored what would happen if we had raised marginal tax rates on the highest income households from 39.6 percent to 50 percent. This change by itself has a tiny effect on the overall distribution of income, reducing the after-tax Gini coefficient from 0.574 to 0.571. (The Gini is a summary index of inequality that is equal to 1 when all of society's income goes to just one person and to 0 when there is complete equality.) Now imagine that all the revenue collected from this change was distributed evenly to the bottom 20 percent. The total revenue raised is $95.6 billion and allows each household at the bottom to have an extra $2,650 in post-tax income. The Gini now falls to 0.560, not terribly different from the 0.574 where we started. This leads the authors to conclude, "That such a sizable increase in the top personal income tax rate leads to a strikingly limited reduction in overall income inequality speaks to the limitations of this particular approach to addressing the broader challenge. It also reflects the fact that the high level of U.S. income inequality is characterized by a wide divergence in income between higher-income households and those at the middle and below."[28]

None of this should be interpreted to mean that there is nothing to be gained by raising top tax rates. For example, under the scenario just described, the ratio of top to bottom incomes (the 90/10 ratio) falls from 16.7 to 12.5. Because the action is at the tails of the distribution, this latter measure (of the ratio between incomes) may be a better guide to understanding the effects of the policy than the Gini Index alone.[29] We could debate whether an increase in marginal tax rates to 50 percent is enough. Marginal rates were far higher than this in the 1950s and even in the 1970s. We could also debate whether an income bounce of over $2,650 to those at the bottom is large or small. To my way of thinking, this would be well worth doing, although I agree with the authors that it is not as powerful as many believe.

The examples I have used so far all involve raising tax rates at the top. Other ways to raise taxes on the wealthy include reforming taxes on capital gains and on estates. They also include eliminating or capping many deductions, such as mortgage interest, the sheltering of retirement income, state and local taxes, the exclusion of employer-provided health benefits, or charitable contributions. Most experts believe that broadening the base of the tax system is preferable on equity and efficiency grounds to only raising rates. Unfortunately, some of those base-broadening reforms were used in 2017 to pay for a very large corporate tax cut.

If there is one opportunity-enhancing tax reform that cries out for attention, it is the estate tax. Republicans want to repeal it entirely, despite the fact that only 0.2—yes, that's two-tenths of 1 percent—of all estates paid any tax at all under the rules in effect in 2017.[30] Even fewer will be liable as the result of the Tax Cuts and Jobs Act of 2017. The transfer of large sums of wealth from one generation to the next is inconsistent with the American belief in providing a more equal opportunity for each new generation to succeed on the basis of hard work and talent rather than on who their parents are. I return to this theme in the next chapter. For now, I simply want to flag the fact that a revitalized estate tax or some other way of reducing the large transfer of wealth between generations makes enormous sense. (Eliminating the so-called step-up in the basis or valuation of wealth transferred at death is another option.) These transfers are contributing over the longer run to the rising concentration of wealth—not a healthy prospect in a democratic nation.

Before leaving the topic of taxation, two other options are worth considering: a value-added tax (VAT) and a tax on carbon. Depending on how the proceeds were used, they could, on net, be progressive. In fact, when one compares inequality in the United States, after counting taxes paid and benefits received, to that found in other advanced countries, the surprise is that it is not so much our tax system that creates an unequal distribution of income as it is the way we spend the proceeds. Unlike most European countries, we rely far less on sales or value-added taxes. That makes the U.S. tax system more progressive, but it also means we have less revenue to spend on helping the bottom ranks. Why not enact a value-added tax similar to that found in every other Organisation for Economic Co-operation and Development (OECD) country?

A VALUE-ADDED TAX

Imagine a presidential candidate promising to not just simplify the income tax but also eliminate it entirely for everyone in the middle and working classes. This is an idea that has been suggested by Yale law professor Michael Graetz. As he puts it, "For the vast majority of Americans, April 15 would be just another spring day."[31]

Such a promise is entirely feasible. We would replace the income tax with a value-added tax for everyone except those with six-figure incomes. The top ranks would continue to pay income taxes as they do now.

A VAT is a flat tax levied on sales at each level of production and eventually passed on to consumers in the form of a higher retail price. It is the equivalent of a national sales tax. Depending on the tax rate, it could both replace the income tax for most families and provide the needed revenue to support a children's allowance, an expanded EITC, or other measures designed to help the forgotten Americans.

The European Union requires countries to levy a VAT of at least 15 percent. That same rate could raise over $1 trillion a year in the United States.[32]

The advantages of a VAT compared to the income tax are many. First, it is simple and easy to administer. Like any tax, it can be avoided—for example, by buying and selling on a black market. But with an increasing proportion of sales moving online, it makes sense to impose a national sales tax rather than multiple state sales taxes. Second, it would encourage savings as opposed to consumption. It would only tax people on what they took out of the economy instead of on what they contributed to it. Those who worked hard and saved a larger portion of their earnings would pay less in taxes. This should encourage both more saving for retirement and economic growth. Third, it can be adjusted at the border, making exports less expensive and imports more so (depending on any compensating changes to the value of the dollar). Finally, it generates a lot of revenue with minimal pain—the reason that small-government conservatives have been loath to support it.

It is true that a VAT tends to be regressive. However, if necessities are excluded (food, clothing, shelter, etc.), an income tax retained for those with six-figure or higher incomes, and the proceeds used in a progressive manner, the tax has a lot to recommend it.

A CARBON TAX

A carbon tax is another option. It is almost universally recommended by economists and business leaders as the most efficient and cost-effective way to address climate change. By increasing the price of carbon-intensive goods, a carbon tax would use a price signal to reduce carbon emissions, but it would provide businesses and households with complete flexibility on how to conserve based on their own circumstances. It would accelerate the shift to alternative sources of energy and encourage job-producing investments in clean technologies.[33] It would also raise a lot of revenue (depending, of course, on how successful it was in limiting emissions). A carbon tax of around

$40 per metric ton of CO_2 would raise about $2 trillion over ten years, enough to pay for the children's allowance or for an expanded EITC, for example. Alternatively, to get even more public buy-in, the revenue could be used to provide rebates to all households, not just those with children. It could also be targeted to low-income households and communities particularly vulnerable to the effects of a hike in the price of carbon (for example, coal-dependent communities).[34]

A carbon tax has been proposed by a group of well-known Republicans (led by former secretary of state James A. Baker III). It would set a carbon price of $40 per ton, and the revenue would be used to provide a "carbon dividend" to all Americans. The dividend would amount to an estimated $2,000 per year for the average four-person family.[35] The American Opportunity Carbon Fee Act, proposed by Senator Whitehouse (D-RI) and Senator Schatz (D-HI) in July 2017, would set a carbon price of $49 per ton, increasing annually at 2 percent over inflation.[36] The Treasury Department estimates that a similar program (a $49 per ton carbon tax coupled with a $583 per person rebate) would produce a net financial gain for the bottom 70 percent of the population. Notably, those in the bottom decile would experience nearly a 9 percent increase in after-tax income, and those between the tenth and twentieth percentiles would experience almost a 5 percent increase in their after-tax incomes.[37] So far, such a policy has proven difficult to enact, but public opinion appears to be moving in the right direction, with many Democrats and now some leading Republicans endorsing it.

My own sense is that we should pursue all three of these revenue-raising options—taxing wealth, a VAT, and a carbon tax—but not be naïve about how difficult it will be to succeed. That also leads me to suggest we focus not just on a fairer distribution of taxes and benefits but also on jobs.

The Importance of Work

Work provides people with an income but it does much more than that. It provides self-respect, a sense of contributing, an identity, and a connection to others. So, joblessness (or perhaps even the fear of it) undermines human dignity and self-worth. Policies that simply redistribute income do nothing to counter that fact. As the journalist Noah Smith puts it, "The U.S.

has moved away from the idea of a social compact with work at its core. That's something that deserves to be reversed."[38]

A similar plea comes from Arthur Brooks (president of the American Enterprise Institute), and the Dalai Lama writing for the *New York Times*. They both note that senior citizens who didn't feel useful to others were nearly three times as likely to die prematurely; that those who are engaged in helping others are happier than those who are not; and that meaningful work is essential to human flourishing. Why, they ask, are people in prosperous countries so anxious and politically frustrated? The problem, they believe, is "not a lack of material riches. It is the growing number of people who feel they are no longer useful, no longer needed, no longer one with their societies."[39]

Some scientific support for this thesis exists. In his research, the psychologist Mihaly Csikszentmihalyi has investigated how people use their time and which activities they enjoy the most, based on a methodology called "experience sampling."[40] The most satisfying experiences, he found, involved active engagement and attention to achieving a set of goals well aligned with one's skills. It also helps if the individual faces a set of challenges, receives feedback on his or her achievements, and if the work requires a level of concentration that eclipses awareness of self and of life's frustrations. He called this type of experience "flow," and it is correlated with other measures of happiness or well-being. It can be activated while at work or during periods of leisure. (A common leisure activity that creates flow is driving a car.) What he and his colleagues found that surprised them was the amount of time people experienced flow while at work and how little they experienced it at other times. Although people in his experiments reported wanting to work less, the quality of their experiences at work were superior to their experiences when not at work. That seeming paradox, he argued, can be explained by social conditioning that labels work as bad and leisure as good. Of course, there are some kinds of work that are demeaning, brutal, or boring. Nor is it just paid work that leads to the experience of flow—any structured and goal-focused activity can do so. Autonomy and effort expended at work also matter—one reason the gig economy and contract work may be a much more positive development than many have assumed. So paid work isn't a panacea. Nonetheless, in these studies it was not just surgeons or managers but also those in more routine, blue-collar, or clerical jobs who had some of their most positive experiences at work. It seems that people long for leisure, but when they have it they don't know what to do with it. When it is unstructured and ill defined, it actually takes considerable effort to make it enjoyable.

These studies on flow are further confirmed by research suggesting that a lack of work is correlated with all kinds of social problems, from depression to addiction. Granted, it has been difficult in these cases to distinguish cause and effect, but the research at least suggests that a lack of work can have serious consequences for people's health and well-being.[41]

The forgotten Americans who are the focus of this book may be suffering less from a lack of income than from a lack of meaningful work that would restore their dignity and self-respect. They have been caught in an economic system that has destroyed the jobs they used to hold and the communities in which they live.

This leads me to suggest that a better alternative to a universal basic income might be to provide what my colleagues Mark Muro and Joseph Parilla call "a universal basic adjustment benefit."[42] In chapter 6, I suggest something very similar. Compared to a UBI, the proposal for a universal basic adjustment benefit—what I call a GI Bill for America's workers—is far less expensive. Note that if we were to spend 1 percent of our GDP—or ten times as much as we do now—on such adjustment policies, it would still be cheaper than providing everyone with even a modest UBI. It would also be more consistent with the desire of most people to feel like they are contributing. They want to be masters of their own lives, take pride in what they know how to do, and not feel like they are redundant or irrelevant. They want jobs, not handouts.

More broadly shared growth is a worthy goal, but it would be a mistake to rely on redistribution as the only or even the major way to achieve a better-functioning economy and society. For this reason, in the next few chapters I suggest that we turn our attention to much more direct ways of helping people secure good jobs and higher wages.

6

A GI Bill for America's Workers

IF BRINGING BACK MANUFACTURING JOBS, restricting trade and immigration, and paying people not to work are the wrong approaches, and if a big redistribution of income or much faster economic growth aren't in the cards, what should be done? There are no easy answers here. The impacts of automation, trade, and other changes have been devastating for many families and communities. One reason that the public is vulnerable to false explanations and tends to blame the wrong culprits is because no one has proposed an agenda that adequately deals with the decline of jobs for the less skilled. But in defense of this apparent lacuna in our policy discourse, it must be said that the answers are far from obvious. Progressives gravitate too readily to redistributing income, while conservatives think it's just about reducing taxes and regulation to spur growth. Both have some role to play, but neither is likely to prove sufficient, and both avoid dealing with what seems to me to be the central problem: a lack of decently paid jobs.

In the next three chapters, I suggest some ideas for addressing these issues. This particular chapter focuses on the need to reskill the workforce. The next chapter explores whether the government should create jobs and boost wages for the lowest paid. The limits of government policy in these arenas lead me to look much more closely in chapter 8 at the need for a bigger role for the private sector in training workers and in sharing profits, so that any gains from growth are more broadly shared.

If there is a theme to these chapters, it's that success depends not just on a more effective set of public policies but also on engaging the private sector in the task of improving skills and earnings. Without private sector engagement, I doubt that we can be successful. The public, including the forgotten Americans, does not look favorably on a much larger federal role and the taxes needed to pay for it. By putting the private sector in the driver's seat, but under a set of incentives that will encourage them to be not just job creators but major builders of the skills that are necessary for future success, we can leverage our public resources, improve our global competitiveness, and move toward inclusive growth in the process.

The big losers in the United States have been those without much education or skill. In the long term, the right solution is to improve their prospects by strengthening families and investing in the education of the next generation, as argued in chapter 3. But that effort will take time, perhaps a generation or more, and the biggest unanswered question in this area is what happens to those left behind in the meantime. This chapter attempts to address that question.

The Original GI Bill and National Service

The country has faced the need to upgrade its workforce in the past. The GI Bill, enacted in 1944, provided generous benefits to World War II veterans, covering college tuition and a stipend for living expenses. The benefits were not conditioned on income or ability, only on military service, and often covered as much as four years of college. The program appears to have boosted the education of its participants.[1] Similar, if less generous, benefits have been offered to the veterans of subsequent wars. I revisit this history here because I believe national service has the potential to address not just a lack of practical skills among the youngest generation, but our cultural divides as well.

In the 1960s, the idea of extending national service to include more than just military service was championed by President Kennedy. This led to the creation of the Peace Corps and later VISTA (Volunteers in Service to America), its domestic equivalent. President Clinton expanded on the idea by establishing the Corporation for National and Community Service (CNCS), an agency overseeing AmeriCorps and other volunteer agencies that still exist today.

The idea of national service has, up to now, had strong bipartisan backing. Supporters have included conservatives such as both presidents Bush, Mitt Romney, John Kasich, John McCain, and liberals such as President Obama, Hillary Clinton, and many other Democrats. The program is also popular with voters of all stripes.[2] Nonetheless, the program has faced budgetary challenges from the start. The number of people applying to serve greatly exceeds the number of slots the agency can provide, and many nonprofit and local community groups are very dependent on national service program volunteers.[3] Anyone who is a U.S. citizen or legal permanent resident, age seventeen or older, can apply for AmeriCorps. Volunteers typically serve for a year and receive a living allowance, priority hiring at about 450 companies, and the equivalent of a Pell grant to go to college if they complete a year of service. Most of the funding is channeled through state commissions and used for a variety of projects related to education, the environment, disaster relief, antipoverty efforts, and health. It has provided volunteers for Teach for America, Youth Build, the Boys and Girls Clubs, the Red Cross, and many other well-known organizations. It easily passes a benefit-cost test, according to at least one analysis, because it provides useful services at very low cost.[4] But for those who are skeptical, another way to pay for national service is to make eligibility for Pell grants or other higher education financing conditional on service and to encourage, whenever feasible, young people to continue to live with their parents or other adult relatives. Those moving to a new community might live with an unrelated family that volunteered to open its home to a national service corps member much like some of today's families have done with students from abroad. These foreign exchange programs have helped to build bridges between countries; we now need to rebuild bridges between communities within our own country. Both the host families and the young volunteers might benefit.

In sum, while expanding national service should not be the only way to help young people bridge the gap between high school and college or a career, it could play a role, not only in helping young people afford more education or training but, even more importantly, in bringing a divided nation together. The journalist Roger Cohen, for example, recommends a "vastly expanded, even mandatory, national service program that might at once throw Americans of every creed and culture together for a year or two at an impressionable age, fire up civic engagement and even revive the American dream . . . American fracture is advancing by the day because Americans are no longer obliged to look one another in the eye and find solutions."[5] General Stanley McChrystal, another advocate for national service, notes that the idea is timelier than ever because young people want to serve, local community organizations need the help, and the technology platform to make this work efficiently now exists.[6]

Helping Workers Adjust: A New GI Bill for America's Workers

National service is one possible solution, but a broader effort to deal with growing structural joblessness and stagnating wages is needed. The United States has put almost all of its eggs into the college basket, neglected training for careers, left the bottom half stranded, and fallen behind other industrialized countries in the process.

Let me begin with what are often called "active labor market policies." These help workers find jobs by providing information or counseling, training or retraining, or other assistance when they lose a job and are having difficulty finding another one. They have been more commonly used in Europe than in the United States. In the United States, they have been funded under a variety of legislative vehicles, including, most recently, the Workforce Innovation and Opportunity Act and the Perkins Act. Many smaller programs have emerged to deal with specific subgroups or areas. In fact, one common complaint is that we have way too many programs and that some simplification or consolidation is in order. It's a byzantine system that ideally should be scrapped and rebuilt from scratch, though that is easier said than done. When I was in the Clinton administration we tried to simplify and consolidate many of these programs, including those in both the Department of Labor and the Department of Education. I knew I was in trouble the day that the deputy secretaries for these two departments arrived for a meeting, closed my office door, and proceeded to warn me that even attempting such a feat was suicidal.

One argument for active labor market policies is that aggregate demand policies in the form of monetary and fiscal policies can increase the total number of jobs in an economy, but there may still be shortages and surpluses of labor in particular areas or occupations or for selected subgroups. In a large and diverse labor market like the United States, such imbalances are inevitable. They reflect the fact that labor isn't perfectly mobile, that markets are not fully competitive, and, most saliently, that it can take many years for the supply of a particular type of labor to catch up with the demand. Policies that address such frictions and shortages by providing information about where the jobs are, training or retraining workers for available jobs, and providing subsidized work or income support as a last resort are one solution to such imbalances. Done right, these policies can improve productivity, enhance opportunity for the less advantaged, and become springboards for a faster and more inclusive rate of growth.

A second argument for such policies is that the economy is still producing a lot of middle-skill jobs. Although there has been a decline in production and clerical jobs that require only a high school degree, there has been no shrinkage in jobs requiring some postsecondary training if not a BA.[7] My colleague Harry Holzer estimates that fewer than half of U.S. workers have obtained any kind of postsecondary degree, even though such credentials are often a prerequisite for entering and remaining in the middle class.[8] Complaints about the difficulty of finding a plumber, an electrician, a computer technician, or an internet service installer come to mind.

Our current labor market policies are seriously underfunded, less effective than they could be, and in need of streamlining and some devolution to lower levels of government and to private sector intermediaries. What is needed is a much bigger and more serious effort to address pockets of joblessness in distressed areas and among less-skilled workers. But the solutions will need to be tailored to the diversity of the problems and communities, which argues for local involvement. And because the private sector, and not the government, is where most jobs are created, businesses need to play a key role as well.

Right now, active labor market policy in the United States is not very active. In fact, it is in the doldrums. The United States spent about 0.11 percent of GDP on these policies in 2014, down from 0.26 percent in 1985.[9] In

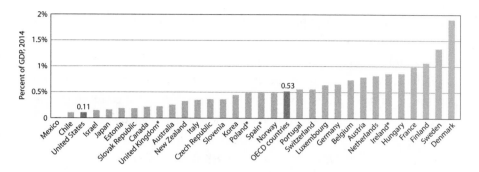

Fig. 6.1. Public expenditure on active labor market policies
Source: OECD, "Public Expenditure and Participant Stocks on LMP,"
http://stats.oecd.org/Index.aspx?DataSetCode=LMPEXP
* indicates that an alternative latest year was used for this figure

terms of total dollar expenditures, that's a decline of about 27 percent in inflation-adjusted dollars.[10] (These figures do not include spending on Pell grants, which enable students to take some technically or vocationally oriented courses at a community college.) For context, we are spending more on prisons. In fact, state and local expenditures on corrections increased 324 percent between 1979–1980 and 2012–2013.[11]

The United States also spends far less on active labor market policies than other advanced nations. In 2014, the total amount spent on active labor market policies across OECD countries averaged 0.5 percent, compared to the 0.11 percent spent in the United States.[12] Only two OECD countries—Mexico and Chile—spent less than the United States (fig. 6.1).

A roughly fivefold increase in spending on training and related adjustment assistance (or about $90 billion per year) would put us in line with the OECD average. If we wanted to match the Swiss, the Germans, the Dutch, or the Danes, it would take a lot more than that.[13] Of course, we don't know how much of this spending is effective right now. However, it's worth noting that labor force participation rates in the United States are considerably lower than they are in most European countries.[14]

One reason the United States may have neglected employment and training is because the emphasis has been on financing higher education. The assumption seems to be that everyone needs to go to college. Yet, many of the students who enroll in college never graduate. About 70 percent of high school graduates enroll in college, but shockingly only about 39 percent of all community college students complete their programs within six years, and among students at four-year schools, only 60 percent graduate within six years.[15] Many of those who enroll but don't graduate require huge amounts of remediation ($2 billion annually at the community college level), and end up with burdensome levels of student debt. At the same time, assessments of what students learn during their first two years of college—especially whether they make gains in critical thinking skills—indicate that these gains are very modest at best and do nothing to reduce initial test score gaps by race or family background.[16]

Contrast the small amount being spent on employment and training with the amount spent on higher education in the form of grants, loans, and tax credits. For the academic year 2014–2015, a total of $162 billion was spent to help people go to college.[17] In contrast, the Department of Education spends about $1.1 billion annually on career and technical education (CTE), primarily through basic Perkins grants to states. Even if we were to combine this investment in CTE with the spending on targeted active labor market policies, we are only spending about $20 billion per year on these work-related programs at the federal level. That $20 billion doesn't count the roughly $30 billion spent on Pell grants, at least some of which finance training, but it still pales in comparison to the funds spent on higher education.

Perhaps we need to shift the emphasis from everyone going to college to a much stronger focus on investing in helping everyone train for and find work. Many mid-skilled jobs require some postsecondary training but not necessarily a four-year college degree.[18] The returns to career and technical education, as we shall see, can be high. To be sure, the returns to a BA degree are still very positive, on average, but averages can be deceiving. The variation in the returns to higher education are enormous, depending not just on whether a student completes the program but also on the selectivity of the school and the student's major.[19] There are many people with BAs who are earning less than those with two-year technical degrees.[20]

We are spending far more on sending people to college than on helping them navigate the labor market and secure decently paid jobs, and this emphasis needs to shift. I don't mean to imply that colleges, and community colleges in particular, are not engaged in valuable training or that investments in higher education don't provide a reasonable return for most of those who graduate—just keep in mind that many never complete a degree but nonetheless end up burdened with student loans. To be sure, the wage premium for having a BA versus a high school degree increased sharply for many years, making college an attractive investment. However, that premium has been stagnant since 2000 for workers with only a four-year as opposed to a graduate degree.[21] As college degrees have become more common, they have also become less valuable. As more and more people earn these degrees, often in open-enrollment institutions, what they actually learn that is valuable to today's employers is increasingly questionable. One well-known result is that college graduates are taking jobs that don't require a college degree.[22] The college-for-everyone mindset needs to change, and with it the way we allocate public resources.

Principles to Guide a GI Bill for America's Workers

There are a number of general principles that should guide a new GI Bill for America's Workers:

First, and most importantly, the bill needs to be geared to the skills that are in demand and the jobs that are available. Training programs linked to the labor market are often called "pathways" or "sectoral employment" programs. They typically involve partnerships between employers and local educational institutions, in which employers specify the skills or even the curricula needed to produce those skills and a school or community college is charged with producing them.[23]

Second, funding for programs and for training institutions should be based on evidence of effectiveness. Funding could be conditional on the proportion of graduates who secure good jobs. At present, the inventory of effective pathway programs is quite thin, and only about a fifth of high school students participate.[24] Most are being funded at the state level. Although limited right now, some of these pathway programs have produced high rates of return for participants and for employers. A careful evaluation of a CTE program provided by community colleges in California found returns of 12 to 23 percent. Most of the high returns were in health care fields and accrued to women, who dominate this sector.[25]

Third, these programs should be flexible enough to evolve in response to changes in technology or demand in the local labor market. Projecting where the jobs of the future are going to be is an art, not a science. But we know that they are going to demand different and higher levels of skills than in the past. Exposing students at a relatively early age to the kinds of jobs available—and helping them to explore their options and not simply drift into college because it's what their parents and society expect—has to be part of the reset.

Fourth, whenever feasible, programs should include work-based learning, such as apprenticeships. As Larry Good and Ed Strong at the Corporation for a Skilled Workforce point out, "In twenty-first century labor markets, the new norm is interweaving work and learning, starting in K-12, continuing through initial postsecondary learning, and then on through the continuing acquisition of new knowledge and skills throughout a career. Work and learning must happen simultaneously, not sequentially, allowing for learning to have experiential context and for work to be improved by learning."[26] Skills learned in the classroom and on the job are both needed. Effectively integrating academic and practical skills, including social skills, is a challenge but should be the goal. Apprenticeships are an effective form of work-based learning and are far more common in other advanced nations than they are in the United States.[27] The research to date indicates that apprenticeships yield significant benefits to workers, employers, and society.[28] An analysis of apprenticeships in Washington State found that the government netted almost three times its spending on apprenticeships within 2.5 years of the program's completion through increased productivity and higher taxable wages.[29]

Fifth, education and training curricula are moving online. These online programs cannot fully replace in-person education and coaching, but they will permit workers in remote areas or those with existing jobs and family responsibilities to upgrade their skills at home and at their own pace. Federal government funding and marketing of this online infrastructure could be a cost-effective game changer. One problem that must be addressed is the low number of adults who are digitally ready to take advantage of such opportunities. According to a Pew report, only 17 percent of adults are digitally ready, meaning that they have the skills necessary to use online platforms, faith in their own ability to determine the reliability of information retrieved online, and some experience using digital learning tools.[30]

Finally, any training program should produce a certificate or other credential that is competency based and validated and recognized as such within an industry or sector.[31] Tamar Jacoby, the president of Opportunity America, writes, "The rapid growth of both certificates and certifications attests to growing interest in occupational training—instruction designed expressly to prepare students for the world of work."[32] Traditional educational credentials such as AA or BA degrees are no substitute for certifying what someone actually knows how to do. Involving the employer community in the establishment and expansion of these credentials could go a long way toward upskilling the workforce. In the United States, only about 30 percent of all students graduate from a four-year college, and roughly another 20 percent earn an AA degree or a certification with value in the job market. That leaves 50 percent who have no recognized credentials to help them find and retain jobs.[33]

Challenges

I don't want to underestimate the difficulties of building such a training system. The challenges include concerns about the cultural stigma associated with vocational training; the need for collaboration between educational institutions, employers, and government; the difficulty of scaling up existing efforts; the need for many people to relocate or telecommute; and the special plight of older workers for whom retraining often doesn't make sense.

CULTURAL STIGMA

The United States has a history of viewing vocational education as a second-class option for those who can't make the grade in a college prep curriculum. As Anthony Carnevale notes, "A majority of Americans do not think everyone should go to college, but the vast majority of parents think their sons and daughters should go, and the students themselves feel the same way."[34] In response to this set of attitudes, advocates of more skills-based training began calling it CTE rather than vocational education. In fact, in 2006, the federal law that reauthorized funding for vocational education replaced the term "vocational" with "career and technical." Advocates of CTE emphasize that everyone should have the option to learn a specific skill and that doing so should not close off the option of getting a BA. The new framing of this option is *pathways to career and college*. In Switzerland, 70 percent of students are taught a marketable skill through a vocational education and training system, and there is no stigma associated with this route through school.[35]

THE NEED FOR COLLABORATION

A new system needs to be built on partnerships between government (especially at the state level), employers, and schools or colleges. This will not happen unless there is strong leadership and a way to keep everyone at the table. Governors may be ideally placed, and have the biggest incentive to fill this role as it is one way to attract business to their states. They will need the help of intermediaries who can serve as advisers, coordinators, and evaluators.[36]

SCALE

Right now, career and technical education is a stepchild in the education family. A few states, California in particular, have made it a priority. But most programs are still small and their effectiveness at scale remains uncertain. I think we need to expand them, but with a watchful eye on their quality and effectiveness.

JOBLESS COMMUNITIES

No amount of training will solve the problem of people who live in communities where the jobs have disappeared. So, relocation assistance for people in declining communities will need to be a priority. Alternatively, many jobs could be done remotely if good broadband services were available. Improving broadband access in these areas could connect residents to employment opportunities elsewhere.

OLDER WORKERS

Some workers, especially those who have spent a lifetime in a decent-paying manufacturing job, may not be good candidates for either retraining or relocation. For this older age group, wage insurance could supplement their incomes while helping to keep them connected to the job market, albeit in a lower-paying job. A number of experts, including my former colleague Robert Litan, have long argued for this idea, and the Obama ad-ministration supported it as well.[37] President Obama's administration pro-posed a wage insurance program that would have replaced 50 percent of a worker's lost wages for two years (up to $10,000 per year) to workers mak-ing less than $50,000 in their new job, provided they had worked for their previous employer for at least three years.[38] A related idea would be to re-place the largely ineffectual Trade Adjustment Assistance (TAA) program with what my colleagues Mark Muro and Joseph Parilla call a "universal basic adjustment benefit" that would provide job-search assistance, reloca-tion grants, cash grants for training, and wage insurance. Unlike the cur-rent TAA program, this adjustment benefit would be available to all experienced workers suffering job losses related to automation or plant closings, not just those related to trade competition.[39]

Examples of Successful Programs

With these principles and challenges in mind, a brief tour of some suc-cessful programs can provide more insight into what a new system might look like and accomplish.

CAREER AND TECHNICAL EDUCATION

California has made a concerted effort to incorporate CTE into both its secondary and postsecondary education systems, and the evidence to date indicates that these efforts have paid off. In 2005, the State Board of Educa-tion adopted CTE standards for students in grades seven through twelve. These provide guidelines for educators aimed at improving the transition from high school to careers or college in fifty-eight different career paths in fifteen different industries. The CTE standards emphasize coursework tailored to local employment needs and provide a flexible foundation of knowledge and skills adaptable to changing economic conditions. Small learning communities, called California Partnership Academies (CPAs), have been established within larger high schools typically enrolling students in grades ten through twelve. At least half of each incoming CPA cohort must, by law, be "at-risk" students, meaning that they are either econom-ically or educationally disadvantaged. Though there are roughly even numbers of male and female students, the gender composition in certain industry-specific programs do differ—females tend to dominate CPAs that focus on fashion and interior design, while males are far more common in manufacturing and product development programs. Each CPA (there were 467 across the state in 2011) offers students courses in both core academic subjects and career-oriented technical skills related to the academy's career theme. A study comparing CPA student outcomes to statewide outcomes for all public high school students found participants were more likely to graduate (95 versus 85 percent) and more likely to have completed the full set of courses required for admission to the state's public universities (57 versus 36 percent).[40] This latter result demonstrates that these programs need not "track" students into a vocational route, but can also offer them the option of pursuing a traditionally academic degree.

CTE is deeply embedded within California's community colleges as well as its high schools. Their community college system is the largest in the country. Two-thirds of the state's college students—about 2.3 million individuals—attend a community college. About half of the awards issued to community college graduates are CTE degrees. As noted earlier, returns on CTE certificates and degrees can be as high as 23 percent.[41] Nationwide, community colleges have a critical role to play in providing the kind of training that workers need. However, their efforts need to be both improved and better resourced. Students need better guidance or more structured programs to help them navigate a more successful path through college. And institutions need to be judged (and provided resources) based not on total enrollments ("seat time") but instead on degree completion and student success in the labor market or in transferring to four-year schools.[42]

APPRENTICESHIPS

Though still relatively scarce in the United States, apprenticeships have a good track record of improving labor market outcomes for participants and boosting productivity at hosting firms.[43] By its very nature, an apprenticeship offers on-the-job training in skills relevant to employers in specific industries, and it enables participants to earn wages while they refine these skills. South Carolina offers the most extensive state apprenticeship program, inspired by the state's recognition that it lacked skilled workers in high demand. The state government annually directs $1 million to the initiative, offering employers a tax credit of $1,000 per apprentice. The program is credited with doubling the number of apprentices in the state at a time when the number of apprenticeships was declining nationwide. Over half of apprentices receive some portion of their training from a technical college, which means that the education being provided by the technical colleges is well integrated with that needed in the workplace.[44]

SECTORAL TRAINING PROGRAMS

New York City has been a hub of innovation for education and training programs. WorkAdvance, for example, offers low-income workers in New York City "demand-driven" sectoral training and advancement, including job placement and counseling. WorkAdvance focuses on employer needs and industry-recognized certifications. A rigorous evaluation conducted by the Manpower Demonstration Research Organization (MDRC) found that WorkAdvance helped participants complete their training, acquire a valuable credential, and boost their earnings compared to a control group, particularly in programs teaching skills in high demand.[45] One of these is Per Scholas. Started in 1998, the program has close ties with employers in New York City's information technology sector and offers participants the kind of training and certifications frequently required to get a good job in information technology (IT). The MDRC researchers who evaluated the program credit Per Scholas's intense demand-driven curricula and long-standing ties with the local IT sector for its success.

These results are heartening, and they stand in stark contrast to some of the older job training programs that have historically been criticized for failing to meaningfully improve participants' labor market outcomes.[46] The apparent difference between these older training programs and the more impressive programs emerging today is the fact that successful programs emphasize industry-specific training customized to local labor markets rather than general education. New York is just one place where this approach has worked and IT is only one example of where skills are in high demand.[47]

Paying for the GI Bill

Although it would be desirable, in my view, for the federal government to spend more on training and other forms of adjustment assistance through its existing workforce development programs, states need to play a role as well and could use the current unemployment insurance system to fund needed services.

The unemployment insurance (UI) system was established in the 1930s to help workers cope with the risk of cyclical unemployment. In today's economy, they also need help coping with the risk of structural joblessness, primarily caused by changes in trade and technology. So one option for financing a new GI Bill for America's workers is to reform the UI system in a way that recognizes that these new risks can disrupt labor markets as much as, if not more than, the cyclical ups and downs of the economy. That means expanding the purposes of the law to cover the costs of various kinds of adjustment assistance, such as training, relocation, wage insurance, and job search counseling.

Right now, the UI system provides cash benefits for a limited time (usually six months) to unemployed workers who have lost a job through no fault of their own. Although the current system has a small federal component, it is primarily a state-based system in which eligibility rules, benefits, and the taxes used to pay for the benefits vary from state to state. Under a reformed system, the allowable purposes of the law would be expanded and new resources made available. States would still have the flexibility to tailor their programs to local conditions. However, a special federal fund might be established to incentivize states to move in this new direction, funded by a limited increase in the small federal component of the unemployment tax. Something similar has been proposed by Harry Holzer and was used during the Obama administration to encourage states to reform their education systems.[48] It was called a "Race to the Top" fund and had some success in encouraging states to improve public K-12 education. Grants to states would be conditional on evidence that their efforts were effective—for example, that training programs were increasing employment and earnings. But most of the financing would be from state UI taxes on employers.

Currently, the UI system in many states is underfunded, and states need to raise their UI taxes to deal with the solvency issue. In the process, they should be encouraged to go beyond that goal. The best way to do this would be to require them to use a much higher wage base for their UI taxes. Right now, the federally mandated wage base is only $7,000, and it has not been adjusted since 1983. As a result, the typical state wage base is quite low, and the tax imposed on that base is therefore very regressive, making low-wage workers more expensive to hire and retain than higher-paid ones. If we want the winners from trade and technology to share the benefits with the losers, then these taxes need to be not just higher but also much more equitably distributed.

The argument for a federal rather than a state role in paying for training is that workers are mobile and could leave the state where they were trained. The benefit of a state financing option is that it encourages each state to find a way to help its workers, consistent with its own history, politics, and economy. As I have argued throughout this book, we are a diverse country and need to honor that diversity and rebuild our democracy from the bottom up. States would have the option to use the UI system to provide grants to local communities for training or other types of adjustment assistance. They should also be encouraged to see this as one way to develop business and new jobs for their state. The South Carolina apprenticeship program discussed earlier in this chapter is a good example.

There are many ways to reform and fund an expanded work-based system, and the plan outlined above is only one such option. In general, the principles guiding these reforms should be a system repurposed to deal with structural as well as cyclical joblessness; a state-based rather than a federal one-size-fits-all system; and a more equitable financing mechanism that ensures that the winners from trade and technology are sharing the benefits with the losers.

Moving the Forgotten Americans to Growing Sectors of the Economy: New Gender Norms

The most rapidly growing sectors of the economy are education, health care, and administration. All these jobs require skills, but they are not necessarily STEM jobs (science, technology, engineering, and math). They are instead what Richard Reeves and I have called HEAL jobs (health, education, administration, and literacy).[49]

Occupations in these fast-growing industries often involve difficult and nonroutine interactions with other people (students, patients, consumers, and supervisors), strong communication skills, creativity or flexibility, and empathy. Right now, many of these jobs are considered "women's work" and are, in fact, overwhelmingly done by women. As production-oriented jobs decline, service-oriented jobs are booming. While jobs making stuff are relatively easy to automate, jobs caring for people are not. And as our incomes grow, we spend a rising portion of them on services and less of them on goods. Some of the most rapidly growing jobs are as health aides, which are about 90 percent female.[50] While women are moving into previously male-dominated jobs, such as doctors, lawyers, pharmacists, and engineers, men are still a very small fraction of kindergarten or preschool teachers, registered nurses, and social workers.[51]

These traditionally female jobs tend to be low paid, even though they are far from unskilled. This fact, together with cultural norms about appropriate kinds of work for men, is inhibiting men from considering career paths in these fields. But if they don't, they are going to be left further behind.

Claire Cain Miller, a correspondent for the *New York Times,* interviewed a man who had been a welder in St. Clair, Missouri. He lost several jobs due to either offshoring or automation but was unwilling to think about moving into the health field. Miller quotes him as saying, "I ain't going to be a nurse; I don't have the tolerance for people. I don't want it to sound bad, but I've always seen a woman in the position of a nurse or some kind of health care worker. I see it as more of a woman's touch." He is instead living on disability insurance because of his rheumatoid arthritis.[52]

This problem is exacerbated by the gender gap in education. Women are now better educated than men. More of them graduate from high school, from college, and even from graduate school. As noted earlier, when a team of researchers studied California's CTE programs, they found very high rates of return for those who took courses in the health field, but these earnings gains were overwhelmingly obtained by women, not men.[53]

These educational and cultural gaps may explain why joblessness among women has not risen in the same way it has for men. It's not that there aren't many women among the forgotten Americans, but they may be better able to adapt and to take advantage of the jobs that are still growing. They are also willing to work for lower wages. And for a variety of reasons (mostly cultural, in my view), they are more comfortable with the idea of taking care of other people.

Until men seize opportunities in these "pink-collar" sectors, they will continue to lose out in this growing area of the labor market. Unless the gender imbalance in the thirty fastest-growing occupations changes, women will take up a million jobs that would otherwise have gone to men.[54]

This may sound like a zero-sum game with men replacing women in these growing sectors, but it doesn't have to be. First, the demand for teachers and health care workers and personal assistants isn't fixed. These fields are providing a growing number of openings. Second, an entire generation of women is retiring from these jobs, and complaints about shortages of teachers and nurses abound, opening up spaces for moderately educated men to find rewarding careers. In the meantime, the women who used to populate these sectors are moving further up the ladder. Well-educated women who used to be teachers and nurses and secretaries will in the future be doctors, lawyers, and executives. (I started my own career as a secretary after my father gave me a course in shorthand as a wedding present. At least he understood that such skills were in high demand at the time.)

Economists tend to focus on market imperfections related to a lack of competition, incomplete information, and adjustment lags. But another problem is the way in which social norms or attitudes affect labor markets. As long as men find themselves unwilling to move into what they consider to be "women's work," all the market-based solutions to close this gap will be inadequate at best. The answer isn't affirmative action as much as it is depictions of men and women in nontraditional roles in the media, in school curricula, and by those in leadership positions. We need more examples of men doing "women's work." When Mark Zuckerberg took two months of leave from his job to care for his newborn daughter, Max, people took notice.[55] Research has shown that behavior is influenced by what one's peers are doing, so as more men take up teaching or nursing, others will follow suit, especially if we invent new labels for traditional jobs. Stewardesses are no longer stewardesses; they are flight attendants, and many are now men. Similarly, nurses might be called "health attendants," and men encouraged to join their ranks.

As someone who grew up in the 1950s and 1960s, I can attest to the fact that progress is not just possible; it has been dramatic. As the only woman in most of my graduate school classes, and as one of a tiny cadre of female economists at that time, I definitely felt a bit out of place. The chairman of one well-regarded economics department to which I had applied for graduate work said he had never had "a housewife in the program" and thus wondered "how it might work out." I chose to enroll at another university. Everything "worked out" just fine.

7

Creating Jobs and Rewarding Work

BECAUSE WORK IS CENTRAL TO BOTH self-respect and earning a living, this chapter explores what role government might play in creating jobs and rewarding work. Many people remember the New Deal programs that put millions of people to work building roads and creating parks, and ask why we couldn't do that again. A majority also supports a higher minimum wage or other policies that would raise the paychecks of those at the bottom.

I explore the pros and cons of such policies. My most important proposal is to boost wages for the bottom half of the earnings distribution by enacting a worker tax credit. I also stress the importance of full employment and favor a small jobs-based safety net at the bottom, a modest increase in the minimum wage, and an expanded tax credit for child care. All of these are predicated on work.

Creating Jobs

Many people look at the disappearance of well-paid jobs in manufacturing or elsewhere and conclude that there are simply not enough jobs to employ everyone who wants to work. Their implicit view of the world is that there are a fixed number of jobs, and that with so many disappearing, it will be impossible to supply everyone with a reasonable livelihood. Economists call this "the lump of labor" fallacy.

Why is this a fallacy? The number of jobs in the economy depends on how much people are spending; that is, on the total demand for goods and services. There are no limits to how much they are willing to spend. Instead of one or two pairs of jeans, we may want a pair for every different occasion. In *The Rise and Fall of American Growth*, Robert Gordon explains how as recently as a century and a half ago, it would have been unusual for most people to have had more than one or two outfits.[1] Now our closets are jammed with clothes. And don't forget about services. Even if we don't need more cars, cell phones, or blue jeans, we may want to have access to better health care and education, go to baseball games, or enjoy greener parks and cafés with exotic food. Yes, it's going to be difficult to teach a steel worker to be a nurse or a gourmet cook, but that's a different issue than the argument that we don't have enough jobs.

In this context, almost nothing could be more important than maintaining full employment. There is no better way to get more inclusive growth than by tightening the labor market. As Jared Bernstein has shown, tight labor markets raise wages, hours worked, employment, and thus incomes far more for the working and middle classes than almost anything else we could do.[2] My own analysis suggests something very similar.[3] Tight labor markets cause companies to do a lot more training, leading to a badly needed upgrading of worker skills.[4] Yet, over the 1980 to 2016 period, we managed to keep unemployment at or below CBO's measure of full employment only 29 percent of the time, according to Bernstein's analysis. This contrasts to 72 percent of the time from 1949 to 1979.

As this book went to press, the job market was beginning to look very healthy, with an unemployment rate at or near historically low levels. That said, there are still some reasons to be concerned. As already noted, labor force participation rates among prime-age adults have fallen since 2000, especially among less-educated men. One possibility is that the job market is not quite as tight as it seems. If we pressed further on the accelerator, they might flow back into jobs, leading to a hoped-for higher growth rate.[5]

Despite my view that a high-employment economy is the best solution to the lack of jobs in the aggregate, many will be unpersuaded. As a result, some progressives are proposing a universal jobs guarantee.[6] One example comes from the Center for American Progress (CAP).[7]

The rationale for a guaranteed jobs program, as articulated by its advocates, is quite compelling. By setting a floor on wages and guaranteed access to jobs, the program would increase the bargaining power of all workers, not just those who took the public jobs. The workers could be employed in building or repairing infrastructure, providing child or elder care, beautifying parks and neighborhoods, and so forth. In theory, there is no shortage of worthy projects that might be funded. Advocates like to point to the eight million people employed during the Works Progress Administration (WPA), along with the 650,000 miles of roads and 78,000 bridges they created, as well as many other enduring legacies, between 1935 and 1943.[8]

One big problem with a guaranteed jobs program is that those who want but fail to find jobs in a full employment economy typically have a variety of barriers that give employers, including public or nonprofit employers, pause. Those barriers may include lack of skills or experience, lack of reliability, inability to get along with others, a criminal background, problems with substance abuse, and so forth. Those barriers make it likely that many will be unable to perform well in their public jobs. Building and repairing infrastructure takes skills that many jobless workers don't have, and taking care of children or the elderly requires a different set of skills that are no less important. In addition, taxpayers and those in regular jobs will not like the idea of using their money to fund what many will consider make-work jobs or boondoggles in the public sector. And those taking the jobs may similarly feel as if they are not in "real" jobs that provide the dignity and respect they are looking for.

Although I think a large-scale public jobs program would be a mistake, there are two other ideas more deserving of support. The first is an independent investment bank, capitalized by the government and led by a board and chair appointed by the president, similar to the Federal Reserve. An independent and professional staff would then select for funding investments in infrastructure and basic research.[9] The investment projects would be selected and approved in advance on their merits but could then be timed to align with downturns in the private economy. Those making the selections would be engineers and analysts with the requisite expertise to consider both costs and benefits and, on that basis, prioritize the investments.

The second idea is to provide a very limited jobs-based safety net for those needing public assistance. It should be viewed as a way to help people transition to a regular job, especially ex-felons or others who need to demonstrate their competence and reliability, and not as a permanent source of employment. It could be combined with a work requirement for those seeking various government benefits. With such a job on offer, we would have a chance to see just how many people are unable to find regular employment and how many are simply holding out for better pay and benefits or have personal reasons for not working. My expectation is that the take-up rate for such an offer would not be very high, and that the cost would therefore be affordable, funded in part by safety-net savings.

Rewarding Work

There are always going to be low-paid jobs in services, retail trade, and other areas. As argued in the last chapter, we should not give up on upskilling these jobs. Child and elder care, for example, is a growing source of new jobs. Creating career ladders and better training for workers in these sectors can enhance their wages and their prospects for upward mobility. But if we care about the value of work, whether it is a fast-food worker, or the person who collects and disposes of our trash, we must also do more to reward low-paid workers for the jobs they are doing right now. One reason they deserve to be paid more is because their jobs are often difficult or disagreeable. Despite my view that there is dignity in work, some jobs confer more dignity than others.

There are three well-known mechanisms for helping workers in low-paid jobs. The first is raising the minimum wage. The second is worker credits, similar to the existing Earned Income Tax Credit, that boost people's earnings through the tax system. The third is providing more child care assistance to families with children, especially single parents, enabling them to work and keep more of their earnings when they do. These policies are not only consistent with the value of individual responsibility and the dignity that work can confer, but they also encourage labor force participation and a higher rate of economic growth. They will, in short, produce more broadly shared prosperity.

A Higher Minimum Wage

The erosion of the real value of the minimum wage since its peak in the late 1960s is one reason for growing gaps between wages at the bottom and those at the top. The big issue, of course, is whether a higher minimum would, by raising business costs, lead to less hiring.

Twenty-nine states and the District of Columbia have raised their minimum wage well above the federal level of $7.25 an hour. Despite fears that this would depress hiring and employment, there is little evidence of that occurring. A much-cited study by the economists David Card and Alan Krueger, looking at fast-food businesses in adjoining states with different minimum wages, found no indication that a higher minimum wage reduced employment.[10] A meta-analysis by Hristos Doucouliagos and T. D. Stanley considered sixty-four different U.S. minimum-wage studies and found that the most precise estimates were heavily clustered at or near zero employment effects.[11]

The Congressional Budget Office modeled the employment and income effects of an increase in the federal minimum wage, and found that raising it to $10.10 would reduce employment by about half a million nationwide but simultaneously improve the incomes of over 16 million workers. The increased earnings for low-wage workers from a higher minimum wage would total around $31 billion.[12] I would count this as a big net gain—the benefits of the higher incomes for so many families outweighing a very small (and statistically uncertain) reduction in jobs for the least skilled, many of them teenagers.

Increases in the minimum wage have two other favorable effects. First, they encourage higher rates of pay for those just above the minimum. Second, they reduce dependence on government benefits, such as food stamps or the Earned Income Tax Credit, leading to major budgetary savings and more dignity for the recipients, who become fully or partially self-supporting.[13]

These studies of the minimum wage rarely provide guidance on just how high one can raise the minimum before having a substantial negative effect on employment. Indeed, my colleagues Harry Holzer and Gary Burtless have both argued that a $15 federal minimum wage may be too high. Given the significant variation in living costs across the country and the fact that some local labor markets have a disproportionate number of less-educated workers, it may be best to allow states and cities to establish their own minimums.[14]

One example is Seattle, which raised its minimum wage in 2015 from $9.47 to $11, and again in 2016 to $13 an hour. A study conducted by researchers at the University of Washington found that these increases did have some adverse effects.[15] That study didn't go uncontested.[16] These kinds of dueling studies make it difficult to know what to believe, but there is likely a wage at which the policy's negative employment effects outweigh its positive impacts on wages.

Still, the vast majority of research in this field suggests that the impacts of minimum wage increases on employment so far have been negligible. All public policies have benefits and costs. To me, raising the federal minimum wage to around $12 an hour and indexing it for inflation seems like a policy whose benefits outweigh its possible costs.

An Expanded EITC or Worker Credit

Another approach to helping the bottom of the income distribution would be to expand the Earned Income Tax Credit (EITC) to cover more lower-income, working households. One of the benefits of the EITC is that it only helps those who help themselves. It is conditioned on work. It simply tops up your wages. That has led such disparate political figures as Ronald Reagan, Bill Clinton, Paul Ryan, and Barack Obama to endorse it at various times.

The EITC is a complicated program. Workers receive a refundable credit (a subsidy that is sent to the family, much like a tax refund). The subsidy is based on an employee's earnings, his or her family size, and his or her marital status. The subsidy phases out at higher income levels. For a single parent with two children, working fulltime at the minimum wage and earning $15,000 a year, the EITC boosted his or her income in 2016 by $5,572 per year. Among childless workers, the benefits are meager.[17]

The EITC promotes work and reduces poverty.[18] In combination with a higher minimum wage, a more generous EITC could be a budget-neutral proposition.[19] The reason is because a higher minimum wage reduces dependence on government benefit programs, freeing up resources that can then be devoted to wage subsidies that help people become self-supporting. Liberals have always supported the EITC; some conservatives have as well, but even more might endorse such measures if they understood the role that both minimum wages and wage subsidies play in encouraging work and in reducing dependence on other government programs, such as food stamps or TANF (welfare).

A proposal from Senator Sherrod Brown and Representative Ro Khanna would both increase the value of the EITC and dramatically expand its reach to childless workers.[20] According to the Tax Policy Center, this proposal would increase the after-tax income received by those in the bottom 20 percent of the income distribution by 6.6 percent.[21]

To be sure, proposals of this sort would be expensive. Researchers from the Tax Policy Center and the Center on Budget and Policy Priorities have analyzed them and shown that something like the Brown-Khanna proposal would cost a little over $1.4 trillion over a decade.[22] As Neil Irwin, who initially suggested an analysis of this approach, wrote in the *New York Times,* "even if you conclude that a radical expansion of tax credits for working-class Americans is desirable, the politics of paying for it are somewhere between hard and impossible."[23]

Despite its popularity, the EITC has a number of shortcomings. The first is that it is very complicated, and for this reason has been plagued with error rates and some fraud. The second is that it discourages marriage. The third is that, by basing benefits on the number of children in a family, it puts too little emphasis on the responsibility of parents to limit the size of their family to what they can afford.

For these reasons, I prefer a much simpler worker pay credit, similar to one suggested by the Tax Policy Center's Elaine Maag in 2015.[24] It would provide a 15 percent raise to every working American up to a maximum of $1,500 per year. The credit would then phase out as earnings rose up to around $40,000 per year. Because this would be based on individual income (and not household income, like the EITC), a couple could earn far more than this by pooling its earnings. This makes the proposal very marriage friendly, in addition to rewarding work. The credit would be delivered as part of an individual's paycheck, offsetting payroll taxes and reinforcing the idea that it is not only an earned benefit but also a form of tax relief for working families.

Paying for the Worker Credit

As noted, a modest expansion of the EITC or of its first cousin, a worker credit, combined with a higher minimum wage, need not be expensive.[25] A much larger expansion, similar to Brown-Khanna, would be. Although Neil Irwin is undoubtedly right about the political feasibility of such an expansion, there is an obvious and compelling way to pay for it. It is by taxing wealth, not work.

Wealth is even more unequally distributed than income. Both the concentration of wealth and the concentration of income have reached record highs in recent years, but wealth more so than income.[26] The baby boom generation, the most affluent generation in history, will, over the next few decades, pass on $30 trillion of their wealth to the next generation.[27]

The inheritance of wealth is inconsistent with basic American values. The American dream rests on the assumption that we live in a meritocracy, where a combination of skill and hard work, rather than inherited class or privilege, is the road to a better future. The estate tax is one of the few mechanisms available to limit inherited wealth. Many members of Congress are proposing to eliminate it.[28] If they don't want to be seen as favoring the rich and powerful, and instead want to be seen as favoring work over inherited wealth, they should adjust their stance.

The tax's power to promote intergenerational mobility has eroded very badly over time. The estate tax is paid by a tiny fraction of American estates—about 2 out of every 1,000 deaths. That contrasts to the 1970s, when there were over 70 taxable estates for every 1,000 deaths.[29] Most of that decline reflects the rising exemption level. In the 1970s, the exemption was $60,000 (about $280,000 in today's dollars, or over half a million per couple). The Tax Cuts and Jobs Act of 2017 doubled the exemption level for the estate tax, so that every estate smaller than $11.2 million (or $22.4 million per married couple) will be exempt. Not only are very few estates subject to the tax, but contrary to what many believe, even fewer of them are small businesses and family farms (about 80 in 2017, and this value will be even lower under the new tax law).[30]

Despite the fact that they will never be hit by the estate tax, the majority of Americans still think that we should eliminate it.[31] This is largely due to misconceptions about who pays the tax. Of surveyed respondents who favor eliminating the tax, about 70 percent believe that it will affect them, and three-quarters believe that it might force the sale of a small business or a family farm.[32]

Republicans have framed the estate tax as a "death tax." This confuses the timing of the tax with whom it affects. *Dead people don't pay taxes.* The main burden of the estate tax is on those who receive bequests. The reason it's important to be clear about this is because it is often argued that the estate tax involves taxing the same people twice. But it doesn't. In effect, it involves taxing two different people just once. Moreover, because unrealized capital gains make up a significant and growing share of larger estates, and the cost basis for taxing these gains is stepped up at death, much of this wealth is never taxed even once.[33] And because most recipients of large bequests are themselves wealthy and did nothing to earn their inheritance, these bequests are, in essence, welfare for the rich.[34] Some economists argue that the prospect of making a gift, or the anticipation of receiving one, changes behavior—for example, the incentive to save—but evidence that such changes are empirically important is scant.[35] Although the anticipation of being able to make a bequest might increase saving on the part of donors, the anticipation of receiving one might reduce saving on the part of the recipient. And regardless of its impact on savings, the receipt of large inheritances is a big work disincentive.[36] If we are going to worry about work disincentives in welfare for the poor, we should also worry about work disincentives in welfare for the rich.

Because of the rise in the exemption level and the drop in rates, revenue from combined estate and gift taxes has plummeted from what it was in the 1970s (see fig. 7.1).[37]

In 1972, the exemption level was over half a million per couple in today's dollars, and the top marginal tax rate was 77 percent, but that rate only applied to estates worth more than $10 million in 1972 dollars (about $58

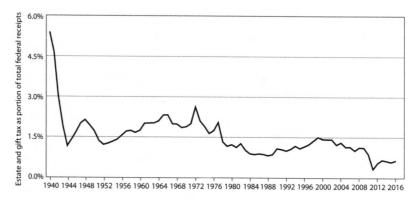

Fig. 7.1. Estate and gift tax revenue as a portion of total federal receipts has declined
Source: Office of Management and Budget, "Historical Tables," tables 2.1 and 2.5,
https://www.whitehouse.gov/omb/budget/Historicals

million today).[38] If the combined estate and gift taxes were to generate the same share of federal revenue as they did back then, they would have produced about $85 billion in 2015. The nearly $1 trillion that this could generate over a decade would be roughly enough to provide a substantial pay raise to the working class.

In combination with a higher estate tax, a worker pay credit would prevent America from becoming more of a class-based society than it already is. It would simply ask each new generation to earn their own way. It would provide bigger paychecks to a group of Americans who have been falling behind. And it would honor the importance of work—not welfare or windfalls—for boosting one's income.

As Franklin D. Roosevelt declared to Congress in 1935, "The transmission from generation to generation of vast fortunes by will, inheritance, or gift is not consistent with the ideals and sentiments of the American people."[39]

Instead of repealing the estate tax, perhaps it's time to use it to reward and encourage work.

Subsidizing Child Care

Another way to encourage work and increase take-home pay is to help families pay for child care. It is by far the largest expense associated with earning a living. Of those who report paying for child care, mothers with at least one child under age fifteen spend an average of about $7,000 per year on child care, or 7 percent of family income. For families living below the poverty level, child care expenses are nearly one-third of income. Families with younger children spend even more—those with children under five spent an average of $9,300 per year on child care, or over 10 percent of family income.[40] Reducing the costs of child care not only increases the disposable income available to these families, it also increases the employment of both married and single mothers.[41]

Currently, there are two major sources of government support for child care. The first is a federal block grant program that provides funds to states to cover the child care expenses of working families with below-average incomes. Eligible families must have incomes below 85 percent of the state's median income, but the program has never received sufficient funds to serve all families in need.

A second source of funding is a child care tax credit (CCTC) that allows families to subtract from any income tax liability a portion (typically 20 percent) of their child care costs (up to $6,000 a year for two children). The credit is only available to parents who are working or in school.[42] The biggest problem with the credit is that it is not refundable. Since most lower-income families don't have any income tax liability (although they do pay hefty payroll taxes), it doesn't help them at all. It primarily benefits the affluent. In fact, most of the benefits go to families with annual incomes between $100,000 and $200,000 a year.[43] In 2016, only about 13 percent of families with children benefited from the CCTC, and families in the lowest income quintile rarely received any help at all.[44]

I have long argued that child care subsidies are a good way to encourage work, enhance women's prospects, and provide safe and stable care for children. They are the policy equivalent of a hat trick. They make it possible for single parents to support their families and for more two-parent families to bring in a second paycheck. Simply making the CCTC refundable would largely benefit families who need it most. The Tax Policy Center estimates that two-thirds of the benefits of refundability would go to families with less than $30,000 in cash income—a group that receives only 6 percent of the total benefits of the existing program.[45] The bipartisan

PACE Act of 2017, sponsored by representatives Kevin Yoder (R-KS) and Stephanie Murphy (D-FL), would make the CCTC fully refundable, raise the credit rate, and index it to inflation.[46] Some have argued for an expanded child tax credit—to be distinguished from a child *care* tax credit.[47] The existing child tax credit was expanded to $2,000 as part of the Tax Cuts and Jobs Act. One advantage of the child tax credit is that it gives families the choice to either work or be stay-at-home parents. But that choice exists only for the more affluent portions of the population and not for most of the forgotten Americans.

Finally, where it is possible to provide a high-quality preschool experience to the children from such families while their parents work, that would enhance children's prospects as well. Such programs tend to cost more but cover all four bases—work, women's prospects, safety, and children's development. They are, in short, a home run!

Conclusion

Jobs and wages are important, and we must find ways to improve both. The Earned Income Tax Credit has been a popular response and needs to be both simplified and expanded. But government tax credits to shore up wages at the bottom are not a sufficient long-term strategy. Instead, we need to reskill the workforce, as argued in chapter 6. In addition, a big new government program may not be in the cards, and even if it were, it would be a mistake to not ask the business community to play a larger role in training and rewarding workers. The private sector needs to get involved for the sake of social cohesion, the health of our democracy, and, as I will show in chapter 8, even for the sake of its own bottom line.

8

A Bigger Role for the Private Sector

THE PRIVATE SECTOR IS RESPONSIBLE FOR nearly 85 percent of all jobs in the economy and for most of the income that ends up in people's pockets.[1] In addition, businesses are one of the few institutions that are still trusted by a majority of the public.[2] If we want to restore broadly based growth, we must engage the business community in that task.

This chapter calls for a new approach, one that could lead to more job growth and more sharing of rewards with workers. My hope is that this approach will become more common simply because it is usually a win-win for both businesses and their workers. However, business practices are sticky, and there are social benefits beyond those that accrue to individual companies. For these reasons, changes in the tax system may be needed to get the country moving in the right direction.

Many supporters of the Tax Cuts and Jobs Act of 2017 believe it will have the effect of creating jobs and raising wages. Others are highly skeptical. Advocates believe that corporations will share their higher after-tax profits with workers and use the higher return on investment to expand their businesses and create jobs. They believe the law will make the United States more competitive with other countries, encouraging more businesses to locate or remain in the United States.

Skeptics note that businesses had trillions of dollars of profits to invest before the law was enacted. They have been using those profits primarily to purchase their own stock or provide higher dividends to shareholders. The

2017 law left most corporate tax loopholes untouched, and made an already complicated set of rules even more complex and open to gaming. Critics further note that corporations are freer than ever to seek out tax havens abroad in a "territorial system" in which taxes depend on where the income was earned. They also argue that the huge increase in debt occasioned by the bill will slow growth over the longer run.

On the other hand, these looming deficits make it likely that some corrections will be needed down the road. When President Reagan reduced taxes in 1981, ballooning deficits, it required several additional tax laws to restore some semblance of fiscal health. That fact, together with the lack of any Democratic support for the bill, makes it likely that we will see another tax law to correct the flaws in the recent one. Assuming the law is revisited, that will provide an opportunity to nudge the private sector toward a more inclusive form of capitalism.

Why a New Approach Is Needed

One reason that growth has not been broadly shared in recent decades is because earnings for the forgotten Americans have stagnated. Productivity (output per hour) has improved, but workers' wages have not increased in

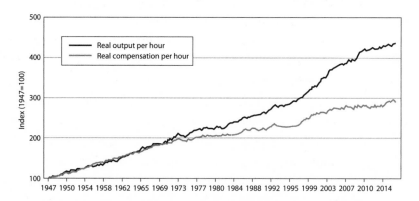

Fig. 8.1. Productivity has increased more rapidly than compensation

Source: Author's analysis of Bureau of Labor Statistics,
Series ID COMPRNFB and Series ID OPHNFB, FRED (Federal Research Bank
of St. Louis), accessed June 11, 2017, https://fred.stlouisfed.org/series/
Note: Real output per hour and real compensation per hour are for
the nonfarm business sector. Both are seasonally adjusted.

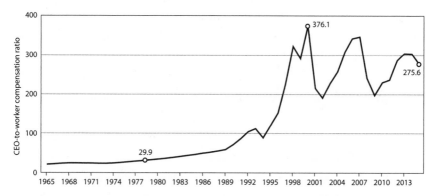

Fig. 8.2. CEO-to-worker compensation ratio has increased since 1980s
Source: Mishel and Schieder, "CEOs Make 276 Times More than Typical Workers," figure C
Note: CEO annual compensation is computed using the "options realized" compensation series, which includes salary, bonus, restricted stock grants, options exercised, and long-term incentive payouts for CEOs at the top 350 U.S. firms ranked by sales.

tandem as they once did (see fig. 8.1).[3] Instead, the benefits of growth have accrued primarily to those at the top of the distribution, including CEOs and shareholders.

Consider what has happened to executive pay. In 2014, on average, CEOs earned $16.3 million annually, over 300 times as much as a typical employee. That contrasts with only 30 times the salary of the typical employee as recently as the late 1970s.[4] The big fluctuations since then (see fig. 8.2), reflect the growing popularity of performance-based pay in the form of stock options. These big increases at the top may have come at the expense of pay levels for other workers or of needed investments in the longer-term growth of a company and the economy.

As it was, the share of income received by the top 1 percent more than doubled from 9 percent in 1976 to 22 percent in 2015. Top incomes have risen in most countries, but the United States stands out in the degree to which rewards have flowed overwhelmingly to the rich. This pattern suggests that institutional or policy differences are playing a key role. It may be that as taxes on high earners were reduced in the United States and members of this group got to keep more of their own money, they had more incentive to bargain for higher pretax compensation. Corporate boards may have responded to these demands, and social norms about what executives "should" earn appear to have shifted (beginning in the 1980s).[5]

The private sector has, at the same time, become overly focused on short-term profits rather than long-term investments, including investments in training. These are constraining a higher level and more inclusive form of growth.

For these and other reasons, labor's share of national output has fallen. Whatever the size of the pie, a much bigger slice than in the past is going to the owners of capital and less of it to the workers who helped create it.

These facts suggest that something is amiss. Under certain assumptions, free markets are the best way to deliver broad-based prosperity. But markets are neither moral nor infallible. Incomplete information, imperfect competition, established norms and practices, the sluggish mobility of capital or labor, and other frictions may be the rule rather than the exception. In addition, what's good for General Motors is not necessarily good for the country. A focus on short-term profits may satisfy activist investors but undermine long-term productivity. Underinvesting in worker training, given that workers often leave to go to another firm, may be rational for an individual company but not beneficial for the economy at large. Similarly, if every company thinks their CEO is above average and pays him or her accordingly, it can lead to the upward spiral in executive pay (see fig. 8.2). So, government has a role to play if we want a more productive and inclusive form of capitalism.

In what follows, I focus on two of the areas in which a new approach is needed: encouraging businesses to invest for the longer term and sharing more gains with workers. The first should create more jobs; the second should boost worker pay.

Investing for the Long Term

Excessive focus on the short term is a growing problem in the United States. Too many businesses are sacrificing long-term gains for short-term success.

Capital markets exist to transfer savings into investment, and, in principle, decisions about how to allocate spending between short- and long-run purposes should be based on a comparison of relative rates of return discounted for delay and uncertainty. If there are profits to be had from more long-term investment, one might ask, why doesn't competition eliminate the gap? The answer may be because both capitalists and managers are myopic. Both classical economists and contemporary behavioral scientists have emphasized this problem. Alfred Marshall famously said that too many people are like "children who pick the plums out of their pudding to eat them all at once."[6] Potential losses from long-term investment are weighted more heavily than gains (another phenomenon emphasized by behavioral research). In addition, executives may believe, with some merit, that their reputations and compensation are tied to how they do in the short run. Activist investors and traders encourage companies to keep an eye on quarterly profits. Once certain practices are established—for example, issuing quarterly earnings guidance—it may be difficult for any individual CEO to break with that tradition or ignore the pressures imposed by both their boards and their investors. This has given rise to companies buying back their own stock, financial manipulation or creative accounting to move earnings from one quarter to another, and cutting back or neglecting longer-term investments in order to boost short-term profits or stock prices. The data on these practices are sobering. Almost 80 percent of chief financial officers at 400 of America's largest public companies say they are willing to sacrifice the long-term value of the firm if it helps them achieve their quarterly profit targets.[7] Business investment in recent decades has been weaker than warranted based on expected returns over the past thirty years, and short termism appears to be one important reason.[8] Analysis of implicit rates of return on investment shows that firms are leaving profitable initiatives on the table.[9] A growing portion of profits is being used for stock buybacks and dividends instead of for investments in workers, in equipment, and in new markets and products, and the average stock holding period has fallen from eight years in 1960 to eight months in 2016.

Most striking of all are the results from a recent study by McKinsey and Company, a management consulting firm.[10] The study shows that there has been a rise in companies that focus on short-term performance, especially since the financial crisis. It further shows that companies that focus more on the long term consistently perform better on a variety of metrics.[11] Between 2001 and 2014, these long-term-oriented companies experienced higher revenue, greater earnings growth, and larger economic profits. They

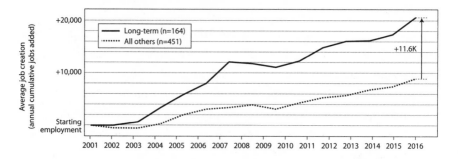

Fig. 8.3. "Long-term companies contribute more to employment
and economic output than other firms"
Source: Barton et al., "Measuring the Economic Impact of Short-Termism," 7, exhibit 4

were able to return more to their shareholders, despite giving less emphasis to quarterly earnings. The study's authors note that the "potential value
unlocked by companies taking a longer-term approach was worth more
than $1 trillion in forgone US GDP over the past decade; if these trends
continue, it could be worth nearly $3 trillion through 2025."[12] Not only did
companies with longer time horizons reap greater profits but they also created far more jobs (see fig. 8.3).[13]

My colleagues William Galston and Elaine Kamarck conclude that the
increasing focus on boosting shares at the expense of capital investments
could "doom our economy to a new normal of slow growth."[14] They cite a
number of business leaders who are concerned about the tendency of
today's companies to borrow money to boost dividends and increase share
buybacks at the expense of capital investment and other long-term strategies. Galston and Kamarck call for a number of sensible reforms to reduce
stock buybacks, curb executive pay, and broaden corporate reporting to focus more on the longer term. Another oft-cited reform would include a
capital gains tax rate that is high for speculators but lower on longer-held
assets, and possibly a financial transactions tax as well.

The findings reported above are eye-opening. They suggest that competition alone and lower corporate tax rates are not going to maximize growth,
much less inclusive growth. Unless the private sector pays more attention
to the longer term and to the welfare of workers as well as shareholders, there
will be too little growth, with most of its benefits going to the fortunate few.

If myopia is widespread, if current practices and norms are sticky, and if there are social benefits to more rapid job growth and more investment in worker training, then market forces alone will not correct the problem. Public policy has a role to play. As Paul Polman, the CEO of Unilever and one of the leaders of the Aspen Institute's American Prosperity Project, said, "If ultimately the purpose of a company is maximizing shareholder return, we risk ending up with many decisions that are not in the interest of society."[15] Or as Dominic Barton, the head of McKinsey, has put it, "We can reform capitalism, or we can let capitalism be reformed for us, through political measures and the pressures of an angry public."[16]

Sharing Gains with Workers

Back in the early postwar period, corporations tended to follow what many call a stakeholder—or what I call an "inclusive"—model of capitalism. It involved paying attention not just to shareholders, but other stakeholders as well, including workers, customers, or the community. Granted, in that era, businesses didn't have to worry as much about foreign competition and did have to worry more about unions.

Inclusive capitalism remains a successful strategy for many companies. They have showcased what can be accomplished when the private sector focuses on motivating workers—whether in the form of profit sharing, training, or providing a variety of benefits such as health care or paid leave. Without such an approach, it will be difficult to achieve broadly based economic growth. It would simply require too much redistribution after the fact, as argued in chapter 5. Instead, *we need a less unequal distribution of market incomes brought about by changing private sector practices.* Done right, this can be a win-win for workers and shareholders alike. And, as many forward-looking business leaders now recognize, if current trends continue, the public may demand something far less palatable.

In the past, workers relied on unions to bargain for higher pay and better benefits and working conditions. Half a century ago, the typical worker at General Motors earned $35 an hour in today's dollars. Compare this to the $11 an hour that the typical Walmart worker earns. As Robert Reich notes,

"This does not mean the typical GM employee a half century ago was 'worth' more than three times what the typical Walmart employee in 2014 was worth . . . The real difference was that GM workers a half century ago had a strong union behind them that summoned the collective bargaining power of all autoworkers to get a substantial share of company revenues for its members."[17] But union membership is now a fraction of what it once was, and it is not likely to return to its heyday in the face of global competition, the decline of manufacturing, and an increasingly professional and white-collar workforce. The proportion of workers who are members of unions has fallen from its mid-1950s peak of 35 percent to about 6 percent now.[18] Despite unions' depleted numbers, all is not lost; companies such as Costco, Trader Joe's, Patagonia, Southwest Airlines, Publix grocery stores, and Ben & Jerry's have made progressive labor policies a major part of their business practices, and have thrived while doing so. Business tax reforms that encourage similar commitments among other companies may help catalyze others to follow their lead.

One common argument against such progressive policies is that they are inconsistent with maximizing profits and serving the interest of shareholders. But there is increasing evidence that this is wrong.

Steven Pearlstein, a business columnist with the *Washington Post*, put the argument as follows:

> In the recent history of management ideas, few have had a more profound—or pernicious—effect than the one that says corporations should be run in a manner that "maximizes shareholder value."
>
> Indeed, you could argue that much of what Americans perceive to be wrong with the economy these days—the slow growth and rising inequality; the recurring scandals; the wild swings from boom to bust; the inadequate investment in R&D, worker training and public goods—has its roots in this ideology.
>
> The funny thing is that this supposed imperative to "maximize" a company's share price has little foundation in history or in law. Nor is there any empirical evidence that it makes the economy or the society better off. What began in the 1970s and '80s as a useful corrective to self-satisfied managerial mediocrity has become a corrupting, self-interested dogma peddled by finance professors, money managers and over-compensated corporate executives.[19]

These are strong words, and there are, as always, two sides to the story. Corporations are not evil, and managers must deal with competing goals even when they don't subscribe to the shareholder-first philosophy.

Many people still believe that shareholders come first, as a matter of law. That's wrong. As Lynn Stout, a prominent legal scholar on this subject, writes, "contrary to popular belief, the managers of public companies have no enforceable legal duty to maximize shareholder value. Certainly they can choose to maximize profits, but they can also choose to pursue any other objective that is not unlawful, including taking care of employees and suppliers, pleasing customers, benefiting the community and the broader society, and preserving and protecting the corporate entity itself. Shareholder primacy is a managerial choice—not a legal requirement."[20] Corporations are not owned by anyone; they own themselves. They are the equivalent of "persons"—as we should all know in the wake of Citizens United. The only rights held by shareholders are the right to vote for directors and the right to any residual value of the corporation in the case of dissolution or sale.[21]

I think Pearlstein and Stout are right about both the law and the evidence. What may be good for any one company is not necessarily good for society; those social benefits create a strong case for government intervention. Why not structure the next round of business tax reform in a way that recognizes these social benefits? I can even imagine some bipartisan agreement around such measures. Delivering these benefits through the private sector should please conservatives. Acknowledging the social benefits and the need for more inclusive growth should please liberals.

Later in this chapter, I suggest some ways in which business tax reform could nudge the private sector in a better direction. But first I want to emphasize the implications of this view of the world for workers and their wages. From the time of Henry Ford, employers have recognized that whether we are talking about wages, benefits, or working conditions, minimizing employment costs is not always the best strategy. In 1914, Ford introduced a $5-per-day wage at his automobile factory, doubling the daily wage while simultaneously reducing the average workday from 9 hours to 8 hours. His company was rewarded with improved worker productivity, reduced turnover, and higher profit margins. The business historian Daniel

Raff and Harvard economist Lawrence Summers estimate that productivity gains ranged from 30 to 50 percent as a direct result of these increased wages.[22] Prior to the wage increase, Ford's company had some of the worst worker retention and highest absenteeism rates in the industry. Raff and Summers suggest that the improved productivity and profitability resulting from the implementation of this policy is evidence of "efficiency wages," wherein offering workers higher wages increases employee effort, reduces turnover and absenteeism, and improves morale.[23] Thus, productivity and profitability can be, within some range at least, an increasing function of wages—a counterintuitive notion, to be sure.

Of course, one can take this principle to an extreme. In 2015, Dan Price, the CEO of a Seattle-based credit card processing company announced that he was going to pay all his employees a minimum of $70,000 a year. The figure was chosen on the basis that it was what most people needed to live comfortably. The CEO temporarily slashed his own paycheck from $1 million to $70,000 to help pay for his new experiment. Price was an instant celebrity, flooded with new customers, and lauded by grateful employees. However, not everyone was happy. Some employees groused that it wasn't fair to pay everyone the same regardless of their skills and contributions, and some key employees left. Other businesses in the area worried that he was setting a standard that would bankrupt most of them. Meanwhile, Price was steeped in a lawsuit (that he ultimately won), which was filed by his brother, a minority shareholder of the company. Three years later the company is doing well. Revenues and employment have both expanded, despite the higher pay.

The moral of these stories is that employers have a choice: they can run a stakeholder or a shareholder company. A stakeholder employer doesn't need to go as far as either Henry Ford or Dan Price to treat their employees well. These companies reaped the benefits of being first movers among their peers, and these benefits may not be sustainable or scalable. Clearly, there are limits and trade-offs, but the point at which better pay and benefits for workers become inconsistent with higher profits isn't as clear as your Economics 101 textbook suggests. Employers, like the rest of us, are sheep. They pay what the competition pays. When unionized workers successfully raised wages in the 1950s, nonunion firms followed suit. That behavior has economic boundaries, to be sure, but also a socially defined component. Within some ill-defined range, the cost of labor doesn't determine the ability of a firm to be successful. When unions were stronger than they are now, they bargained for higher wages, and unionized workers earned what economists like to call "rents"—meaning more than they were supposedly worth. It helped, of course, if bargaining was industrywide and if there was little or no competition from other countries. But the benefits were also clear: middle-class communities with stable families and a broadly based prosperity that created plenty of demand for the goods the workers were producing.

Contrary to what many economists preach, wages are not set by demand and supply alone. There are wide differences in pay for equally skilled workers across firms—something that is only possible in a less than fully competitive market.[24] Workers are heterogeneous, their productivity is hard to assess, and replacing existing workers can be costly. Wage-setting norms matter, and bargaining over shares of a firm's profits occurs. As noted above, in recent decades, efforts to minimize costs and maximize short-run profits have led to too much of the surplus going to executives. However, the variation in practices and productivity across firms is wide, and appears to be growing wider, despite the fact that competition is supposed to eliminate these gaps. The most successful firms on the frontiers of practice in an industry are still experiencing increased productivity, while the majority of firms in each industry are lagging badly, putting a drag on total productivity growth for the economy at large.[25] One likely reason is that economic concentration is also growing, and, with greater monopoly power, firms are less bound by the market and freer to choose a management style and division of rewards that suits their preferences.[26] The rising share of income going to capital at the expense of labor is, in part, the result of this rising concentration.[27] The decline of unions has also opened up opportunities to reallocate income from workers to owners and managers. It would be nice if union power could be restored, but there are other ways to ensure that more of the gains from any enterprise go to the workers who produce them. Profit sharing is one of them.

Joseph Blasi and Douglas Kruse at Rutgers and Richard Freeman at Harvard have done extensive research and writing on the topic of sharing rewards with workers. Their book, *The Citizen's Share,* describes various ways of giving workers a stake in the success of their companies. These include—in addition to profit sharing—employee ownership, gain sharing (for example, pay linked to group performance), and broad-based stock options.[28]

Profit sharing is the most common form of shared capitalism. These shares can be paid out as cash bonuses on a yearly or more frequent basis, and they depend on company profitability. Worker compensation is thus partly tied to how well the company does and can fluctuate quite a bit as a result. On average, firms that have adopted this practice provide a cash bonus that is 5 percent of an employee's annual compensation. In 2016, Ford hourly workers received an average profit-sharing check of $6,900.[29] Southwest Airlines' record profits in 2015 allowed them to pay out profits of about 16 percent of the average employee's compensation to over 49,000 employees.[30]

Employee ownership is another form of shared capitalism. About 20 percent of all private sector workers own stock in their own company.[31] The value of this ownership is modest but not insignificant. The average private sector employee with stock owned over $45,000 in company stock in 2014.[32] There are many large corporations offering their employees a stock ownership plan (ESOP). These include Google, Procter & Gamble, and Southwest Airlines. Some companies are entirely owned by their employees. A good example is Publix Super Markets, a grocery store chain with over 180,000 employees. It has been an employee-owned company since 1974. Their plan awards free shares of stock to employees who have stayed for at least a year and have accrued more than one thousand hours with the company. These shares are valued between 8 and 12 percent of an employee's annual compensation.[33]

These various forms of shared capitalism are much more commonplace than might be expected: 47 percent of all for-profit employees participate in some form, with the greatest number (36 percent) participating in profit sharing.[34] Many companies use combinations of shared capitalism—for example, profit sharing to motivate workers in the short term and stock ownership to motivate them in the longer term.

Economic theory might predict a number of problems with various forms of shared capitalism. First, any extra benefits to workers from inclusive capitalism might simply be at the expense of regular compensation with no net benefit to the worker. Second, an inefficient allocation of capital can occur if a firm is employee owned and thus less subject to the discipline of external capital markets. (Of course, high levels of retained earnings shield many companies from that discipline in any case.) Third, employees may be exposed to too much risk if their savings are primarily invested in their own company. Fourth, basing rewards partly on factors over which workers have little or no control (for example, the business cycle or energy prices) is inconsistent with the idea of pay for productivity. Related to this, it also makes an employee's compensation somewhat dependent on the productivity of his or her coworkers and can lead to free riding. (Why bother to work harder if profits are shared equally among workers and your effort constitutes a tiny fraction of the total?)

On the other side of the argument, tying compensation to profits can better align the interests of workers and managers, leading to higher productivity, less turnover or absenteeism, and higher returns to shareholders. It can lead to more employees monitoring each other's performance, more engagement in the enterprise, and a corporate culture that values employee participation and ideas, leading to greater teamwork and innovation.

There are now hundreds of studies on the effects of various forms of shared capitalism, including meta-analyses that attempt to extract some general lessons from all the individual studies. Typically, the studies look at the output or value added by a firm and try to determine how much difference some form of shared capitalism makes, after holding constant or adjusting for as many other firm differences as possible or by matching similar firms with and without employee ownership or profit sharing. As always, the findings are mixed but strongly suggest the following:

1. The effects on output or productivity are typically positive.[35]
2. Profit sharing has larger effects than employee ownership.[36]
3. Financial gains to workers do not come at the expense of their regular pay; they usually add to it.
4. Firm profits and share prices are either not affected or given a boost.[37]

5. Any positive effects are usually small when averaged across firms. Negative effects are very uncommon.

6. When ESOPs are adopted not to improve incentives but for other reasons, such as preventing a takeover, the results can be negative.

7. Sorting out cause and effect has been difficult. Are successful firms more likely to share their profits or does profit sharing help to make them more successful? It is likely that both are true. At least one study identified the causal direction by randomly assigning twenty-one fast-food franchises to one group that shared profits and another group that did not. The study found that those franchises randomly assigned to the profit-sharing group experienced greater productivity and profitability and reduced employee turnover.[38]

Given this extensive evidence, why, then, is profit sharing or some other form of shared capitalism not more widespread? The answer may be simple inertia, lack of knowledge about its benefits, or some continued skepticism about how to interpret the evidence. It may be related to the kind of short termism and increased monopoly power discussed earlier. And it may simply be ideological, reflecting the strong belief, among economists and many business leaders in particular, that markets will ensure that both labor and capital markets are efficient and that widening gaps in incomes and earnings, with the top ranks pulling away from everyone else, are the result of competitive forces. With increases in the scale of global markets and the size of corporations, for example, a winner-take-all bidding up of top salaries may have occurred. On the other side of the argument, increasing levels of industry concentration and other noncompetitive forces, along with evolving social norms and close ties between top managers and their boards, may be creating unearned economic rents. A greater role for workers and broader sharing of such rents need not harm the performance of a company or of the economy at large. In fact, in many cases, it would improve it.

If a larger role for the private sector in producing inclusive growth makes economic sense, what about the politics of moving further in that direction?

It turns out that the idea of employee ownership has some bipartisan support. Conservatives support employee ownership because it gives workers a stake in capitalism, and liberals support it because it reduces inequality among employees. As John Case puts it in the *Atlantic*, "The left favors spreading the wealth. The right wants to create more capitalists. With employee ownership, they can both get their way."[39]

The value of inclusive capitalism has deep roots in our history. As Blasi, Freeman, and Kruse note, the founders, from George Washington to Madison and Jefferson, all believed that democracy would not survive and flourish unless property ownership was widespread. In their day, the major form of property was land. The Homestead Act of 1862 and other laws were intended to encourage land ownership. Tax preferences for home ownership have a similar aim. But in an industrial or postindustrial era, the major form of property is financial capital, and we are seeing a growing concentration of such capital in the hands of a very small number of very wealthy people.[40]

In 1974, with the strong backing of Senator Russell Long, Congress enacted the Employee Retirement Insurance and Security Act (ERISA). It included tax preferences for the creation of ESOPs.[41] Again, the purpose was to spread the wealth. Currently, such plans receive numerous tax benefits. Broad-based profit sharing, which, as we have seen, is even more beneficial, has not been given a similar push.

There are any number of ways to address this and in the process to create a more worker-friendly form of capitalism. One idea is to change a provision in the Internal Revenue Code, Section 162(m).[42] The section was initially motivated by excessive executive pay. Until the enactment of the Tax Cuts and Jobs Act of 2017, executive pay in publicly held companies above $1 million per year could not be deducted unless that pay was performance based. The 2017 law scrapped the performance-based exclusion, meaning that all executive pay above $1 million is now nondeductible. It is thus subject to corporate taxation, albeit at the much lower rate of 21 percent.

Section 162(m) could be further amended to encourage more profit sharing. For example, a business with a broad-based profit-sharing plan could be allowed to take a credit for the portion of its profits shared with its employees (up to some wage or salary cap). Thus corporate or business taxes would only be levied effectively on the share of profits reserved for shareholders—or owner/managers in closely held corporations or partnerships.

Based on the evidence summarized above, profit sharing should be encouraged. Of all the types of inclusive capitalism, it poses the least amount of risk to employees, requiring no prior knowledge about the stock market. It also comes in the form of temporarily increased wages rather than stock ownership, and can be spent immediately if an employee needs to do so. ESOPs and stock options provide the opportunity for employees to earn more over the longer run, but they take much longer to vest, can be difficult to understand, and are subject to market volatility.

Flexibility is important, however. One practical solution would be for firms to enroll employees in at least two shared capitalism plans: one that poses little risk and provides immediate payout (profit sharing), and one that would allow for employees to invest in their company in the longer term through stock ownership, albeit in slightly riskier fashion.

Investing in Training

Broader ownership of financial capital and greater sharing of the rewards from enterprise would help to ameliorate inequality. But human capital is also more valuable than ever. While complaints of a "skills gap" are common among executives, few invest substantially in workforce training.[43] So, another way to help workers adjust to a rapidly changing economy would be to make corporate tax reductions conditional not just on a broader sharing of the wealth but also on corporate investments in education and training. These investments could be outsourced to community colleges or other training entities or provided by the company itself. Because the training would be closely linked to what companies need, and not to what providers or the government believe to be appropriate, there is a greater chance that employer-sponsored training would enhance wages, productivity, and upward mobility.

AT&T is one of a growing number of large companies that decided to invest more in its employees as a matter of economic competitiveness. Remaining on the frontlines of the telecommunications industry requires a highly skilled and innovative workforce trained to use the most modern technologies, but such a workforce doesn't evolve on its own. It requires company investments in employee development and motivated workers. As Thomas Friedman documents in *Thank You for Being Late,* AT&T felt increasing pressure to upskill its workforce from its competitors and the technological advances inherent to the industry. So it decided to assist its employees to become lifelong learners.[44] As *Fortune* describes it, "AT&T has embarked on what may be the most ambitious retraining program in corporate American history."[45] Its "Workforce 2020" program first identified skills necessary to remain competitive in a dynamic industry and established a goal of hiring as many people as possible from within the company. The company launched a self-service platform that enables individuals to develop skills, and tracks their progress and company outcomes.[46] An external hire can cost as much as $200,000, so the company prioritizes promotion and mobility within the company. As Bill Blase, the head of AT&T's human resources, explains, this "is more cost-effective and will generate more employee engagement and productivity, which means employees will go the extra mile so customers will be served better and shareholder value will increase. The companies with the most highly engaged workforces earn three times those with less."[47]

AT&T is practicing its own brand of inclusive capitalism with a focus on the long run. One way that AT&T assists its employees with lifelong learning is through partnerships with traditional and online universities to provide specific degrees and training credentials relevant to the company's work. It reimburses employees up to $8,000 per year and $30,000 across the employee's tenure with the company for pursuing such credentials. It then prioritizes hiring from within, thus incentivizing its workforce to pursue these opportunities. In 2016, the company filled more than 40 percent of its 40,000 job openings with existing employees.[48] John Donovan, the company's chief strategy officer, says, "you can be a lifelong employee if you are ready to be a lifelong learner. We will give you the platform but you have to opt in."[49]

AT&T is a great example, but it is large (with over 300,000 employees) and atypical. Most companies have little incentive right now to provide more training because workers are mobile and often leave the company that trained them. The return on such training might be high, but it cannot be captured by any one company.[50] The decline in lifetime employment with the same company and a lot more job switching by individuals have further eroded employer incentives to train their employees.[51] For their part, workers cannot normally afford to invest in their own training and may make poor choices even when they can. These market failures lead to underinvestment in skill building. At the same time, the performance of the U.S. economy and the well-being of most workers depend heavily on whether we can find a way to reskill the labor force in line with today's demands.

Employer-based training takes two major forms.[52] Informal, on-the-job training is usually provided by a more experienced worker to a new employee, while more formal training may take place in a classroom setting but with funding and curriculum supplied by the employer. Most on-the-job training only takes a few months to complete, but the vast majority of middle-skilled jobs require at least some training. Formal, classroom-based training is most common in STEM fields, health care, and certain blue-collar industries, especially those that require occupational licenses or certifications. Workers with a college degree are nearly twice as likely as high school graduates to receive formal employer-based training.[53]

The data on the current scope of worker training are admittedly inadequate. The last federally sponsored nationally representative survey on the subject was conducted in 1995.[54] Differing definitions of training can lead to widely varying estimates. Does a one-time information technology training session designed to update workers on the intricacies of Microsoft Office count as "training"? Or are we primarily talking about larger investments in skills that reap longer-term payoffs? In a review of the data on employer-sponsored training, Urban Institute economist Robert Lerman notes that estimates of the proportion of employed men and women ages twenty-five to sixty-four who received training in the last twelve months ranged from 21 percent to 56 percent.[55] According to the Survey of Income and Program Participation (SIPP), conducted by the U.S. Census Bureau, employers are offering less training than they did in the past (fig. 8.4).[56]

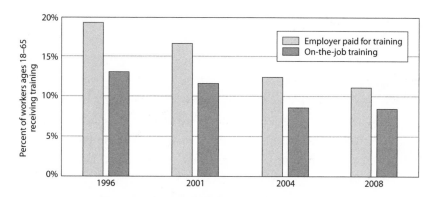

Fig. 8.4. Workers are receiving less employer-sponsored training than in the past
Source: Council of Economic Advisers, "Economic Report," figure 3-27
Note: Includes workers ages 18–65 receiving training of any duration in the prior year.
Values reflect CEA analysis of Census Bureau, SIPP Employment and
Training Topical Module.

While the scope of employer-sponsored training is hard to pin down, the empirical research shows that the benefits are positive for both firms and workers, with the training of less-skilled or less-educated workers creating the largest gains.[57]

Very few public dollars are invested in subsidizing employer training. As noted in chapter 6, federal spending on training has decreased. State spending is modest as well.[58]

Some state and local governments have experimented with offering training tax credits or grants to employers. For example, the New York State Employee Training Incentive Program offers a refundable income tax credit to businesses that invest in upgrading, retraining, or improving the productivity of employees or interns in certain advanced technology programs. The credit is 50 percent of the training costs, up to $10,000 per employee and up to $3,000 per intern. New York City also funds a Customized Training Program, awarding up to $400,000 per business and covering between 60 and 70 percent of eligible training costs.[59] The Massachusetts Workforce Training Fund allocated $107 million to 2,258 companies training more than 157,000 workers between 1999 and 2005. A study of the program found substantial rates of return to workers, firms, and the state.[60] States often adopt these training subsidies to attract business, but unlike most other subsidies employed for this purpose, those that improve worker productivity are not a zero-sum game for the economy as a whole, doing nothing more than reallocating jobs from one state to another. Instead, they can induce a positive-sum game, or "race to the top," as states compete to see who can provide the most support for worker training initiatives.

One way to scale up such investments would be to raise unemployment insurance taxes as proposed in chapter 6 and to allow the proceeds to be invested in worker training. A federal-match program would likely be more efficient than one that is entirely federally financed, as states and localities have more motivation and stronger relationships with local labor markets than the federal government. They would also reap the most immediate benefits from a more skilled workforce. However financed, given the broader benefits of training to workers and to society, training subsidies deserve greater support. Yes, they will be gamed (how does one measure how much training actually occurs that would not have occurred anyway?), but a little "windfall" of this sort may be the price one must pay to create a more competitive and better-paid workforce.

One way to avoid the windfall problem is to target any subsidies or tax credits on *increases* in training above some base level. In May 2017, scholars at the Aspen Institute proposed a worker training tax credit designed to do just that. It mirrors the policy design of the popular R&D Tax Credit—businesses would establish a base expenditure level on qualified training expenses based on the average amount spent in the three preceding years. The credit would cover 20 percent of the difference between the current expenditures on these qualified training activities and the base expenditure level, and it would not cover training expenses for highly compensated workers (making more than $120,000 per year).[61] Such a policy is attractive in that it is targeted to those who need it the most (low- and middle-wage workers), and it incentivizes investments in training on the margin.

While the empirical research has not come to a consensus about the optimal level of employer-sponsored training, its social benefits combined with very low levels of public subsidy suggest it is seriously underfunded. A major point of consistency across studies is that training is more common for higher-skilled workers and at larger firms. This skewed level of investment acts to perpetuate or worsen wage inequality.

Encouraging investments in human capital, particularly among America's less-skilled workers, is critical to reversing the wage stagnation among the forgotten Americans discussed in this and previous chapters. It could also improve productivity, generating more economic growth in the process.

Most jobs are in the private sector and most income comes from those jobs. Combine this with the fact that a new or greatly expanded federal program is unlikely to be approved anytime soon, no matter who sits in Congress or the White House, and we have a recipe for continuing stagnation of middle-class incomes. And the more those incomes stagnate, the more the electorate will blame its elected officials for failing them once again.

For the most part, the ball is in the court of the private sector, but it could use a little nudge delivered primarily through a reformed tax law. This isn't to say that many companies are not already practicing an inclusive form of capitalism. I was surprised to learn how many companies are sharing their profits, and how many, such as AT&T, have made training a priority—but there are still social benefits to be had here at a relatively low public cost. Long-term business strategies produce real results both for businesses and the overall economy, in terms of greater revenues, higher returns for shareholders, and more jobs. Putting the public thumb on the corporate scale here may at least signal what society values and what the longer-term health of our democracy requires.

9

Updating Social Insurance

IF THE LAST CHAPTER WAS ABOUT MAKING capitalism more inclusive, this chapter is about making capitalism more resilient—that is, better able to meet today's challenges. I propose two new social insurance funds. One is for lifelong learning and "fresh starts" for working-age Americans. Another is for paid leave to help workers struggling to balance their obligations to family with those of earning a living. To pay for these changes and put the system on a fiscally sustainable trajectory, retirement benefit growth needs to be slowed and payroll taxes increased, especially for higher-income Americans. We need a system that is fairer—both between and across generations—but also one that is affordable and fiscally sustainable.

This chapter begins with three fundamental questions. First, why do we need social insurance at all? Why shouldn't we be expected to save for various contingencies and future needs? The short answer is because we are shortsighted. We place far too much emphasis on our present as opposed to our future well-being.

Second, why, if we are so much more prosperous, are we not devoting less time to earning a living and more time to other worthy pursuits? We work far more hours than our European counterparts.[1] The usual answer to this question is that many people, especially those with limited incomes, can't afford to take more time off. But if we managed to save *collectively* for the purpose of devoting more time to activities other than work, this distributional issue could be solved. The problem is that our institutions, including existing labor laws and the social insurance system, are not well aligned with our ability to afford to work less.

Third and last, do we want to relegate whatever nonworking time we have primarily to our retirement years, or would we rather have some of that time in midlife to raise children, continue our education, or make a fresh start with a new business or a new career? My answer is that it's time to reallocate some resources across the age span.

After addressing these three questions, I review five trends that have reshaped our lives and require an update to social insurance in response. They include greater affluence, the shift to a knowledge economy, greater longevity, the dramatic increase in women's employment and the growth of single-parent families, and rising inequality.

The hallmarks of the new system would be its flexibility and its pivot from only enhancing security to boosting opportunity. It would promise support not just for retirement, but also for other purposes, and it would provide people with the ability to decide between different uses of paid time off. These could include midcareer training and education, and family and medical leave. They could also include (with strict limits) paid time off for starting a new business or engaging in some creative or community-oriented task. If the existing social insurance system is mostly about security and protecting people against risk, the new one would be more about providing opportunities for people to reinvent and reskill themselves and to strike out in new directions. By emphasizing opportunity and not just security, these new benefits might even increase mobility and growth.

Why We Need Social Insurance: The Grasshopper Syndrome

As behavioral economists have emphasized, we are all the victims of myopia. We are very bad at planning for the future. In theory, we should be expected to save enough money to take care of such contingencies as not being able to work in old age, becoming unemployed, or facing a serious illness or injury. Indeed, economists like to argue that, where feasible, individuals should save (self-insure) or buy private insurance to deal with the exigencies of life.[2] But they also recognize that insurance markets or private savings are not always the best option.[3] In practice, we may not be willing to set money aside for various purposes unless we are required to do so. Some believe we should simply allow people to bear the consequences of their shortsightedness. A true libertarian might even argue that those who cannot afford to buy health insurance, for example, should simply be allowed to go without medical care when the need arises.

In one of Aesop's fables, a grasshopper who was too busy singing all summer to collect food for the winter is facing starvation. He begs the ants who have collected a store of food for the winter to help him out. They respond, quite unsympathetically with a simple question: "May we ask what you were doing with yourself all last summer?"[4] An affluent society may similarly disapprove of goofing off all summer and of society's "moochers," but it is nonetheless unlikely to allow people to starve when hard times come. Social insurance requires the grasshoppers to save up for hard times through a system that spreads the risk and provides some extra help to those most in need, but it also asks them to contribute something. It is not outright charity, and it can be designed to provide incentives for people to work or save.

Private insurance has other drawbacks. Even were it available, only those facing the biggest risks (who often know who they are) will purchase the insurance, leading to a system that fails to spread the risks widely enough to make it affordable. (This is the issue of adverse selection that has played such a big role in debates about the Affordable Care Act and why coverage was made mandatory.) Finally, there is merit in spreading the burden of such costs across the entire population in an equitable fashion, recognizing that some of us will be lucky and some unlucky. We may not know in advance who among us is going to live for a long time and who is going to die early, but we can gain some peace of mind by insuring collectively against the risk of outliving our savings or incurring very large medical expenses, for example.

Then there are the risks created by changes in the economy that no one can predict. An individual who has worked hard for many years in a manufacturing plant, only to find his or her job has been made obsolete by automation or trade, can't buy insurance or save enough to deal with such misfortune. He or she needs help finding a comparable new job, but this might require taking time off to obtain new skills, move to another area, or start his or her own business.

Why We Need a New System

Imagine you are a young woman just graduating from high school and starting your first job. You will immediately notice that payroll taxes are deducted from your paycheck. You will discover that they are mainly for retirement and wonder if you will ever see those benefits many decades from now. As time goes on, you continue to pay these taxes but have any number of pressing needs: a new baby that requires your care, the desire to take a course at a community college to enhance your job prospects, a broken leg or a bout with cancer that necessitates taking time off to recover. Your income is essential to you and your family, yet there is no way to replace it unless you saved a lot out of your relatively meager pay. You know that you should be saving more, but it's hard. It takes discipline and planning—attributes that few people have in abundance, especially in a culture that is consumer oriented and credit card fueled. That's why payroll tax deductions make sense; they change the default from not saving enough to saving more, which is what you want to do even though you find it hard in practice. But you would like it to be for purposes you value and understand. Shouldn't there be an option to use some of your savings for something other than your old age, which, after all, is a long way away and filled with uncertainty? Will you still be alive? Will Social Security still exist?

Later, you discover that your payroll tax money is not going into a personal account, as you originally thought, but instead into a general "trust fund" at the Treasury Department that pays benefits to *today's* elderly. (Your benefits, in turn, will be paid by today's children when they become adults, in a giant Ponzi scheme.) Some of today's elderly, you can see, clearly need the money; others don't. And what about your own needs? Wouldn't it be nice to have the ability to receive some benefits before you reach retirement age?

In short, you have some very good reasons to question the current system. A lot has changed since it was first established in the 1930s. Let's take a tour of those changes.

Greater Affluence (and Why It Has Not Produced More Time Off)

We are more prosperous than ever, but very little of that prosperity has been devoted to expanding time off from work during one's prime working years. The assumption is that most people will spend virtually their entire lives on the job, from the time they leave school to the time when they retire, around age sixty-five. At that point, they may live another twenty years before they die.[5] They will receive generous benefits, courtesy of Social Security and Medicare—roughly $2 million per couple for the millennial generation, according to Eugene Steuerle.[6]

Because people are living longer than in the past, they are, for this reason alone, consuming more leisure over a lifetime. But if we were reinventing the system to fit today's economic and social realities, is retirement where we would want to concentrate our nonworking time? Does it make sense to work nonstop from the time one enters the labor force to the time when one reaches normal retirement age in one's mid- to late sixties? Why is it that none of our greater prosperity has been devoted to making more time available for other purposes, such as taking care of one's family, life-long learning, starting a new business, or easing various transitions and setbacks along the way?

As an economy becomes more prosperous, the relative scarcity and value of time becomes greater. If we value leisure by what we give up by not working, leisure is getting more expensive. Thus the phrase "time is money." On the other hand, with greater affluence, one might imagine people wanting to use some of their newfound prosperity to work less rather than more. Historically, it has been the wealthy who have been the leisured class.

After a century of progress in the United States that has increased GDP per capita at least fivefold, we are still working more or less as much as we did when the Fair Labor Standards Act of 1938 established the norm of a forty-hour workweek. Women are working more for pay, and if we were to include *unpaid* work in the home, as some time researchers do, we would find that there has been some decline in hours spent on paid and unpaid work combined.[7] This was made possible by smaller families, more labor-saving devices, and more market substitutes for home-produced goods. But if we focus on paid work outside the home, it's hard to see any decline at all.

Why? Is it because we can't bear to give up the extra income that work provides? Is it because business demands our full commitment, and the countervailing power of unions and government to restrain them—or to restructure work in ways that are better aligned with today's realities—has weakened? Is it because we really like to work?

Probably all of these have played a role, but the biggest reason we work so much is because our desire to consume more rises with our ability to do so and with what we see others enjoying. And with rising inequality, the consumption standards of the rich have produced a hamster wheel for everyone else, intensifying the unending struggle to keep up.

Although time can't be accumulated, money can be, and those who save are able to acquire more inter-temporal flexibility. With a nest egg or accumulated savings, they can buy time off from work to go back to school, to quit a job, or to sustain themselves through a period of unemployment or extensive job search. In this context, the lack of saving among the youngest generation seems especially troublesome. In a survey conducted by the Federal Reserve in 2016, 44 percent of Americans reported that if faced with a $400 emergency expense, they would either need to borrow, sell something to cover the expense, or not be able to come up with the money at all.[8] They are not just living paycheck to paycheck; they are in danger of becoming time slaves to work. In short, those who value autonomy should think about giving greater priority to saving. We cannot control the ups and downs in our lives, the opportunities and the setbacks, but we can be better prepared for dealing with them when they arrive, as they inevitably will. And if myopia rules, then we need a social insurance system that allows for these contingencies.

I don't want to omit from this discussion one important factor of why we continue to work as much as in the past: the intrinsic value of work. Psychologists who have studied these issues suggest that an engaged life, including one with meaningful work, has great benefits for our sense of well-being. Too much free time can lead to an unhealthy rumination or excessive anxiety about life's inevitable ups and downs. In chapter 5, I discussed the work of Mihaly Csikszentmihalyi whose book *Flow* argues that work can be a highly satisfying way to spend one's time.

The happiest people are those who have found a balance. In one survey, people who reported not feeling rushed but also being fully engaged (having no excess time) were twice as likely to report being very happy than the rest of the population. As John Robinson wrote for *Scientific American,* "there seems dysfunction in having either too much or too little free time. In a society that otherwise seems obsessed with speed and the latest IT gadgets, this would seem to offer a path to a more contented lifestyle."[9] Or, as James Gleick says in his smart and witty book *Faster,* time is something we all have. We must choose how to use it. "You can drift in its currents or you can swim."[10] Or, as the *Economist* magazine put it, time is "most highly valued when it is gone. No one has ever complained of having too much of it. Instead, most people worry over how it flies, and wonder where it goes. Cruelly, it runs away faster as people get older."[11]

Time, in fact, is the ultimate scarcity. It is also the great equalizer. We each have exactly 24 hours per day, 7 days per week, and 365 days per year. True, some of us live longer than others, and it is notable that the gap in longevity between those with higher and lower incomes has increased— one reason why I believe that the social insurance system needs to be adjusted to restore some of its earlier progressivity.

Work has great value, but we may need a better balance between paid work and other activities. We could easily afford that balance with the right social insurance system, one that works for those whose personal economic circumstances don't make that balance possible at the present time.

A New Economy

Not only were we much less affluent in the first part of the twentieth century when social insurance was enacted than we are now, but we also had an industrial economy. The deindustrialization of the economy and the effects of trade and technology on less-educated workers were given extensive treatment in earlier chapters. What I want to reiterate here is the importance of addressing the plight of these workers—the group I have called the forgotten Americans. The younger ones need better education and training, along with assistance to relocate. The older ones may need wage insurance, a worker tax credit, or other forms of assistance. More opportunities for lifelong learning will not only help workers adjust to changes in the economy, but they will also improve productivity and the rate of economic growth. Much of that training should, in my view, occur in school or in the workplace, as I argued in earlier chapters—with employers playing a bigger role. But our social insurance system should enable workers to take a certain amount of paid time off to train for a new career or enhance their existing skills to improve their labor market opportunities.

Greater Longevity

A century ago, most families had a single (male) breadwinner who often worked fulltime for one employer for much, if not all, of his working years. He died much earlier than would be the case today and had few (if any) years to enjoy retirement. An average twenty-year-old could be expected to live an additional sixty years in 2014, compared to only about forty-five a century ago.[12]

If one survives to the age of sixty-five today, one's chances of living longer are still greater: today, the average sixty-five-year-old can expect to live almost twenty more years. In 1930, the average sixty-five-year-old could only expect to live about twelve more years.[13] Not only are people living longer but they are also living healthier. Years of quality-adjusted life expectancy have increased largely thanks to the reduced incidence of cardiovascular disease and vision problems, for example, as well as improved functioning for those who do experience various health problems.[14]

These gains in life expectancy have not been evenly distributed. The better educated and those with higher incomes have secured the largest gains, while the less-educated or lower-income individuals have made little progress. The result is that gaps in longevity at older ages have widened sharply. For example, average life expectancy at age fifty for women born in 1920 was about 3.5 years higher for those in the top tenth of the income distribution than for those in the bottom tenth; twenty years later, the gap was closer to 10 years.[15]

There are several implications of these trends. First, a far larger proportion of the elderly should be able to work longer than in the past, especially those who are well educated and work in professional or white-collar jobs. They have been moving in this direction, as health and longevity have allowed, but policy has not kept pace.[16] The so-called full retirement age when one is eligible for full Social Security benefits was sixty-five for those born in or before 1937. It then gradually increased to sixty-six for those born between 1943 and 1954, and finally to sixty-seven for those born after 1960.[17] These retirement ages are not fully aligned with rising longevity, improved health, or the fact that work is less physically demanding than in the past. Further, many people want to work parttime or to retire gradually. Social Security should be adjusted accordingly, an issue that I return to below.

A second implication is that the divergence in longevity by income and education means that Social Security benefits are less progressive than in the past.[18] Although the system is designed to provide greater replacement of annual earnings for lower- than for higher-wage workers, those who live the longest collect benefits for a longer number of years than those who die early.[19] This is an argument for adjusting benefits in a way that recognizes the rising gap in life expectancy between the high-paid and the low-paid and the divergent circumstances of workers in white-collar jobs versus those doing physically demanding work.

The third implication is that a burgeoning population of the very old, those in their eighties and nineties, will increase the need for elder care. Even when such care is provided by home health workers or in an institution, families will be responsible for organizing or coordinating such care and spending time helping with a variety of tasks associated with having aging parents. For some, it will mean having to take time off in order to look after a parent. Paid leave proposals should take this need into account and allow leave to be used to care for aging relatives. In the end, this will be both more cost-effective and more humane than putting people in nursing homes.

More Employed Women and Single-Parent Families

Today, the majority of married couples with children have more than one earner.[20] In fact, women are not just contributing to family income but are over 40 percent of all *primary* breadwinners in America.[21] These primary breadwinners include single parents and married women who earn more than their husbands.

The story about women's increased labor force participation is well known. The proportion of mothers with young children who work has doubled just since 1970.[22] Gone is what the Washington Center for Equitable Growth's Heather Boushey calls "the American Wife."[23] She not only took care of any children in the household, but also attended to all the other details of everyday life, from shopping to home maintenance, cooking and cleaning, attending to sick or elderly family members, and volunteering in the community. She was, in Boushey's words, the "silent partner" of every business firm, making it possible for men to work long hours without worrying about their children, a variety of domestic details, or civic obligations.[24] Now, of course, the American wife is also working long hours at a paid job.

The increase in women's employment and earnings has been critically important to middle-class families. Middle-class incomes have grown slowly since the late 1970s, but without the contribution of a second earner they would have declined.[25] Women's contributions to the economy are now a major feature of most advanced societies.[26] However, the labor force participation of women has stalled in the United States since about 2000, and many European countries now have higher participation rates, in part because these European countries have social insurance systems that provide far more time off for family care.[27]

If we focus just on two-earner families, hours of market work have risen.[28] In Boushey's words, "we've lost lots of family time but not gained a lot of money."[29]

The big increase in work among women has been fueled not just by the need for a second earner to make ends meet but because many more of them are the sole breadwinners for their families. The proportion of children under the age of eighteen who live with only one parent rose from just under 10 percent in 1960 to over 27 percent in 2016.[30] Single parents have no choice but to work. In the past, many collected a welfare check, but in 1996, welfare was reformed and it is now a miniscule program with strong work requirements and time-limited benefits.

The rise of dual-earner families and of single parenthood has created a new problem: how to balance work and family life. Regardless of what has happened to hours of work in general, the group most affected by a time squeeze is working parents. It would be easy to suggest that they simply not work and instead stay home with their children. But this is not a feasible alternative for single parents and would require a sharp drop in living standards for two-earner families.

These changes in women's employment rates and in family composition make the need for some form of paid leave much greater than in the past. Putting the burden on employers to provide such leave would be a mistake; it might lead to discrimination against parents, especially mothers. A more sensible strategy is to ask employees to help pay for such leave through payroll taxes.

Growing Inequality

Still another reason to restructure the current social insurance system is the sharp increase in inequality in American society (see chapter 3). Although the social insurance system is somewhat redistributive, it is less redistributive than in the past.[31] As already noted, there is a rising gap between the mortality rates of higher- and lower-income individuals, with the result that the former receive benefits for many more years than the latter.[32] In addition, higher-wage workers (because they are healthier, work in white-collar jobs, and can afford to wait before claiming a Social Security check) are retiring later, which enables them to continue to earn income well past the normal retirement age and to collect higher annual benefits by delaying receipt of Social Security.[33] Anyone who chooses to retire at sixty-two may do so and still collect benefits, but at a discount of about 30 percent relative to the monthly benefit they would receive if they waited until the normal retirement age. In addition, those who wait until age seventy to retire earn a "delayed retirement credit," which adds roughly another 24 percent to their monthly benefit relative to what it would be at their normal retirement age.[34] What this means, in effect, is that the "maximum benefit age" is age seventy. Anyone retiring before seventy pays a penalty. Or, to state it in reverse, retiring at seventy provides a large boost to one's monthly benefit, compared to retiring at sixty-two. For example, a worker entitled to $1,000 a month by delaying to age seventy would only get $568 if she retired at age sixty-two. Yet nearly half of workers today retire at age sixty-two.[35]

Because those with more education and higher earnings are more likely to be able to take advantage of delayed retirement, while the least advantaged may need to retire early due to disability or the nature of their jobs, the monthly benefits of more advantaged workers are likely to be much higher for this reason alone, and not just because they earned more over a lifetime. If they also live longer, this will add to their advantages.

Not only are Social Security and Medicare less progressive than in the past, but they are also large and are growing so rapidly that they are crowding out spending in the federal budget on programs targeted to the young and the poor.[36] To be sure, we could raise taxes to pay for both, but if this remains politically infeasible, growing spending on the elderly is preventing the kind of investments in children and in working-age adults that might improve their prospects and the economy's productivity. If we want more inclusive growth, we need to restructure the benefits of the social insurance system over the longer run, so that more of them accrue to both the less advantaged and those of working age.

Time for Reform

Each of these developments—more affluence, a more knowledge-based economy, greater longevity, new types of families, and rising inequality—suggests the need to rethink our social insurance system.

At the most fundamental level, the question is how much of our economic growth do we want to devote to ever-higher levels of income and how much to working less over a lifetime, so that more time can be devoted to such activities as investing in new skills and caring for families? Put differently, how should a fixed number of lifetime hours be allocated over the life span? How much to paid work, how much to lifelong learning or family care, and how much to a leisurely retirement? For many people, less paid work when young and more of it when old would make a lot of sense, thus freeing up time for mid-career investments in education and family without necessarily increasing the cost of social insurance.

Each new generation is going to need more education than the last, and not all of that education needs to be acquired before one starts to work. Lifelong learning may be the better concept. Finally, later retirement for some may be appropriate now that we are living longer and healthier lives.

At the same time, work-life balance is a much bigger issue than in the past, now that there are more two-earner families and more single parents. We need to focus on paid leave in cases where someone needs to stay home to care for a child, or to care for their own or another close family member's illness.

The watchword here should be flexibility. The old lockstep pattern of getting an education from ages six to seventeen, working from ages eighteen to sixty-five, and then retiring, no longer makes sense. We should open up new options that permit a much more flexible use of people's time, enabling them to better combine work, family, education, retirement, and leisure in new ways.

The Current Social Insurance System

The three major risks covered by today's social insurance system include (1) temporary loss of a job through no fault of one's own, (2) long-term inability to work due to illness or injury, and (3) inability to work due to old age. The current system was originally enacted in 1935 as a response to the Depression. Its first rendition included unemployment insurance (UI) and old age and survivors insurance (OASI), more commonly known as Social Security, as well as some means-tested welfare programs. In 1956, protection against the risk of disability was added (social security disability insurance, or SSDI).[37] And in 1965, health care coverage for the disabled and the elderly was provided (Medicare).[38] In 2016, the federal government spent over $1.5 trillion on the entire system—$910 billion on Social Security (OASI and SSDI combined), $588 billion on Medicare (net of offsetting receipts), and $33 billion on unemployment compensation.[39] States also participate extensively in funding and administering UI.[40]

Social Security (or OASDI, encompassing both OASI and SSDI) has been remarkably successful both at providing an income to vulnerable groups, the aged and disabled in particular, and at maintaining its political popularity as a contributory system. This is a good base on which to build. But it leaves out a lot. It does not cover short-term disability or the need to care for a family member (family and medical leave). It also does not cover long-term joblessness caused by changes in technology, trade, or other shocks to the economy. Ironically, joblessness is covered in the short run but not the long run, while disability is covered in the long run but not in the short run. (Some states and private employers have taken up some of this slack but have left gaping holes, especially for low-wage workers.)

The social insurance model was first introduced by Otto von Bismarck, chancellor to Germany, when the nation adopted its program in 1889. Importantly, he viewed it as a way to make his conservative policies more acceptable.[41] President Franklin Roosevelt and his Committee on Economic Security had similar ideas.[42] A free enterprise economy that does not provide any safety nets for those who lose out in the market will have difficulty sustaining its democratic form. Eventually a socialist such as Eugene Debs or a populist such as Donald Trump will challenge the system and threaten to destroy its foundations. Such populist uprisings have not yet done too much damage, but they have deep roots in discontent among those left behind in nations that have achieved a certain level of affluence but failed to share that success widely. A twenty-first-century economy can afford a more extensive set of protections than what was put in place back in the 1930s when real GDP per capita was about one-fifth what it is now.[43] As a fiscal hawk, I have argued in the past for reining in entitlement spending; but I am increasingly of the view that, with some reallocation of the benefits, an expanded and improved social insurance system can contribute to growth and well-being while reducing today's political discontents.

Elected officials in the United States have always given lip service to the need to compensate the losers from trade and technology, but they have not done much to make this a reality. If we want to preserve both free markets and democracy, we must rethink how we can reconcile the two in a world turned upside down by globalization, new technologies, and new demographic realities.

Failure to reform or update our social insurance system will have another consequence. It could lead to policies that are far more damaging to the economy. These could include restrictions on trade and immigration or burdensome and costly mandates on employers to pay higher wages or provide more generous benefits. They could also include regulations that protect today's business or employee interests against tomorrow's more efficient competitors as people struggle to hang onto what they already have. And finally, they could include small additions to an already byzantine social welfare bureaucracy, encompassing about eighty means-tested programs, that applies more and more complicated Band-Aids to the wounds of those left behind.

Social Insurance for the Twenty-First Century

The system I envisage would, like the current system, be contributory and linked to work experience. It is not welfare. It would be financed by payroll taxes. As such, it would be far more efficient and popular than the maze of government programs that now serve disadvantaged and dislocated workers.

There would be, as part of this proposal, two new purposes for social insurance and two new trust fund accounts: first, a lifelong learning account for those pursuing education or training, and, second, a paid leave account for family and medical leave.

Lifelong Learning Account

Eligibility for funds in the lifelong learning account might require considerable years of prior work experience (for example, ten years) and a proposed education or retraining plan with an approved education or training provider. The funds could be used for living expenses during the period of training and potentially be supplemented by Pell grants or student loans for tuition.[44] It might be limited to two years and be subject to an earnings test.

The lifelong learning account can be a selling point for an updated social insurance system and serve to broaden the constituency for reform among young adults skeptical that they will ever see any benefits from Social Security. Whether seen as a "second chance" for those who fall on hard times or as a "fresh start" for those who simply need a new beginning, it could provide just the kind of psychological and creative boost that many people need in midlife.

Paid Leave Account

Eligibility for the paid leave account would also require some prior labor market experience, perhaps a year or two. This leave could be used to care for a new or adopted baby, to recover from one's own extended illness, or to care for a sick family member. The benefit would be proportional to wages up to a cap and might be available for up to twelve weeks. Again, it is not my intent to prescribe a particular program design, only to suggest what it *might* look like.

The United States is the only advanced country that does not mandate that workers be given paid time off for these purposes. Some Americans currently have access to paid leave through their employers or state programs, although every survey or study on the subject concludes that higher-income professionals are far more likely to have access than lower-income, less-skilled workers. According to the BLS National Compensation Survey, workers in the highest 10 percent of weekly wages are nearly six times more likely to have access to paid family leave than workers in the lowest 10 percent.[45]

The companies that offer paid leave benefits to their workers do not report that these benefits pose a burden on their profitability or productivity.[46] In fact, most companies with a formal paid family and medical leave policy suggest that the policy has positive effects on employee morale, turnover, profitability, and productivity. While the policy's cost or its administrative burden are frequently cited concerns prior to implementation, 71 percent of employers offering paid family and medical leave report that it has a positive effect on employee productivity, and 63 percent report that it has had a positive effect on profitability. Even among smaller employers with fewer than one hundred employees, nearly half reported that the policy had a positive effect on profitability.[47]

Even accounting for some likely bias in such surveys (why suggest that you adopted a policy that turned out to be more costly than expected?), the now-extensive evidence on paid leave suggests it imposes little if any significant burden on employers. Put differently, this is one more data point in the argument about efficiency wages made earlier in this book. More generous compensation, whether in the form of pay or in the form of enhanced benefits, may increase productivity with no untoward effects on profits.

Paid parental leave also improves attachment to the labor force, especially among mothers. Francine Blau and Lawrence Kahn found that nearly one-third of the decline in U.S. female labor force participation relative to other OECD countries can be attributed to America's lack of family-friendly policies, including parental leave.[48] Fathers are more likely to be involved in child care throughout the child's life when they have access to paid paternity leave.[49] Further, many experts have documented that access to paid leave is associated with improvements in children's healthy development.[50]

Paid parental leave is widely supported by the American public. A Pew study in 2017 found that 82 percent support paid maternity leave, 69 percent support paid paternity leave, and 85 percent say that workers should be able to take paid leave to recover from their own serious health conditions.[51]

Paid leave has recently received a lot of attention. Both presidential candidates in 2016 put forth their own proposals, legislation has been introduced in Congress, and some modest business tax incentives for private employers who provide paid family and medical leave were included in the Tax Cuts and Jobs Act of 2017.[52] An AEI-Brookings expert working group (that I cochaired) also spent a year studying the topic of paid parental leave and put forward a proposal of its own.[53] It would offer eight weeks of paid parental leave to both mothers and fathers at a wage replacement rate of 70 percent of the employee's previous wages, up to a cap of $600 per week. While some working group members favored more generous benefits and others wanted to target them to low-wage workers only, all agreed that the United States needs a federal paid parental leave policy. There was also unanimous agreement that the cost of such a policy should not be imposed on businesses who might then discriminate against those of childbearing age, women in particular. The majority of the group favored a modest addition to employee payroll taxes as the preferred financing mechanism. The AEI-Brookings working group is now studying family and medical leave in addition to parental leave and plans to report on their work late in 2018.

All these benefits would need to be costed out and the specific design of the new benefits carefully considered in light of these costs and the extended purposes of the law. But like Social Security itself, these new benefits would be "earned" in a universal contributory system in which the most generous benefits were provided to those with limited earnings. Some flexibility to reallocate one's benefits across these different purposes could be allowed (as long as this didn't risk leaving people impoverished in old age).

Challenges

There are three major issues with my proposed agenda. The first is that it could be expensive and would require an increase in payroll taxes (or other offsetting savings) to fund it at a time when those taxes are insufficient to cover currently promised benefits.[54] The second is that it could lead to moral hazard, allowing people to take advantage of the system for reasons that are not appropriate. The third is that it might be difficult to administer. Unlike the current Social Security system, which simply mails checks to everyone once they reach a certain age, it would require some eligibility screens that could be costly to implement as well as open to abuse.

Affordability

Social Security is currently underfunded. There are plenty of good ideas for how to reform the system to restore its solvency, but so far efforts to do so have gone nowhere due to political opposition to cutting benefits or raising taxes.[55] One advantage of the kind of reform I envisage is that it would provide some new benefits, thus sweetening the package and changing the framing of any new proposal. The new benefits might have wide appeal, especially to the younger generation, and could be used to sell a package that, in the process of offering new benefits, also restored the solvency of the system.

The currently retired, or those about to retire, would be grandfathered into the current system; it would not be fair or politically wise to change the rules of the game midstream. In fact, any changes should be phased in gradually so that people would have time to adjust.

There are any number of ways to pay for the reforms and simultaneously put the system on a more solid fiscal footing. First, we could encourage later retirement among those who can work well beyond their normal retirement age. Second, we could slow the growth of benefits for those with a lifetime of high earnings. They are more likely to have private retirement savings and to have already reaped big tax advantages from money invested in 401(k) plans and IRAs. Third, we could phase out or reform the spousal benefit that provides additional benefits to the spouses and survivors of retired, disabled, and deceased workers. Stay-at-home spouses are a declining phenomenon, and providing extra benefits to these families is decidedly unfair given that, unlike two-earner families, they have paid far less into the system (only one set of payroll taxes instead of two).[56] Fourth, we could change the cost-of-living adjustment (COLA) in a way that better reflects, according to most experts, the true impact of inflation. Finally, we could raise payroll taxes through some combination of increasing the rate and the earnings level subject to the tax.[57]

I believe all these proposals have merit and that, in combination, they could both restore solvency and finance some new benefits. A complete analysis of costs and benefits will need to be undertaken. But to give the reader a sense of the magnitudes, restoring the long-run solvency of Social Security without changing benefits would require an immediate increase in the payroll tax of about 3 percentage points, from 12.4 percent (6.2 percent on each the employer and the employee) to 15.4 percent.[58] Much of that payroll tax increase could be avoided if the wage base (currently $127,000) was raised substantially or eliminated. (The Medicare payroll tax cap was eliminated in 1994.) The other reforms listed above would add further to the savings, leaving room to fund some new purposes. A mix of tax increases and benefit savings are the most likely to command bipartisan support.

Taxes are never popular, but payroll taxes are better tolerated than most. Because they are earmarked for specific benefits, people feel like they are getting something in return. And the fact is that they are. Even if they never use the benefits, the existence of a contributory system provides peace of mind for oneself and one's family. Moreover, they are collected in a relatively painless way, before people take the money home in their paychecks. Some of the costs can be borne by employers, as is the case now, although most economists believe these costs are actually "passed along" to employees in the form of lower wages. Still, the perception that business is paying part of the cost makes such taxes more acceptable. For any one individual, we should think of these taxes as forced savings for worthy purposes— purposes they are not saving enough for now, even though they know they should.

Proposals to raise the retirement age also make great sense. They are needed to put the system back into fiscal balance, and they are consistent with our longer and healthier lives. The elderly are the new leisured class.

They are healthier and wealthier than ever.[59] For this reason, their claim on leisure time is, in my view, less compelling than that of dual-earner and single-parent families, and working-age adults who need additional schooling or are seeking expanded horizons by training in a new field.

With the combined Social Security OASI and DI trust funds now projected to run out of sufficient funds to pay full benefits in 2034, many fiscal hawks are proposing to raise the retirement age to seventy.[60] Some also want to index benefits for longevity.[61] Indexing in this context means that as life expectancy lengthens, Social Security retirement age would rise in tandem, thereby keeping lifetime benefits roughly constant over time and helping to balance the books.

Keep in mind, however, that raising the retirement age would disproportionately benefit the affluent. The reason is because, as noted earlier, high earners are expected to live longer than low earners. Thus, raising the retirement age across the board would cut lifetime benefits of low-wage workers by a larger percentage than those of high-wage workers.[62] There are several ways to deal with this problem. One is to offer a minimum benefit that does not depend on lifetime earnings or the timing of retirement (after the age of sixty-two). Another is to encourage much later retirement among high earners while reducing the penalty for early retirement among low earners.[63]

Right now, the solvency of the Social Security system and the amount of private savings people have put aside for retirement are huge issues. As the economist Alicia Munnell argues, the solution needs to include, among other things, encouraging people to work longer.[64] This will have a number of benefits. It will enable them to earn and save for more years and increase their benefits when they do retire. It will also reduce the number of years for which some combination of private savings, employer-based retirement benefits, and Social Security is needed.

Misuse of the New Benefits

As for the third challenge, the fear that these new benefits will lead to "abuse" is real although likely exaggerated. The idea that social insurance reduces personal responsibility has at least some empirical support. Most of us are ants, but grasshoppers do exist. Unemployment insurance can increase the duration of unemployment, SSDI has likely contributed to a small proportion of the decline in male labor force participation, and Social Security might reduce personal savings.[65] We have to get at this challenge by designing and administering any new program well. Time off for new parents might require a birth certificate. Time off for one's own or a close family member's illness might need to be recommended by a doctor. However, states that have provided such leaves are not reporting any significant abuse.[66] We want to provide people with a net and not a hammock, to borrow from the conservative sound bite on this issue. The United States is a large and diverse nation with a set of political and ethical values that tilt conservative. Freeloading is viewed as a sin. Trust in the benign intentions of others is unfortunately in short supply. At the same time, I want to argue that worrying too much about abuse is tantamount to worrying about the deck chairs when there is an iceberg looming on the horizon. It assumes that we cannot afford to support a group of people that the economy has treated badly through no fault of their own. They did not automate factories or source their supplies from China. I believe the benefits of trade and technology are positive for the economy as a whole. But we do need to compensate the losers. The lifelong learning funds are designed to do exactly that, and these new benefits are linked to the importance the public attaches to work, to education, and to family.

Administrative Issues

The administrative issues associated with my proposal are also real. The Social Security Administration would need to take them on, creating a new office to administer each of the two new benefit programs.

Another option would be to combine this with some reforms to the SSDI program and to use that structure to administer a new temporary disability fund (paid leave for an extended illness or injury but one that is not likely to be permanent). I suggest this for several reasons. First, some portion of the rapid increase in disability benefits in recent years was likely caused by the difficulty of finding work and not because disability itself has increased. We thus have a program designed to replace income lost due to a serious medical condition now increasingly serving as a program dealing, implicitly if not explicitly, with structural unemployment. The liberalized definitions of disability enacted in 1984 have made the likelihood that an application will be approved based on labor market conditions and not just medical diagnosis much higher.[67] Second, almost every expert who has studied SSDI believes that it discourages reentry into the labor market. If there were a national temporary disability insurance program, many people—now on SSDI because that's the only option—would be encouraged to rejoin the labor force after taking some time off.

While there are fears of abuse and concerns about extending an existing entitlement program, it is the wrong frame for thinking about economic growth and social welfare. It is inconsistent with the idea that some of the benefits of economic growth should be used to provide a better life for all Americans, not just the winners. If some people end up working less (or saving less), perhaps that's not such a high price to pay, especially when one considers the alternatives.

The theme of this chapter is that an inclusive form of capitalism requires helping people navigate the twists and turns in their lives, recognizing that they are not always forward planners. I have argued for policies that are consistent with the values individuals attach to work, to education, and to family. That means ensuring that any new benefits are earned through work and dedicated to education and family care. The reforms I propose would, in addition, reallocate some resources between old and young and between rich and poor—providing a bigger stake in our democracy to both the younger generation and to those who have been left behind.

10

Conclusion

ANYONE CONCERNED ABOUT THE STATE OF AMERICA in the early decades of the twenty-first century should read William Golding's well-known novel *Lord of the Flies*.[1] A group of English schoolboys is marooned on an island. They need to find food, build huts, keep a signal fire burning, and protect the youngest and most vulnerable members of the group ("the littluns"). They elect a leader, a twelve-year-old named Ralph, and even agree on some governing principles. But before long, they lose confidence in their leadership and their rules, begin to believe in an illusory but terrifying beast, form warring tribes, and shift their allegiance to Ralph's rival, Jack. Jack is impulsive, power driven, and lacking in empathy. But he hunts pigs and promises food. In the end, the boys' experiment in governing themselves falls apart. Without grown-ups in charge, without the institutions and norms of the civilization the boys have left behind, disorder and disaster ensue. Eventually violence breaks out and several boys die.

America, much like the boys in *Lord of the Flies*, is in trouble. In *Lord of the Flies*, the boys are eventually saved by a British naval officer—a kind of deus ex machina end to the novel. But who or what is going to save America? The country is experiencing deep divisions and, in the minds of many, a lack of sober leadership.

As I argued in earlier chapters, our society is coming apart. Growing inequality and long-term joblessness are leaving too many people behind, with political consequences that were all too evident in the 2016 election. If we continue on our current path, the center may not hold. The appeal of a populism that flouts long-established democratic norms could do severe damage to our political system. I am under no illusion that the ideas contained in this book will assuage the feeling among too many voters that their elected officials have failed to address their concerns. But something like what I have proposed might send the message that they have been heard. It is time for both parties to face the reality that the biggest problems in America are deep economic and political divisions. I believe we should favor a system in which work is expected and rewarded. But it should also be a system that recognizes the flaws in a pure market system—a system that will only flourish if the flaws are addressed.

Like the boys in *Lord of the Flies*, we need leaders, rules, and norms that enable individuals and enterprises of all kinds to flourish. As long as a majority of the population remains hostile to government, it will be difficult to move forward with a more enlightened set of policies. Breaking the impasse would be easier if we could come together around some moral principles, not just a laundry list of programs—principles that recognize both rights and responsibilities, what individuals must do and what we can only do collectively. In this book, I have argued that three values might command broad support. Those values are the importance of family, education, and work.

Are we, like the boys in *Lord of the Flies*, waiting to be saved by some outside force, or are we capable of electing principled leaders from both parties who care more about being statesmen than about being reelected? Can we repair our government institutions to make voting easier, gerrymandering less prevalent, the electoral system more consistent with the principle of "one man, one vote," and money in politics less influential? Only time will tell. E. J. Dionne, Thomas Mann, and Norman Ornstein suggest some possible political reforms in their book, *One Nation after Trump*.[2] In the meantime, we should be clear about the nature and scope of our economic problems, how they are affecting most Americans, and what we might do. Political reform is very difficult; cultural divisions don't lend themselves to government solutions, but the opinion divide on economic issues is less wide and a solution is more within reach.

In the preceding chapters, I laid out my own ideas for finding common ground in a divided America. Chapter 2 provided a closeup look at the white working class, the group that voted overwhelmingly for Trump. Trump spoke to this group, calling them the forgotten Americans, and although they are not the only ones who have been forgotten, they have real griev-ances. They often vote for those who do not have their interests at heart, a phenomenon we need to understand. They are dismissive of government policies that might help them. They live in their own cultural and informa-tional bubbles, while the professional classes live in others still. One thing seems clear, however. A lack of decent-paying jobs is at the heart of their discontent.

To be sure, culture, and not just economics, drove this group to support Donald Trump. Their conservative cultural values serve as a safe harbor when the economic seas have blown up a storm. If one lives in a merito-cratic society, where merit is defined by distant elites, how does one recon-cile a failure to achieve, whether in education, in work, or in one's family with self-respect? One way is to imagine that other people—for example, immigrants or racial minorities—are "cutting in line," to borrow the meta-phor used by sociologist, Arlie Hochschild. Another way is to blame it on the establishment and an elite political class that has failed to act on one's behalf. Ronald Reagan famously said that government was the problem and not the solution. Many people now agree with him. In chapter 2, I em-phasized the sharp decline in trust of government and the role a portion of the media has played in polarizing the country. But I also suggested that if there is a political opening here, it is on economics, not on culture. Attitu-dinal gaps between liberals and conservatives are narrower on economic than on cultural issues.

In chapter 3, I surveyed the economic landscape—showing that most Americans have not been making much progress. If you were born in 1940, your chances of doing better than your parents were very high; but if you were born in, say, 1980, they are not. The economic escalator enabling each generation to do better than the last has stalled. It has stalled for two reasons: first, because of the slowdown in overall economic growth, but even more importantly, because whatever income growth we have had has flowed primarily to the wealthy. Stagnant incomes for the middle class are a problem, and it turns out that 70 percent of that stagnation is due not to a lack of economic growth but to its maldistribution. I concluded that long-term growth is unlikely to speed up anytime soon, and that inequality has reached virtually unprecedented levels. I showed how a focus on families, education, and work could restore upward mobility. Over 70 percent of Americans would achieve middle-class incomes if they got at least a high school education, worked full-time, and formed stable families before having children. Of these three, full-time work is the major source of higher incomes—at least in the shortrun. And the best way to ensure full-time work is to maintain full employment through appropriate monetary and fiscal policy.

In chapter 4, I addressed the contention that if only we could get the longer-term growth rate from 2 percent to 3 or 4 percent per year, that would translate into jobs for everyone. While it's possible to boost the growth rate temporarily through economic stimulus, that won't necessarily budge it over the longer run. Tax cuts similar to those enacted in late 2017 can give people extra money to spend and provide a quick kick to the economy. But if the stimulus is deficit financed, and does little to encourage public or private investment, it can be a drag on long-term growth. Extra borrowing typically raises interest rates and the value of the dollar, discouraging both investment and exports. My metaphor for economic growth is that it is like a car. Its engine is misunderstood, its speedometer (the GDP) is misleading, and even if we arrive at our destination, we are likely to be disappointed. Money, above a certain level, doesn't buy happiness. The current focus on such remedies as supply-side tax cuts, wholesale deregulation, bringing back manufacturing, or restricting trade and immigration are superficially appealing but flawed.

Given current levels of inequality, redistribution sounds like the right thing to do. But as I argued in chapter 5, the political reality is that even Democrats have been reluctant to call for anything beyond modest reforms to the personal income tax as the best way to compensate for growing inequality. And their proposals have usually gone nowhere even when Democrats were in control of both Congress and the White House. In addition, the reality is that the kind of modest changes that are likely to be politically feasible wouldn't put much of a dent in inequality. On the other

Table 10.1. Key proposals to help the forgotten Americans

Theme	Proposal	Who benefits	Financing	Other notes
Skill building and jobs for the future (6)	**GI Bill:** Increase funding for career and technical education; adjustment assistance including retraining, relocation, apprenticeships, wage insurance	High school/community college students; dislocated, lesser-skilled workers; employers in need of skilled workers	Reform unemployment insurance: matching funds for state innovation; reallocate funding from less-effective programs, including higher education	Many good proposals from experts and examples in states and localities
Creating jobs and rewarding work (7)	**Create jobs:** Maintain full employment; jobs of last resort linked to the use of the safety net	All workers; hard-to-employ workers	Revenues from a high-employment economy; Safety net savings	
	Worker credit: Refundable 15 percent credit to workers up to a maximum of $1,500 per year; phase out as earnings rise to $40,000 per year; delivered as part of paycheck, offsetting payroll taxes	All workers with earnings under $40,000 per year	Increase taxes on estates and gifts to meet level of revenue from 1972 (approx. $1 trillion over a decade); other options include a carbon tax or VAT	Also: expand child care tax credits and increase the minimum wage to $12 per hour

A bigger role for the private sector (8)	**Inclusive capitalism:** Encourage private companies to share profits and ownership and train workers	All private sector workers	Amend tax code so that corporations receive credits if they offer these benefits	
A new role for social insurance (9)	**Lifelong learning account:** New funding for pursuits such as retraining	Mid-career adults who want to retrain, upskill, or pursue a new start	Encourage later retirement for most workers; slow growth of benefits for high earners; phase out spousal benefit; change COLA; raise payroll taxes	Might be combined with reforms to other social insurance programs (like SSDI)
	Paid leave account: New funding for up to 12 weeks of job-protected, paid time off to care for a new child or ill family member or to recover from one's own illness	Workers with some (1–2 years) work experience who need time off to address certain life events		

hand, if we were to replace the income tax on middle- and working-class families with a value-added tax or a carbon tax, we might have more success. These forms of taxation are often rejected on the left because they are regressive. But designed appropriately and combined with a progressive set of benefits, they would help a lot. So, too, would a much steeper estate tax. I showed that if we returned the estate tax to early 1970s levels, we could enable most people to pass on a reasonable amount of wealth to their children tax-free and still raise close to $1 trillion over a decade. That $1 trillion, in turn, could be devoted to giving a pay raise to everyone in the bottom half of the earnings distribution. This policy is consistent with the belief that no one should get a big windfall just because his or her parents are rich. Indeed, one way to think about large inheritances is that they are just another form of welfare—although in this case for the rich and not the poor. Large transfers of wealth are inconsistent with the idea that every generation should earn their own way. Those lucky enough to be born into affluent families already inherit many advantages related to home, school, and neighborhood environments. These children have already won the lottery; they don't need to win it a second time.

My proposal to raise wages at the bottom with a worker credit is big, bold, and consistent with the value of work. The public cares more about earning a decent living than about almost anything else. Work provides dignity, self-respect, a sense of contributing, and a way of connecting with others. Table 10.1 summarizes my key proposals for helping the forgotten Americans obtain jobs and earn decent wages and indicates the chapter in which each proposal appears. A raise for those in the bottom half of the distribution is just one of these proposals.

First, I call for a serious effort to rebuild the skills of the workforce. Although the problems may begin during the school years, we cannot wait for all those problems to be fixed. We need to address the more immediate needs of those adversely affected by trade, and especially by new technologies. The problem is a growing gap between the skills employers need and those held by today's workers. This gap has had serious consequences for those in the bottom half. Many of them have simply stopped working. Others have taken low-paid jobs, uprooted their families, or relied more heavily on disability benefits or a second job. Their economic problems are implicated in the opioid epidemic, rising rates of mortality among middle-aged white Americans, and our political discontents. Eventually the economy will almost surely create new jobs to replace the ones being lost, but it may take a long time and cause great harm in the interim. Much of this effort will need to be subsidized by the government, especially state and local governments, but all of it should be done in cooperation with the private sector. Government training programs do not have a great record of success, but good results have been achieved when there is a public-private partnership focused on the actual skills and know-how that employers need. That means less emphasis on the idea that everyone should go to a four-year college and more on career and technical education in high schools and in community colleges; it also means more work-based learning such as apprenticeships. And a new norm of universal national service would help as a way to give young people new skills and a chance to broaden their social networks. It could also reduce cultural misunderstandings in the process.

Next, I argue that we cannot wait until the skill-rebuilding process gains traction to do something about low wages. A tax cut—or worker credit—for the bottom half is in order. A worker credit is similar to the Earned Income Tax Credit but based on personal earnings and not on family income, eliminating any disincentive to marry and the complexity of the EITC. It will be expensive—roughly $1 trillion over a decade—but, as noted, could be paid for by taxing estates or unearned wealth at 1970s levels.

I then suggest that the private sector do its part. Wages have not kept pace with productivity, while executive compensation has skyrocketed. The portion of our national income earned by workers has shrunk dramatically, and businesses are doing less training than in the past. Something is amiss here. A large part of the problem is the failure of business leaders to understand that an excessive focus on the short term versus the long term and on shareholders versus workers is leading to a cramped and unhealthy version of capitalism. If history is a guide, the Tax Cuts and Jobs Act of 2017 will need to be modified in the coming years, creating an opportunity to reform business and corporate taxes in a way that recognizes the needs of workers as well as owners and shareholders. Drawing on research by the consulting firm McKinsey, I show in chapter 8 that businesses' longer time horizons and greater attention to workers are not inconsistent with maximizing shareholder value; in fact, they often enhance it. The trick is to find the right balance between different corporate goals. Right now, too many businesses are obsessed with their quarterly earnings rather than with creating value for the longer run.

Although work and wages are central to addressing our current divisions, we must honor families and education along with work. That means allowing people to take time off when work interferes with the care of family members or with learning a new skill. For these reasons, in chapter 9, I suggest an update to our existing social insurance system with two new funds: one for family care and one for lifelong learning. All this would require either some increase in payroll taxes or later retirement for most of us. Reforming Social Security is a big political lift, to be sure, but made easier by the inclusion of new benefits for younger Americans along with a fairer and more fiscally sustainable system.

In conclusion, the problem is a lack of economic progress and too few decently paid jobs for the forgotten Americans. More economic growth or a redistribution of existing incomes could help, but they are insufficient, and the rhetoric around them creates false hopes. Instead, we need a new skills-building program for America's workers, a boost in their after-tax wages, a bigger role for the private sector in rewarding and training workers, and an updated social insurance system. This agenda should appeal to most of the public because they are more moderate than their elected officials. And more importantly, it should appeal to Americans because they want to work and they want to be self-sufficient. What they need from the government is a hand-up—a path to success.

The agenda is based on three principles: first, a focus on the values almost everyone can endorse—the values of family, education, and work—but especially work; second, policies that can be delivered by broad-based and trusted institutions such as businesses and community colleges; and third, a recognition that times have changed and that managing that change is critical to keeping America strong.

Unless we reorient our economic policies to focus less on the amount of economic growth and more on who benefits from it, we will not necessarily make most people better off and may only add to their political discontents.

Put most simply, the goals should be rewards for everyone, not just a few, and rewards through work rather than through redistribution.

Embedded in this agenda is the need to bring the forgotten Americans back into the mainstream of economic and political life through the dignity that skills and work can provide. I believe that is our best shot at reducing not just our economic divisions, but our cultural and political ones as well.

Is enacting this agenda or something like it even remotely feasible? Are we, like the boys in the *Lord of the Flies*, doomed to form warring tribes, or can we bind up our divisions, rebuild trust in institutions, and behave like grown-ups who know how to govern ourselves? The future of our democracy may well depend on the answer.

NOTES

Chapter 1. Introduction

1. Quoted in "'Welfare Queen' Becomes Issue in Reagan Campaign," *New York Times,* February 15, 1976, http://www.nytimes.com/1976/02/15/archives/welfare-queen -becomes-issue-in-reagan-campaign-hitting-a-nerve-now.html.

2. The reconciled version of the bill (Public Law No. 115-97) is called an "Act to provide for reconciliation pursuant to titles II and V of the concurrent resolution on the budget for fiscal year 2018." However, for simplicity, I refer to it throughout the book as the "Tax Cuts and Jobs Act" (TCJA).

3. Eduardo Porter, "Do Oil Companies Really Need $4 Billion per Year of Taxpayers' Money?" *New York Times,* August 5, 2016, https://www.nytimes.com/2016/08/06 /upshot/do-oil-companies-really-need-4-billion-per-year-of-taxpayers-money.html.

4. See Brink Lindsey and Steven Teles, *The Captured Economy: How the Powerful Enrich Themselves, Slow Down Growth, and Increase Inequality* (New York: Oxford University Press, 2017).

5. Yphtach Lelkes, "Mass Polarization: Manifestations and Measurements," *Public Opinion Quarterly* 80, no. S1 (2016): 392–410.

6. Isabel V. Sawhill, "Creating Opportunity for the Forgotten Americans," in *Brookings: Big Ideas for America,* ed. Michael E. O'Hanlon (Washington, DC: Brookings Institution Press, 2017), 185–193. Also, see chapter 3.

7. General Stanley McChrystal, "Securing the American Character," *Democracy,* no. 33 (Summer 2014), https://democracyjournal.org/magazine/33/securing-the -american-character/.

Chapter 2. The Forgotten Americans

1. Author's analysis of the American National Election Studies 2016 Time Series Study, American National Election Studies, Stanford University and University of

Michigan, "ANES 2016 Time Series Study" (Ann Arbor, MI: Inter-university Consortium for Political and Social Research, 2017).

2. Donald J. Trump, Speech to the Republican National Convention (Cleveland, Ohio, July 21, 2016), https://assets.donaldjtrump.com/DJT_Acceptance_Speech.pdf.

3. Guy Molyneux, "A Tale of Two Populisms," *American Prospect*, June 1, 2017, http://prospect.org/article/tale-two-populisms.

4. Author's analysis of the American National Election Studies 2016 Time Series Study, American National Election Studies, "ANES 2016 Time Series Study."

5. Lynn Vavreck, "The Ways That the 2016 Election Was Perfectly Normal," *New York Times*, May 1, 2017, https://www.nytimes.com/2017/05/01/upshot/the-ways-that-the-2016-election-was-perfectly-normal.html.

6. Stanley Greenberg, "The Democrats' 'Working-Class' Problem," *American Prospect*, June 1, 2017, http://prospect.org/article/democrats%E2%80%99-%E2%80%98working-class-problem%E2%80%99.

7. For a sampling of these views, see *American Prospect* (Summer 2017), which includes articles by a number of political analysts.

8. One exception is Mark Lilla, *The Once and Future Liberal: After Identity Politics* (New York: HarperCollins, 2017).

9. Molyneux, "Tale of Two Populisms."

10. Jack Goldsmith, "Will Donald Trump Destroy the Presidency?" *Atlantic*, October 2017, https://www.theatlantic.com/magazine/archive/2017/10/will-donald-trump-destroy-the-presidency/537921/.

11. On this point, see Max Ehrenfreund and Jeff Guo, "If You've Ever Described People as 'White Working Class,' Read This," *Washington Post*, November 23, 2016, https://www.washingtonpost.com/news/wonk/wp/2016/11/22/who-exactly-is-the-white-working-class-and-what-do-they-believe-good-questions/?utm_term=.c2eef57c8931.

12. Lee Drutman, "Political Divisions in 2016 and Beyond" (Washington, DC: Democracy Fund Voter Study Group June 2017), https://www.voterstudygroup.org/publications/2016-elections/political-divisions-in-2016-and-beyond.

13. See David Baldassarri and Andrew Gelman, "Partisans without Constraint: Political Polarization and Trends in American Public Opinion," *American Journal of Sociology* 114, no. 2 (2008): 408–446; Matthew S. Levendusky and Neil Malhotra, "(Mis)perceptions of Partisan Polarization in the American Public," *Public Opinion Quarterly* 80 (2015): 378–391.

14. Ross Douthat, "In Search of the American Center," *New York Times*, June 21, 2017, https://www.nytimes.com/2017/06/21/opinion/in-search-of-the-american-center.html.

15. See Norm Ornstein, "The Eight Causes of Trumpism," *Atlantic*, January 4, 2016, https://www.theatlantic.com/politics/archive/2016/01/the-eight-causes-of-trumpism/422427/.

16. In the wake of the Trump election the media has tended to focus on the white working class (because that's who voted overwhelmingly for Trump) and to use a

variety of ways of defining that group. The most common definition is whites without a college or BA degree. I also considered other definitions, looking at income, occupation, and where people live. In the end, I chose education as the simplest and most stable characteristic with which to describe the white working class. Education is also highly correlated with most of the other variables one might want to consider. Thus, unless otherwise specified, "white working class" refers to non-Hispanic whites with less than a BA and who are between the ages of twenty-five and sixty-four. Because a lack of jobs is a core problem for the forgotten Americans, I leave out the under-twenty-five-year-olds because they may still be in school and the over-sixty-four-year-olds because they are likely to be retired.

17. Most data reported in this section were derived from the Census Bureau's Current Population Survey (March ASEC samples). However, other survey data are included to supplement these descriptive characteristics. The definitions of the white working class across these various sources vary but not enough to invalidate combining the insights they provide.

18. Daniel Cox, Rachel Lienesch, and Robert P. Jones, "Beyond Economics: Fears of Cultural Displacement Pushed the White Working Class to Trump," *PRRI* and the *Atlantic*, May 9, 2017, https://www.prri.org/research/white-working-class -attitudes-economy-trade-immigration-election-donald-trump/.

19. For more details, see Eleanor Krause and Isabel Sawhill, "What We Know and Don't Know about Declining Labor Force Participation: A Review" (Washington, DC: Brookings Institution, May 2017), https://www.brookings.edu/research/what -we-know-and-dont-know-about-declining-labor-force-participation-a-review/.

20. Carol Graham and Sergio Pinto, "Unhappiness in America: Desperation in White Towns, Resilience and Diversity in the Cities" (Washington, DC: Brookings Institution, September 2016), https://www.brookings.edu/research/unhappiness -in-america-desperation-in-white-towns-resilience-and-diversity-in-the-cities/.

21. See Annie Lowrey, "2016: A Year Defined by America's Diverging Economies," *Atlantic*, December 30, 2016, https://www.theatlantic.com/business/archive /2016/12/2016-diverging-economies/511838/.

22. Anne Case and Angus Deaton, "Mortality and Morbidity in the 21st Century," *Brookings Papers on Economic Activity*, March 23–24, 2017.

23. See Cox, Lienesch, and Jones, "Beyond Economics."

24. Jeff Guo, "Death Predicts Whether People Vote for Donald Trump," *Washington Post*, March 4, 2016, https://www.washingtonpost.com/news/wonk/wp/2016 /03/04/death-predicts-whether-people-vote-for-donald-trump/?utm_term= .833f70ff574b.

25. On this final point, see Cox, Lienesch, and Jones, "Beyond Economics."

26. Ibid.

27. Arthur C. Brooks, "How Donald Trump Filled the Dignity Deficit," *Wall Street Journal*, November 9, 2016, https://www.wsj.com/articles/how-donald-trump -filled-the-dignity-deficit-1478734436.

28. Thomas Frank, *What's the Matter with Kansas?* (New York: Metropolitan Books, 2004); Thomas Frank, *Listen, Liberal* (New York: Metropolitan Books, 2016).

29. J. D. Vance, *Hillbilly Elegy: A Memoir of a Family and Culture in Crisis* (New York: HarperCollins, 2016); Arlie Russell Hochschild, *Strangers in Their Own Land: Anger and Mourning on the American Right* (New York: The New Press, 2016).

30. Vance, *Hillbilly Elegy,* 207.

31. Ibid., 192–193.

32. Ibid., 244–245.

33. Ibid., 127.

34. Ibid., 245.

35. Hochschild, *Strangers in Their Own Land,* 146.

36. Ibid., 144.

37. Ibid., 145.

38. Isaac Shapiro, Danilo Triso, and Raheem Chaudhry, "Poverty Reduction Programs Help Adults Lacking College Degrees the Most" (Washington, DC: Center on Budget and Policy Priorities, February 2017), https://www.cbpp.org/research/poverty-and-inequality/poverty-reduction-programs-help-adults-lacking-college-degrees-the-most.

39. Hochschild, *Strangers in Their Own Land,* 150.

40. Ibid., 159.

41. Jennifer Silva, *Coming Up Short: Working-Class Adulthood in an Age of Uncertainty* (New York: Oxford University Press, 2013).

42. Monica Prasad, Steve G. Hoffman, and Keiran Bezila, "Walking the Line: The White Working Class and the Economic Consequences of Morality," *Politics and Society* 44, no. 2 (2016): 281–304.

43. Robert Leonard, "Why Rural America Voted for Trump," *New York Times,* January 5, 2017, https://www.nytimes.com/2017/01/05/opinion/why-rural-america-voted-for-trump.html.

44. Katherine J. Cramer, "For Years, I've Been Watching the Anti-Elite Fury Build in Wisconsin: Then Came Trump," *Vox,* November 16, 2017, https://www.vox.com/the-big-idea/2016/11/16/13645116/rural-resentment-elites-trump.

45. Katherine J. Cramer, *The Politics of Resentment: Rural Consciousness in Wisconsin and the Rise of Scott Walker* (Chicago: University of Chicago Press, 2016), 131.

46. Ibid.

47. Joan C. Williams, *White Working Class* (Boston: Harvard Business Review Press, 2017), 33.

48. Joan C. Williams, "What So Many People Don't Get about the U.S. Working Class," *Harvard Business Review,* November 10, 2016, https://hbr.org/2016/11/what-so-many-people-dont-get-about-the-u-s-working-class.

49. Ibid.

50. See Bill Bishop, *The Big Sort: Why the Clustering of Like-Minded America Is Tearing Us Apart* (New York: First Mariner Books, 2009).

51. Quoted in Thomas Edsall, "Reaching Out to the Voters Left Behind," *New York Times,* April 13, 2017, https://www.nytimes.com/2017/04/13/opinion/reaching-out-to-the-voters-the-left-left-behind.html.

52. Lowrey, "2016: A Year Defined."

53. William H. Frey, "Census Shows Nonmetropolitan America Is Whiter, Getting Older, and Losing Population," Brookings Institution, June 27, 2017, https://www.brookings.edu/blog/the-avenue/2017/06/27/census-shows-nonmetropolitan-america-is-whiter-getting-older-and-losing-population/.

54. Gregor Aisch, Josh Katz, and David Leonhardt, "Where Men Aren't Working," *New York Times,* December 11, 2014, https://www.nytimes.com/interactive/2014/12/12/upshot/where-men-arent-working-map.html.

55. Jonathan Sallet, "Better Together: Broadband Deployment and Broadband Competition," Brookings Institution, March 15, 2017, https://www.brookings.edu/blog/techtank/2017/03/15/better-together-broadband-deployment-and-broadband-competition/.

56. See Chris McGreal, "America's Poorest White Town: Abandoned by Coal, Swallowed by Drugs," *Guardian,* November 12, 2015, https://www.theguardian.com/us-news/2015/nov/12/beattyville-kentucky-and-americas-poorest-towns.

57. Eleanor now works with me at Brookings and has contributed enormously to the contents of this book, so she deserves all kinds of credit for that reason alone.

58. James N. Maples, Brian G. Clark, Ryan Sharp, Braylon Gillespie, and Katherine Gerlaugh, "Economic Impact of Rock Climbing in the Red River Gorge, KY," Eastern Kentucky University, March 2016, https://www.accessfund.org/uploads/RRG-EIS-final.pdf.

59. See Dayna Bowen Matthew and Richard V. Reeves, "Trump Won White Voters, but Serious Inequalities Remain for Black Americans," Brookings Institution, January 13, 2017, https://www.brookings.edu/blog/social-mobility-memos/2017/01/13/trump-won-white-voters-but-serious-inequities-remain-for-black-americans/.

60. Author's analysis of Current Population Survey, Bureau of Labor Statistics, "Current Population Survey, 2017 ASEC Supplement" (Washington, DC: BLS, 2017).

61. Pew Research Center, "Public Trust in Government Remains Near Historic Lows as Partisan Attitudes Shift," Pew Research Center, May 3, 2017, http://www.people-press.org/2017/05/03/public-trust-in-government-remains-near-historic-lows-as-partisan-attitudes-shift/.

62. Ibid.

63. Pew Research Center, "Political Polarization in the American Public," Pew Research Center, June 12, 2014, http://www.people-press.org/2014/06/12/political-polarization-in-the-american-public/.

64. Jim Norman, "America's Confidence in Institutions Stays Low," Gallup, June 13, 2016, http://www.gallup.com/poll/192581/americans-confidence-institutions-stays-low.aspx.

65. On the resentment of elite colleges, see Cramer, *Politics of Resentment*. For an excellent summary (and data) on community colleges and the white working class, see Ronald Brownstein, "Why Some Cities and States Are Footing the Bill for Community College," *Atlantic*, April 20, 2017, https://www.theatlantic.com/politics/archive/2017/04/community-college-tuition-free/523587/.

66. Yuval Levin, *The Fractured Republic: Renewing America's Social Contract in the Age of Individualism* (New York: Basic Books, 2016), 5.

67. George A. Akerlof and Robert J. Shiller, *Phishing for Phools: The Economics of Manipulation and Deception* (Princeton, NJ: Princeton University Press, 2015).

68. Eric Hedberg, Thom Reilly, David Daugherty, and Joseph Garcia, "Voters, Media, and Social Networks," ASU Morrison Institute for Public Policy, April 2017, https://morrisoninstitute.asu.edu/sites/default/files/content/products/Media%20Report%202017.pdf, 1.

69. Ibid., 4. In a study of Arizona voters, the authors found that 79 percent of Republicans cited Fox News as their main source of information, with much lower proportions (around 50–54 percent) citing any other source. Among Democrats, CNN was the most popular, with 76 percent saying it was their main source, but it competed with many other sources that were almost as popular (with ratings of over 68 percent). These other sources included NBC, PBS, ABC, and CBS.

70. Jieun Shin and Kjerstin Thorson, "Partisan Selective Sharing: The Biased Diffusion of Fact-Checking Messages on Social Media: Sharing Fact-Checking Messages on Social Media," *Journal of Communication* 67, no. 2 (2017): 233–255.

71. Gregory J. Martin and Ali Yurukoglu, "Bias in Cable News: Persuasion and Polarization," *American Economic Review* 107, no. 9 (September 2017): 2565–2599.

72. For an interesting description of four case studies of voter manipulation by effective political advertising, see Kathleen Hall Jamieson, "Implications of the Demise of 'Fact' in Political Discourse," *Proceedings of the American Philosophical Society* 159, no. 1 (March 2015): 66–84.

73. Jack Goldsmith, "Will Donald Trump Destroy the Presidency?" *Atlantic*, October 2017, https://www.theatlantic.com/magazine/archive/2017/10/will-donald-trump-destroy-the-presidency/537921/.

74. Pew Research Center, "In Changing News Landscape, Even Television Is Vulnerable," Pew Research Center, September 27, 2012, http://www.people-press.org/2012/09/27/in-changing-news-landscape-even-television-is-vulnerable/.

75. Ibid.

76. Bishop, *Big Sort*, 39.

77. For a depressing but very interesting and provocative exegesis on the flaws in a democracy, including data on how misinformed and biased voters are, see Jason Brennan, *Against Democracy* (Princeton, NJ: Princeton University Press, 2016).

78. Yphtach Lelkes finds that Republicans and Democrats increasingly dislike one another. He calls this "affective polarization" and finds that it increased by 8 points on a 101-point scale between 1978 and 2012. Yphtach Lelkes, "Mass Polar-

ization: Manifestations and Measurements," *Public Opinion Quarterly* 80, no. S1 (2016): 392–410.

79. Ibid.

80. Walter Scheidel, *The Great Leveller: Violence and the History of Inequality from the Stone Age to the Twenty-First Century* (Princeton, NJ: Princeton University Press, 2017).

81. Sheryll Cashin, *Loving: Interracial Intimacy in America and the Threat to White Supremacy* (Boston: Beacon Press, 2017), 163.

Chapter 3. What Went Wrong?

1. As William Galston warns, "If economic growth and well-being are in jeopardy, so are our political arrangements." He notes that a strong and stable middle class has been critical to maintaining a stable constitutional democracy ever since Aristotle's times. Benjamin Friedman similarly warns that when a population does not experience the prosperity resulting from economic growth, the central faith in democracy may be at risk. When enough individuals lose the sense that they are getting ahead, a society may "retreat into rigidity and intolerance." William A. Galston, "The New Challenge to Market Democracies" (Washington, DC: Brookings Institution, October 20, 2014), https://www.brookings.edu/research/the-new-challenge-to-market-democracies-the-political-and-social-costs-of-economic-stagnation; Benjamin Friedman, *The Moral Consequences of Economic Growth* (New York: Random House, 2005).

2. Raj Chetty, David Grusky, Maximilian Hell, Nathaniel Hendren, Robert Manduca, and Jimmy Narang, "The Fading American Dream: Trends in Absolute Income Mobility since 1940," *Science*, April 24, 2017.

3. Between the 1981–82 and the 2016–17 school years, the average tuition and fees for both public and private nonprofit four-year institutions increased by about 300 percent in constant 2016 dollars (from $2,390 to $9,650 for public institutions and from $10,810 to $33,480 for private institutions). "Tuition and Fees and Room and Board over Time, 1976–77 to 2016–17, Selected Years," College Board, accessed February 7, 2017, https://trends.collegeboard.org/college-pricing/figures-tables/tuition-and-fees-and-room-and-board-over-time-1976-77_2016-17-selected-years.

4. In 1960, 72 percent of adults over age eighteen were married; by the year 2000, only 57 percent were. See D'Vera Cohn, Jeffrey S. Passel, Wendy Wang, and Gretchen Livingston, "Barely Half of U.S. Adults Are Married—A Record Low," Pew Research Center, December 14, 2011, http://www.pewsocialtrends.org/2011/12/14/barely-half-of-u-s-adults-are-married-a-record-low/.

5. Chetty et al., "Fading American Dream."

6. Karlyn Bowman, Jennifer Marsico, and Heather Sims, "Is the American Dream Alive? Examining Americans' Attitudes" (Washington, DC: American Enterprise Institute, 2014).

7. Author's calculations based on data from the Bureau of Economic Analysis, "National Income and Product Accounts" (Washington, DC: U.S. Department of Commerce, 2016). Note that real GDP grew by about 3.2 percent over this same time period.

8. Elizabeth Arias, "United States Life Tables, 2011," Centers for Disease Control, *National Vital Statistics Reports* 64, no. 11 (2015).

9. Robert J. Gordon, *The Rise and Fall of American Growth* (Princeton, NJ: Princeton University Press, 2016).

10. Erik Brynjolfsson and Andrew McAfee, *The Second Machine Age: Work, Progress, and Prosperity in a Time of Brilliant Technologies* (New York: W. W. Norton, 2014).

11. Steve Lohr, "Why the Economic Payoff from Technology Is So Elusive," *New York Times*, June 5, 2016, https://www.nytimes.com/2016/06/06/business/why-the -economic-payoff-from-technology-is-so-elusive.html?_r=0.

12. Anthony B. Atkinson, Thomas Piketty, and Emmanuel Saez, "Top Incomes in the Long Run of History," *Journal of Economic Literature* 49, no. 1 (2011): 3–71.

13. Data retrieved from World Wealth and Income Database, "Top 10% Share," United States, http://wid.world/country/usa/. The WID database is a free, on-line database of world wealth and income series reported in the scholarly work of Thomas Piketty, Gabriel Zucman, Emmanuel Saez, and other economists on the historical evolution and distribution of income and wealth.

14. Claudia Goldin and Lawrence F. Katz, "Long-Run Changes in the Wage Structure: Narrowing, Widening, Polarizing," *Brookings Papers on Economic Activity* 2 (2007): 135–167.

15. For a good review of the reasons for rising inequality, see Timothy Noah, *The Great Divergence: America's Growing Inequality Crisis and What We Can Do about It* (New York: Bloomsbury, 2013).

16. There are two controversies about inequality in the United States that are worth mentioning. The first is that some analysts who focus on consumption rather than income believe that the rise in inequality has been exaggerated. (For a review of the literature on both sides of this argument, see Thomas Edsall, "The Hidden Prosperity of the Poor," *New York Times*, January 30, 2013, https://opinionator .blogs.nytimes.com/2013/01/30/the-hidden-prosperity-of-the-poor/.)

The second controversy is how to value health benefits. Take Medicaid or Medicare. If one values the insurance they provide to the poor and the elderly at its market value, they are worth a lot. If they are counted as "income" to the poor and the elderly, they can double or more than double those incomes and make many people at the bottom of the distribution appear to be quite well off. And as the price of health care continues to outpace other prices in the United States, the value of that insurance rises as well, even if these high costs fail to deliver much improvement in health outcomes. The dilemma for CBO and other analysts is how to treat these health benefits. The benefits themselves are clearly valuable. At the same time, they may not be doing as much as we might like to improve health. More importantly, unlike cash, they aren't fungible. That is, they cannot be used to buy food or move to a better neighborhood, which might be as important to one's well-being and even one's health as access to health care. My own view is that this leads to an overestimate of what CBO calls pretax incomes (incomes after the inclusion of benefits but before taxes) for bottom-half families, and especially for the poorest.

17. See Uri Dadush, Kernal Davis, Sarah P. Milsom, and Bennett Stancil, *Inequality in America: Facts, Trends, and International Perspectives* (Washington, DC: Brookings Institution Press, 2012).

18. Branko Milanovic, *Global Inequality: A New Approach for the Age of Globalization* (Cambridge, MA: Harvard University Press, 2016).

19. Richard Reeves, *Dream Hoarders: How the American Upper Middle Class Is Leaving Everyone Else in the Dust, Why That Is a Problem, and What to Do about It* (Washington, DC: Brookings Institution Press, 2017).

20. Bureau of Labor Statistics, "Table 18. Employed Persons by Detailed Industry, Sex, Race, and Hispanic or Latino Ethnicity," Labor Force Statistics from the Current Population Survey, accessed August 7, 2017, https://www.bls.gov/cps/cpsaat18.htm.

21. Binyamin Appelbaum, "The Jobs Americans Do," *New York Times,* February 23, 2017, https://www.nytimes.com/2017/02/23/magazine/the-new-working-class.html?_r=0.

22. For an excellent review of artificial intelligence and its implications, see "Special Report on Artificial Intelligence," *Economist* print edition, June 25, 2016. Also, see Darrell M. West, *The Future of Work* (Washington, DC: Brookings Institution Press, 2018).

23. Matt Peckham, "What 7 of the World's Smartest People Think about Artificial Intelligence," *Time,* May 5, 2016, http://time.com/4278790/smart-people-ai/.

24. Jason Furman, John P. Holdren, Cecilia Muñoz, Megan Smith, and Jeffrey Zients, "Artificial Intelligence, Automation, and the Economy" (Washington, DC: Executive Office of the President, December 2016), 23.

25. Peckham, "What 7 of the World's Smartest People."

26. Ibid.

27. Brynjolfsson and McAfee, *Second Machine Age.*

28. Carl Benedict Frey and Michael A. Osborne, "The Future of Employment: How Susceptible Are Jobs to Computerisation?" Oxford University, 2013. The OECD is less pessimistic and sees only 9 percent of jobs being automated across its twenty-one-member countries. See Steve Lohr, "Robots Will Take Jobs, but Not as Fast as Some Fear, New Report Says," *New York Times,* January 12, 2017, https://www.nytimes.com/2017/01/12/technology/robots-will-take-jobs-but-not-as-fast-as-some-fear-new-report-says.html.

29. James Manyika, Michael Chui, Mehdi Miremadi, Jacques Bughin, Katy George, Paul Willmott, and Martin Dewhurst, "Harnessing Automation for a Future That Works," McKinsey Global Institute, January 2017, https://www.mckinsey.com/global-themes/digital-disruption/harnessing-automation-for-a-future-that-works.

30. Daron Acemoglu and Pascual Restrepo, "Robots and Jobs: Evidence from US Labor Markets," NBER Working Paper no. 23285, March 2017, http://www.nber.org/papers/w23285.

31. Furman et al., "Artificial Intelligence."

32. See James Bessen, *Learning by Doing: The Real Connection between Innovation, Wages, and Wealth* (New Haven, CT: Yale University Press, 2015).

33. See "Automation and Anxiety," in "Special Report on Artificial Intelligence."

34. Ibid., 10.

35. Tyler Cowen argues, for example, that before most European nations created a welfare state to soften the impact of industrialization in the nineteenth century, there was "a lot of overreaction in other, more destructive directions." He goes on to say, "I like to think we will be more intellectually moderate this time around, but the political developments of the last few years, and the observed global tilt toward the authoritarian, are hardly reassuring." See Tyler Cowen, "Industrial Revolution Comparisons Aren't Comforting," *Bloomberg View,* February 16, 2017, https://www.bloomberg.com/view/articles/2017-02-16/industrial-revolution-comparisons-aren-t-comforting.

36. Michael J. Hicks and Srikant Devaraj, "The Myth and Reality of Manufacturing in America," Ball State University, 2015, http://projects.cberdata.org/reports/MfgReality.pdf.

37. Daron Acemoglu, David Autor, David Dorn, Gordon H. Hanson, and Brendan Price, "Import Competition and the Great US Employment Sag of the 2000s," *Journal of Labor Economics* 34, no. S1 (January 2016): S141–S198. A separate paper by Justin Pierce and Peter Schott considers the effect of trade liberalization on mortality. The authors show that rising imports from China following the liberalization of trade in 2000 has led to both bad employment outcomes and rising suicide rates in the U.S. counties most affected, even after carefully controlling for other possible explanations. Justin R. Pierce and Peter K. Schott, "Trade Liberalization and Mortality: Evidence from U.S. Counties," Finance and Economics Discussion Series 2016-094 (Washington, DC: Board of Governors of the Federal Reserve System, 2016).

38. For a great summary of the academic evidence on all these trade and flexibility issues, see Jon Hilsenrath and Bob Davis, "How the China Shock, Deep and Swift, Spurred the Rise of Trump," *Wall Street Journal,* August 11, 2016, https://www.wsj.com/articles/how-the-china-shock-deep-and-swift-spurred-the-rise-of-trump-1470929543.

39. Quoted in Claire Cain Miller, "The Long-Term Jobs Killer Is Not China: It's Automation," *New York Times,* December 21, 2016, https://www.nytimes.com/2016/12/21/upshot/the-long-term-jobs-killer-is-not-china-its-automation.html.

40. Council of Economic Advisers, "Economic Report of the President" (Washington, DC: Executive Office of the President, February 2015), 144–145.

41. For a detailed review on this topic, see Eleanor Krause and Isabel Sawhill, "What We Know and Don't Know about Declining Labor Force Participation: A Review"

(Washington, DC: Brookings Institution, May 2017), https://www.brookings.edu
/research/what-we-know-and-dont-know-about-declining-labor-force-participation
-a-review/.

42. Francine Blau and Lawrence Kahn suggest that the lack of these family-friendly
policies can explain nearly one-third of the decline in American women's labor
force participation, relative to other OECD countries. Francine D. Blau and Lawrence M. Kahn, "Female Labor Supply: Why Is the United States Falling Behind?"
American Economic Review 103, no. 3 (May 2013): 251–256.

43. Anthony P. Carnevale, Nicole Smith, and Jeff Strohl, "Recovery: Job Growth and
Education Requirements through 2020," Georgetown University Center on Education and the Workforce, June 2013, https://cew-7632.kxcdn.com/wp-content
/uploads/2014/11/Recovery2020.FR_.Web_.pdf.

44. As Tamar Jacoby writes, "at least one third and perhaps half of all jobs coming
online in the next five years will be 'middle skill'—requiring less than a bachelor's degree but more than a high school diploma (in most cases some kind of
technical training)." (Tamar Jacoby, "The Certificate Revolution," in *Education for
Upward Mobility*, ed. Michael J. Petrilli [Lanham, MD: Rowman and Littlefield,
2016], 52.)

45. Daniel P. McMurrer and Isabel V. Sawhill, *Getting Ahead: Economic and Social
Mobility in America* (Washington, DC: Urban Institute Press: 1998), 1.

46. See Isabel V. Sawhill, Julia B. Isaacs, and Ron Haskins, "Getting Ahead or Losing
Ground: Economic Mobility in America" (Washington, DC: Brookings Institu-
tion, February 20, 2008), https://www.brookings.edu/research/getting-ahead-or
-losing-ground-economic-mobility-in-america/; Isabel V. Sawhill and Richard V.
Reeves, "Modeling Equal Opportunity," *Russell Sage Foundation Journal of the Social
Sciences* 2, no. 2 (2016): 60–97; Timothy Smeeding, Robert Erikson, and Markus
Jantti, *Persistence, Privilege, and Parenting: The Comparative Study of Intergenera-
tional Mobility* (New York: Russell Sage Foundation, 2011).

47. Robert D. Putnam, *Our Kids: The American Dream in Crisis* (New York: Simon &
Schuster, 2016).

48. See Isabel V. Sawhill, "Inequality and Social Mobility: Be Afraid" (Washington,
DC: Brookings Institution, May 27, 2015), https://www.brookings.edu/blog/social
-mobility-memos/2015/05/27/inequality-and-social-mobility-be-afraid/.

49. The resulting Social Genome Model is now a partnership among three institutions: the Brookings Institution, the Urban Institute, and Child Trends.

50. For a more extended discussion of the model, its strengths, and its limitations,
see Sawhill and Reeves, "Modeling Equal Opportunity."

51. Richard V. Reeves and Isabel Sawhill, "Social Mobility: A Promise That Could Still
Be Kept," *Milken Institute Review*, June 15, 2015, http://www.milkenreview.org/articles
/social-mobility-a-promise-that-could-still-be-kept.

52. Isabel V. Sawhill, "Creating Opportunity for the Forgotten Americans," in *Brookings: Big Ideas for America*, ed. Michael E. O'Hanlon (Washington, DC: Brookings
Institution Press, 2017).

53. Our estimates are based on a simulation with census data. An astute reader will wonder whether the correlations we model are causal. They are not. However, we have written a technical appendix that explains the approach in detail, along with some limitations of the data. We also review a number of other studies that explore the causality issue and give us reason to believe that our approach gets the general magnitudes right. The analysis shows that work is the biggest driver of success. Reliance on annual data, however, may give work more prominence than it deserves. Over the longer run, family circumstances and especially education may be more important. For more detail, see Isabel Sawhill and Edward Rodrigue, "The Three Norms Analysis: Technical Background" (Washington, DC: Brookings Institution, revised March 2018), https://www.brookings.edu/research/an-agenda-for-reducing-poverty-and-improving-opportunity/.

54. See Isabel V. Sawhill, *Generation Unbound: Drifting into Sex and Parenthood without Marriage* (Washington, DC: Brookings Institution Press, 2014).

55. Wendy Wang and W. Bradford Wilcox, "The Millennial Success Sequence: Marriage, Kids, and the 'Success Sequence' among Young Adults," AEI and the Institute for Family Studies, 2017, https://www.aei.org/wp-content/uploads/2017/06/IFS-MillennialSuccessSequence-Final.pdf.

56. I estimate that the growth of single-parent families since 1970 has increased the child poverty rate by 25 percent. Sawhill, *Generation Unbound;* Isabel Sawhill and Joanna Venator, "Improving Children's Life Chances through Better Family Planning," CCF Brief no. 55 (Washington, DC: Brookings Institution, January 2015), https://www.brookings.edu/research/improving-childrens-life-chances-through-better-family-planning/; Sara McLanahan and Isabel Sawhill, "Marriage and Child Wellbeing Revisited: Introducing the Issue," *Future of Children* 25, no. 2 (2015): 3–9; and Ron Haskins and Isabel V. Sawhill, "The Decline of the American Family: Can Anything Be Done to Stop the Damage?" *ANNALS of the American Academy of Political and Social Science* 667, no. 1 (2016): 8–34.

57. Isabel Sawhill, "Reducing Poverty by Cutting Unplanned Births," *Health Affairs,* August 21, 2015, http://healthaffairs.org/blog/2015/08/21/reducing-poverty-by-cutting-unplanned-births/.

58. Ben Schiller, "Spending $1 Billion on Reducing Unintended Pregnancy Would Deliver $6 Billion to the Economy," *Fast Company,* September 21, 2016, https://www.fastcompany.com/3063555/spending-1-billion-on-reducing-unintended-pregnancy-would-deliver-6-b; Michelle Boyd, Devin Murphy, and Debby Bielak, "'Billion Dollar Bets' to Reduce Unintended Pregnancies: Creating Economic Opportunity for Every American" (Boston: Bridgespan Group, August 2016).

59. National Center for Educational Statistics, "Table 219.10. High School Graduates, by Sex and Control of School: Selected Years, 1869–70 through 2026–27," NCES Digest of Education Statistics, 2015, https://nces.ed.gov/programs/digest/d16/tables/dt16_219.10.asp?current=yes.

60. Christopher B. Swanson, "Closing the Graduation Gap: Educational and Economic Conditions in America's Largest Cities" (Bethesda, MD: Editorial Projects in Education, April 2009).

61. Jeffrey J. Selingo, "Wanted: Factory Workers, Degree Required," *New York Times,* January 30, 2017, https://www.nytimes.com/2017/01/30/education/edlife/factory-workers-college-degree-apprenticeships.html?_r=0.

62. The Executive Office of the President reported in 2016 that "fewer than 40 percent of graduating students scored at college- and career-ready levels in 2013." Furman et al., "Artificial Intelligence." The National Assessment Government Board estimated that, of students in grade 12 in 2013, 39 percent were academically prepared for college in mathematics and 38 percent were prepared in reading. U.S. Department of Education, Institute of Education Sciences, National Center for Education Statistics, "National Assessment of Educational Progress (NAEP), 2013 Mathematics and Reading Assessments."

63. Rebecca Unterman, "Headed to College: The Effects of New York City's Small High Schools of Choice on Postsecondary Enrollment" (New York: MDRC, October 2014); James J. Kemple, "Career Academies: Long-Term Impacts on Labor Market Outcomes, Educational Attainment, and Transitions to Adulthood" (New York: MDRC, June 2008).

64. As my colleagues at Brookings report, "Charter schools with a strong academic focus and 'no-excuses' philosophy that serve poor black students in urban areas stand as contradictions to the general association between school-level poverty and academic achievement. These very high-poverty, high-minority schools produce achievement gains that are substantially greater than the traditional public schools in the same catchment areas. This is further evidence that school quality is a primary mediator of academic achievement rather than the racial or economic makeup of a school's student body." Grover J. "Russ" Whitehurst, Richard V. Reeves, and Edward Rodrigue, "Segregation, Race, and Charter Schools: What Do We Know?" (Washington, DC: Brookings Institution, October 2016), https://www.brookings.edu/research/segregation-race-and-charter-schools-what-do-we-know/.

65. See David Osborne, *Reinventing America's Schools: Creating a 21st Century Education System* (New York: Bloomsbury, 2017).

66. "Excellence in the Classroom," *The Future of Children* 17, no 1 (Spring 2007).

67. Isabel V. Sawhill, "Higher Education and the Opportunity Gap" (Washington, DC: Brookings Institution, October 8, 2013), https://www.brookings.edu/research/higher-education-and-the-opportunity-gap/.

68. Isabel V. Sawhill, "Target Aid to Students Most Likely to Succeed," *Education Next* 14, no. 2 (Spring 2014): 58–64.

69. Department of Education, "Department of Education Fiscal Year 2016 President's Budget," April 29, 2015, https://www2.ed.gov/about/overview/budget/budget16/16pbapt.pdf.

70. The proportion would be higher if we included those disqualified for cosmetic reasons, such as excessive tattoos.

71. Miriam Jordan, "Recruits' Ineligibility Tests the Military," *Wall Street Journal,* June 27, 2014, https://www.wsj.com/articles/recruits-ineligibility-tests-the-military -1403909945.

Chapter 4. Why Economic Growth Is Not Enough

1. Ben S. Bernanke, "When Growth Is Not Enough," remarks prepared for delivery on June 26, 2017, at the European Central Bank Forum on Central Banking at Sintra, https://www.brookings.edu/wp-content/uploads/2017/06/es_20170626 _whengrowthisnotenough.pdf.

2. Robert Solow, "A Contribution to the Theory of Economic Growth," *Quarterly Journal of Economics* 70, no. 1 (February 1956): 65–94.

3. Moses Abramovitz, "Resource and Output Trends in the United States since 1870," *American Economic Review* 46 (1956): 5–23.

4. Author's analysis of U.S. Congressional Budget Office, Real Potential Gross Domestic Product, retrieved on August 2, 2017, from FRED (Federal Reserve Bank of St. Louis), https://fred.stlouisfed.org/series/GDPPOT.

5. Larry Summers believes that we face not just a temporary lack of demand but possibly what he and others have called "secular stagnation." His argument is that there is a global excess of savings that is not being invested. This has led to insufficient demand, slow growth, low inflation, and low interest rates. He believes that unless we spend more—for example, by investing in infrastructure or clean energy—we will continue to have slow growth, and that low interest rates will lead to excessive investment in risky assets with a reoccurrence of the kind of financial bubbles that triggered the last recession. Larry Summers, "The Age of Secular Stagnation: What It Is and What to Do about It," *Foreign Affairs,* February 15, 2016, https://www.foreignaffairs.com/articles/united-states/2016 -02-15/age-secular-stagnation.

6. Quoted in Ylan Q. Mui, "Federal Reserve Chair Janet Yellen: Question Everything," *Washington Post,* October 14, 2016, https://www.washingtonpost.com /news/wonk/wp/2016/10/14/federal-reserve-chair-janet-yellen-question-everything /?utm_term=.7ed586f008a9.

7. See the Joint Committee on Taxation, "Macroeconomic Analysis of the 'Tax Cut and Jobs Act' as Ordered Reported by the Senate Committee on Finance on November 16, 2017," JCX-61-17, November 30, 2017, https://www.jct.gov/publications .html?func=startdown&id=5045.

8. The Simpson-Bowles Commission, formally known as the National Commission on Fiscal Responsibility and Reform, was a bipartisan commission created by President Obama in 2010 to identify solutions to the nation's fiscal challenges. The final report did not reach the vote threshold required to have it sent to Congress for a vote.

9. Michael Porter et al., on behalf of the Harvard Business School, reviewed the state of U.S. competitiveness and found that, among other issues, the U.S. econ-

omy is in an era of "political paralysis" that has restricted progress in Washington and in the private sector. The authors point to Americans' distrust of the U.S. political system and increasing levels of polarization as contributors to slowing growth. Notably, they suggest "that dysfunction in America's political system is now the single most important challenge to U.S. economic progress" (5). Michael E. Porter, Jan W. Rivkin, Mihir A. Desai, and Manjari Raman, "Problems Unsolved and a Nation Divided," Harvard Business School, September 2016, http://www.hbs.edu/competitiveness/Documents/problems-unsolved-and-a-nation-divided.pdf; also see Brink Lindsey and Steven Teles, *The Captured Economy* (Oxford: Oxford University Press, 2017).

10. This broader metric incorporates consumption, leisure, mortality, and inequality. See Charles I. Jones and Peter J. Klenow, "Beyond GDP? Welfare across Countries and Times," *American Economic Review* 106, no. 9 (2016): 2426–2457. Ben Bernanke and Peter Olson extend the analysis first conducted by Jones and Klenow and show that slowing improvements in life expectancy and increased inequality are holding overall welfare in the United States back, compared to other countries. Ben Bernanke and Peter Olson, "Are Americans Better Off than They Were a Decade or Two Ago?" (Washington, DC: Brookings Institution, October 19, 2016), https://www.brookings.edu/blog/ben-bernanke/2016/10/19/are-americans-better-off-than-they-were-a-decade-or-two-ago/.

11. OECD, "Average Annual Hours Actually Worked per Worker," OECD.Stat, accessed August 2, 2017, from https://stats.oecd.org/Index.aspx?DataSetCode=ANHRS.

12. See World Wealth and Income Database, "Top 1% Share," accessed August 2, 2017, from http://wid.world/country/france/ and http://wid.world/country/usa/.

13. Eleanor Krause and Isabel Sawhill, "Should We Try to Live like the French?" (Washington, DC: Brookings Institution, November 10, 2016), https://www.brookings.edu/blog/social-mobility-memos/2016/11/10/should-we-try-to-live-like-the-french/.

14. The U.S. Council of Economic Advisers reports that were it not for the increase in women's labor force participation since 1970, the national economy would be $2 trillion smaller and median household incomes $14,000 smaller. Council of Economic Advisers, "Eleven Facts about American Families and Work" (Washington, DC: Executive Office of the President of the United States, 2014), https://obamawhitehouse.archives.gov/sites/default/files/docs/eleven_facts_about_family_and_work_final.pdf.

15. In 1996, the Boskin Commission released a report that concluded that "changes in the CPI have substantially overstated the actual rate of price inflation, by about 1.3 percentage points per annum prior to 1996." Advisory Commission to Study the Consumer Price Index, "Toward a More Accurate Measure of the Cost of Living," Final Report to the Senate Finance Committee, December 4, 1996, https://catalog.hathitrust.org/Record/003239902.

16. As many economists like to note, this is not necessarily a new problem. GDP was never intended to capture consumer surplus, so this might not be a "measurement issue" at all. But GDP is nonetheless missing rising consumer welfare over time. See Kemal Dervis and Zia Qureshi, "The Productivity Slump—Fact or Fiction: The Measurement Debate" (Washington, DC: Brookings Institution, August 26, 2016), https://www.brookings.edu/research/the-productivity-slump-fact-or -fiction-the-measurement-debate/.

17. For example, the Deepwater Horizon oil spill, despite the fact that it caused disruption of fishing and tourism activities, harm to marine ecosystems, and direct job loss, might have actually increased GDP thanks to the employment gains required to clean up the spill. Luca Di Leo, "Oil Spill May End Up Lifting GDP Slightly," Real Time Economics, *Wall Street Journal*, June 15, 2010, http:// blogs.wsj.com/economics/2010/06/15/oil-spill-may-end-up-lifting-gdp -slightly/.

18. Robert F. Kennedy, Remarks at the University of Kansas, March 18, 1968, https:// www.jfklibrary.org/Research/Research-Aids/Ready-Reference/RFK-Speeches /Remarks-of-Robert-F-Kennedy-at-the-University-of-Kansas-March-18-1968 .aspx.

19. Richard Easterlin, "Does Economic Growth Improve the Human Lot? Some Empirical Evidence," in *Nations and Households in Economic Growth: Essays in Honor of Moses Abramovitz*, ed. Paul A. David and Melvin W. Reder (New York: Academic Press, Inc., 1974).

20. Robert H. Frank, *Falling Behind: How Rising Inequality Harms the Middle Class* (Berkeley: University of California Press, 2007); Robert H. Frank, "The Easterlin Paradox Revisited," *Emotion* 12, no. 6 (2012): 1188–1191.

21. Kahneman and Tversky first proposed the concept of loss aversion in 1979, suggesting that "losses loom larger than gains." The theory has since been widely accepted by behavioral economists conducting experiments in a wide array of research settings. Daniel Kahneman and Alan Tversky, "Prospect Theory: An Analysis of Decision under Risk," *Econometrica* 47, no. 2 (1979): 263–292.

22. The term "Laffer Curve" was actually coined by Jude Wanniski, a journalist at the *Wall Street Journal*, following a 1974 dinner with Arthur Laffer, Dick Cheney, and Donald Rumsfeld, during which Laffer sketched an original iteration of the curve on a restaurant napkin. National Museum of American History, "Laffer Curve Napkin," Smithsonian, http://americanhistory.si.edu/collections/search/object /nmah_1439217.

23. To his credit, in 1986, Martin Feldstein argued that supply-side economics is generally about removing government disincentives for investment and individual initiative, and that "new" supply-side economists posit extravagant claims that reduced taxes will yield dramatic growth, increased tax revenue, increased personal savings, and small reductions in inflation. While he didn't doubt that reducing marginal tax rates favorably influenced GNP and work incentives, he argued that such exaggerated claims gave a bad name to supply-side economics.

Martin Feldstein, "Supply Side Economics: Old Truths and New Claims," *American Economic Review* 76, no. 2, Papers and Proceedings of the Ninety-Eighth Annual Meeting of the American Economic Association (May 1986): 26–30.

24. Center on Budget and Policy Priorities, "Tax Cuts for the Rich Aren't an Economic Panacea—and Could Hurt Growth" (Washington, DC: Center on Budget and Policy Priorities, April 13, 2017), https://www.cbpp.org/research/federal-tax /tax-cuts-for-the-rich-arent-an-economic-panacea-and-could-hurt-growth.

25. See William G. Gale, "State Income Tax Cuts: Still a Bad Idea" (Washington, DC: Brookings Institution, July 28, 2015), https://www.brookings.edu/opinions/state -income-tax-cuts-still-a-bad-idea/; William G. Gale and Andrew A. Samwick, "Effects of Income Tax Changes on Economic Growth" (Washington, DC: Brookings Institution, February 1, 2016), https://www.brookings.edu/research/effects-of -income-tax-changes-on-economic-growth/.

26. Thomas Piketty, Emmanuel Saez, and Stefanie Stantcheva, "Optimal Taxation of Top Labor Incomes: A Tale of Three Elasticities," NBER Working Paper no. 17616 (November 2011), http://www.nber.org/papers/w17616.

27. Michael Tomasky, "Finally, Something Isn't the Matter with Kansas," *New York Times*, June 12, 2017, https://www.nytimes.com/2017/06/12/opinion/finally -something-isnt-the-matter-with-kansas.html; William G. Gale, "States That Cut Taxes Do So at Their Peril," *Real Clear Markets*, July 28, 3015, http://www.real clearmarkets.com/articles/2015/07/28/states_that_cut_taxes_do_so_at_their _peril_101763.html.

28. Gale and Samwick, "Effects of Income Tax Changes," 27–28.

29. The Council of Economic Advisers, "Corporate Tax Reform and Wages: Theory and Evidence" (Washington, DC: Executive Office of the President, October 2017), https://www.whitehouse.gov/sites/whitehouse.gov/files/documents/Tax%20 Reform%20and%20Wages.pdf.

30. Josh Bivens, "Cutting Corporate Taxes Will Not Boost American Wages" (Washington, DC: Economic Policy Institute, October 25, 2017), http://www.epi.org/publication /cutting-corporate-taxes-will-not-boost-american-wages/.

31. These analytical shops include the Congressional Budget Office, the Treasury's Office of Tax Analysis, and the Tax Policy Center. Also, see Jane Gravelle, "Corporate Tax Reform: Issues for Congress" (Washington, DC: Congressional Research Service, September 22, 2017), https://fas.org/sgp/crs/misc/RL34229 .pdf.

32. Eric A. Hanushek, Paul E. Peterson, and Ludger Woessmann, *Endangering Prosperity: A Global View of the American School* (Washington, DC: Brookings Institution Press, 2013), 63.

33. Author's analysis of Bureau of Labor Statistics, "Databases, Tables & Calculators by Subject," Series ID PRS30006093 and Series ID CES3000000001.

34. See Harry J. Holzer, "Building a New Middle Class in the Knowledge Economy," Progressive Policy Institute, April 2017, http://www.progressivepolicy.org/wp -content/uploads/2017/04/PPI_MiddleClassJobs.pdf, 6.

35. Martin Neil Baily and Barry P. Bosworth, "U.S. Manufacturing: Understanding Its Past and Its Potential Future," *Journal of Economic Perspectives* 28, no. 1 (Winter 2014): 3–26.

36. Bureau of Labor Statistics, "Employment Projections," Table 2.3: Industries with the Fastest Growing and Most Rapidly Declining Wage and Salary Employment (Washington, DC: U.S. Department of Labor, 2015).

37. Binyamin Appelbaum, "Why Are Politicians So Obsessed with Manufacturing?" *New York Times Magazine,* October 4, 2016, https://www.nytimes.com/2016/10/09/magazine/why-are-politicians-so-obsessed-with-manufacturing.html?rref=collection%2Fbyline%2Fbinyamin-appelbaum&action=click&contentCollection=undefined&region=stream&module=stream_unit&version=latest&contentPlacement=41&pgtype=collection.

38. "Trade, at What Price?" *Economist,* April 2, 2016, http://www.economist.com/news/united-states/21695855-americas-economy-benefits-hugely-trade-its-costs-have-been-amplified-policy.

39. David Dollar, "Global Value Chains Shed New Light on Trade" (Washington, DC: Brookings Institution, July 10, 2017), https://www.brookings.edu/blog/order-from-chaos/2017/07/10/global-value-chains-shed-new-light-on-trade/.

40. There may be an issue of currency manipulation, however. Greg Ip makes this point in the *Wall Street Journal,* citing a new book by Fred Bergsten and Joseph Gagnon. Greg Ip, "This Time, Trump Is Right about Trade," *Wall Street Journal,* May 31, 2017, https://www.wsj.com/articles/this-time-trump-is-right-about-trade-1496223180.

41. National Academies of Sciences, Engineering, and Medicine, "The Economic and Fiscal Consequences of Immigration" (Washington, DC: National Academies Press, 2017).

42. Ibid.

43. Francine D. Blau and Gretchen Donehower, "President Trump Said a Major Report Found Immigration Hurt the Economy: 2 Authors Respond," *Vox,* March 17, 2017, https://www.vox.com/the-big-idea/2017/3/17/14951590/nas-report-immigration-economy-taxpayers-trump.

44. Ryan Avent, *The Wealth of Humans: Work, Power, and Status in the Twenty-First Century* (New York: Penguin Books, 2016).

Chapter 5. The Limits of Redistribution

1. Several studies have now shown a relationship between inequality and the overall performance of the economy, though not every expert agrees that inequality necessarily inhibits growth. See Raghuran G. Rajan, *Fault Lines: How Hidden Fractures Still Threaten the World Economy* (Princeton, NJ: Princeton University Press, 2011); Frederico Cingano, "Trends in Income Inequality and Its Impact on Economic Growth," *OECD Social, Employment, and Migration Working Papers* no. 163 (Paris: OECD Publishing, December 2014); Jonathan D. Ostry, Andrew Berg, and Charalam-

bos G. Tsangarides, "Redistribution, Inequality, and Growth," IMF Staff Discussion Note, February 2012; Jared Bernstein, "The Impact of Inequality on Growth" (Washington, DC: Center for American Progress, December 2013), https://www .americanprogress.org/wp-content/uploads/2013/12/BerensteinInequality.pdf.

2. Quoted in Sean Illing, "Why We Need to Plan for a Future without Jobs," *Vox*, November 24, 2016, https://www.vox.com/conversations/2016/10/17/13245808 /andy-stern-work-universal-basic-income-technology-artificial-intelligence -unions.

3. One of the best articles on UBI was written by Andrew Flowers for FiveThirty- Eight. Andrew Flowers, "What Would Happen if We Just Gave People Money?" *FiveThirtyEight*, April 25, 2016, http://fivethirtyeight.com/features/universal-basic -income/.

4. BBC News, "Switzerland's Voters Reject Basic Income Plan," *BBC*, June 5, 2016, http://www.bbc.com/news/world-europe-36454060.

5. Charles Murray, "A Guaranteed Income for Every American," *Wall Street Journal*, June 3, 2016, https://www.wsj.com/articles/a-guaranteed-income-for-every-american -1464969586; Anthony Atkinson, "Mind the Gap," *Economist*, June 6, 2015, https:// www.economist.com/news/books-and-arts/21653596-anthony-atkinson -godfather-inequality-research-growing-problem-mind-gap.

6. Robert Greenstein, "Commentary: Universal Basic Income May Sound Attractive but, If It Occurred, Would Likelier Increase Poverty than Reduce It" (Washing- ton, DC: Center on Budget and Policy Priorities, May 31, 2016), https://www .cbpp.org/poverty-and-opportunity/commentary-universal-basic-income-may -sound-attractive-but-if-it-occurred.

7. Irwin Garfinkel, David Harris, Jane Waldfogel, and Christopher Wimer, "Doing More for Our Children: Modeling a Universal Child Allowance or More Generous Child Tax Credit," *Century Foundation*, March 16, 2016, https://tcf.org/content /report/doing-more-for-our-children/.

8. See chapter 2 in Ron Haskins and Isabel Sawhill, *Creating an Opportunity Society* (Washington, DC: Brookings Institution Press, 2009); Alberto Alesina, Rafael Di Tella, and Robert MacCulloch, "Inequality and Happiness: Are Europeans and Americans Different?" *Journal of Public Economics* 88 (2004): 2009–2042.

9. This argument and the data can be found in chapter 12 of Michael J. Graetz and Ian Shapiro, *Death by a Thousand Cuts: The Fight over Taxing Inherited Wealth* (Princeton, NJ: Princeton University Press, 2005).

10. For more discussion of this point, see chapter 2 in Haskins and Sawhill, *Creating an Opportunity Society*.

11. Views about the role of luck are strongly correlated with political leanings, with conservatives believing that people can get ahead if they work hard and liberals much more likely to think that it is circumstances beyond people's control that affect their success. Pew Research Center, "Beyond Red vs. Blue: The Political Ty- pology," Pew, June 26, 2014, http://www.people-press.org/2014/06/26/the-political -typology-beyond-red-vs-blue/.

12. Ingvild Almås, Alexander W. Cappelen, and Bertil Tungodden, "Cutthroat Capitalism versus Cuddly Socialism: Are Americans More Meritocratic and Efficiency-Seeking than Scandinavians?" NHH Department of Economics Discussion Paper no. 18 (2016).

13. Kenneth Scheve and David Stasavage, *Taxing the Rich: A History of Fiscal Fairness in the United States and Europe* (Princeton, NJ: Princeton University Press, 2016).

14. Nicholas Kristof, "What Monkeys Can Teach Us about Fairness," *New York Times*, June 3, 2017, https://www.nytimes.com/2017/06/03/opinion/sunday/what-monkeys -can-teach-us-about-fairness.html.

15. Christina Starmans, Mark Sheskin, and Paul Bloom, "Why People Prefer Unequal Societies," *Nature Human Behaviour* 1, no. 0082 (2017).

16. Note that these data appear to be at odds with the Scheve and Stasavage study and may be due to the way the question was asked and its specificity. Hannah Fingerhut, "More Americans Favor Raising the Lowering Tax Rates on Corporations, High Household Incomes," Pew Research Center, September 27, 2017, http://www.pewresearch.org/fact-tank/2017/09/27/more-americans-favor -raising-than-lowering-tax-rates-on-corporations-high-household-incomes/.

17. While it was introduced as the Tax Cuts and Jobs Act, the final version of the bill was called an "Act to provide for reconciliation pursuant to titles II and V of the concurrent resolution on the budget for fiscal year 2018." For simplicity, I refer to the law by its name as introduced in Congress.

18. Daniel Kahneman and Amos Tversky, "Choices, Values, and Frames," *American Psychologist* 39, no. 4 (1984): 341–350.

19. Based on author's analysis of IRS tax return data.

20. I'm indebted to Professor James W. Sawhill at Washington University for suggesting this calculation.

21. Tax Policy Center, "Distributional Analysis of the Conference Agreement for the Tax Cuts and Jobs Act" (Washington, DC: Tax Policy Center, December 18, 2017), http://www.taxpolicycenter.org/publications/distributional-analysis-conference -agreement-tax-cuts-and-jobs-act/full.

22. Jane Mayer, *Dark Money: The Hidden History of the Billionaires behind the Rise of the Radical Right* (New York: Doubleday, 2016).

23. Thomas B. Edsall, "You Cannot Be Too Cynical about the Republican Tax Bill," *New York Times*, December 21, 2017, https://www.nytimes.com/2017/12/21/opinion /republican-tax-bill-trump-corker.html.

24. Darrell West, *Billionaires: Reflections on the Upper Crust* (Washington, DC: Brookings Institution Press, 2014).

25. Richard Reeves, *Dream Hoarders: How the American Upper Middle Class Is Leaving Everyone Else in the Dust, Why That Is a Problem, and What to Do about It* (Washington, DC: Brookings Institution Press, 2017).

26. Jason Furman, "Inequality: Facts, Explanations, and Policies," Remarks presented at City College of New York, October 17, 2016, https://obamawhitehouse.archives .gov/sites/default/files/page/files/20161017_furman_ccny_inequality_cea.pdf.

27. These are rough calculations based on IRS tax return data and on the more precise estimates published by the Congressional Budget Office. See "Revenues: Option 1" in Congressional Budget Office, *Options for Reducing the Deficit: 2017 to 2026* (Washington, DC: CBO, December 8, 2016), https://www.cbo.gov/sites /default/files/114th-congress-2015-2016/reports/52142-breakout-chapter42.pdf.

28. William G. Gale, Melissa S. Kearney, and Peter R. Orszag, "Would a Significant Increase in the Top Income Tax Rate Substantially Alter Income Inequality?" (Washington, DC: Brookings Institution, September 2015), https://www.brookings .edu/wp-content/uploads/2016/06/would-top-income-tax-alter-income -inequality.pdf.

29. The research team also looked at whether the results would change significantly under the assumption that higher tax rates on upper income households would cause them to reduce their pretax income by quite a lot (with an elasticity of 0.4). This didn't significantly change their conclusions.

30. Chye-Ching Huang and Chloe Cho, "Ten Facts You Should Know about the Federal Estate Tax" (Washington, DC: Center on Budget and Policy Priorities, October 30, 2017), https://www.cbpp.org/research/federal-tax/ten-facts-you-should-know-about -the-federal-estate-tax.

31. Michael Graetz, "Should the U.S. Adopt a Value-Added Tax?" *Wall Street Journal*, February 28, 2016, https://www.wsj.com/articles/should-the-u-s-adopt-a-value -added-tax-1456715703.

32. Author's calculations based on Congressional Budget Office, "Impose a 5 Percent Value-Added Tax," in *Options for Reducing the Deficit: 2017 to 2026* (Washington, DC: CBO, December 8, 2016); Tax Policy Center, Revenue Table T09-0442, 2009, http://www.taxpolicycenter.org/model-estimates/broad-based-value-added-tax/5 -percent-broad-based-value-added-tax-vat-impact-tax.

33. See Noah Kaufman, Michael Obeiter, and Eleanor Krause, "Putting a Price on Carbon: Reducing Emissions" (Washington, DC: World Resources Institute, January 2016), http://www.wri.org/publication/putting-price-carbon-reducing -emissions.

34. See Noah Kaufman and Eleanor Krause, "Putting a Price on Carbon: Ensuring Equity" (Washington, DC: World Resources Institute, April 2016), http://www .wri.org/sites/default/files/Putting_a_Price_on_Carbon_Ensuring_Equity.pdf.

35. James A. Baker III et al., "The Conservative Case for Carbon Dividends," Climate Leadership Council, February 2017, https://www.clcouncil.org/media/TheConse rvativeCaseforCarbonDividends.pdf.

36. Sheldon Whitehouse, "American Opportunity Carbon Fee Act Introduced to Congress," July 26, 2017, https://www.whitehouse.senate.gov/news/release/american -opportunity-carbon-fee-act-introduced-in-congress.

37. John Horowitz, Julie-Anne Cronin, Hannah Hawkins, Laura Konda, and Alex Yuskavage, "Methodology for Analyzing a Carbon Tax," U.S. Department of the Treasury, Office of Tax Analysis Working Paper 115, January 2017, https://www .treasury.gov/resource-center/tax-policy/tax-analysis/Documents/WP-115.pdf.

38. Noah Smith, "The Connection between Work and Dignity," *Bloomberg View*, December 21, 2016, https://www.bloomberg.com/view/articles/2016-12-21/the-connection-between-work-and-dignity.

39. The Dalai Lama and Arthur C. Brooks, "Dalai Lama: Behind Our Anxiety, the Fear of Being Unneeded," *New York Times*, November 4, 2016, https://www.nytimes.com/2016/11/04/opinion/dalai-lama-behind-our-anxiety-the-fear-of-being-unneeded.html.

40. See Mihaly Csikszentmihalyi, *Flow* (New York: Harper and Row, 1990); Mihaly Csikszentmihalyi and Judith LeFevre, "Optimal Experience in Work and Leisure," *Journal of Personality and Social Psychology* 56, no. 5 (1989): 815–822.

41. For more on this set of issues, see Alan Krueger, Daniel Kahneman, David Schkade, Norbert Schwarz, and Arthur A. Stone, "National Time Accounting: The Currency of Life," in *Measuring the Subjective Well-Being of Nations: National Accounts of Time Use and Well-Being*, ed. Alan B. Krueger (Chicago: University of Chicago Press, October 2009). In some research, people's self-reported evaluation of work as opposed to nonwork activities was considerably more negative. How to reconcile the two sets of findings remains unclear.

42. Mark Muro and Joseph Parilla, "Maladjusted: It's Time to Reimagine Economic 'Adjustment' Programs" (Washington, DC: Brookings Institution, January 10, 2017), https://www.brookings.edu/blog/the-avenue/2017/01/10/maladjusted-its-time-to-reimagine-economic-adjustment-programs/.

Chapter 6. A GI Bill for America's Workers

1. John Bound and Sarah Turner, "Going to War and Going to College: Did World War II and the G.I. Bill Increase Educational Attainment for Returning Veterans?" NBER Working Paper no. 7452, December 1999, http://www.nber.org/papers/w7452.

2. TargetPoint Consulting, "Voices for National Service Presidential Battleground Poll," October 19, 2015, http://voicesforservice.org/wp-content/uploads/2016/03/TargetPoint-National-Service-Memo-Final.pdf.

3. Corporation for National and Community Service, "AmeriCorps Week Marked from Coast to Coast," March 23, 2012, https://www.nationalservice.gov/newsroom/press-releases/2012/americorps-week-marked-coast-coast.

4. Clive Belfield shows that the annual social investment in national service totals about $2 billion, and social benefits total about $7.9 billion, for a benefit-cost ratio of 3.9. Clive Belfield, "The Economic Value of National Service," Voices for National Service and Civic Enterprises for the Franklin Project at the Aspen Institute, September 2013, http://voicesforservice.org/wp-content/uploads/2016/03/Sep19_Econ_Value_National_Service-2.pdf.

5. Roger Cohen, "Travel Abroad, in Your Own Country," *New York Times*, March 4, 2017, https://www.nytimes.com/2017/03/04/opinion/sunday/travel-abroad-in-your-own-country.html?mcubz=1.

6. General Stanley McChrystal, "Securing the American Character," *Democracy*, no. 33 (Summer 2014), http://democracyjournal.org/magazine/33/securing-the -american-character/.

7. See Harry J. Holzer, "Building a New Middle Class in the Knowledge Economy," Progressive Policy Institute, April 2017, http://www.progressivepolicy.org /wp-content/uploads/2017/04/PPI_MiddleClassJobs.pdf; Anthony P. Carnevale, Tamara Jayasundera, and Andrew R. Hanson, "Career and Technical Education: Five Ways That Pay Along the Way to the B.A.," Georgetown University Center on Education and the Workforce, September 2012, https://www.insidehighered .com/sites/default/server_files/files/CTE_FiveWays_FullReport_Embargoed .pdf.

8. Holzer, "Building a New Middle Class."

9. A CEA report on this topic notes, "Through the Workforce Innovation and Opportunity Act—the Federal Government's largest job training investment program—only about 175,000 people are trained per year . . . Relative to the overall economy, the United States now spends less than half of what it did on such programs 30 years ago." Council of Economic Advisers, "Artificial Intelligence, Automation, and the Economy" (Washington, DC: Executive Office of the President, December 2016), https://obamawhitehouse.archives.gov/sites/whitehouse .gov/files/documents/Artificial-Intelligence-Automation-Economy.PDF, 3; OECD, "Public Expenditure and Participant Stocks on LMP," OECD.Stat, accessed June 7, 2017, from http://stats.oecd.org/Index.aspx?DataSetCode=LMPEXP.

10. Author's calculations based on OECD, "Public Expenditure."

11. Stephanie Stullich, Ivy Morgan, and Oliver Schak, "State and Local Expenditures on Corrections and Education," U.S. Department of Education, Office of Planning, Evaluation and Policy Development, July 2016, https://www2.ed.gov/rschstat /eval/other/expenditures-corrections-education/brief.pdf.

12. OECD, "Public Expenditure."

13. This recommendation and point were made in Council of Economic Advisers, "Artificial Intelligence."

14. OECD, "Public Expenditure."

15. Bureau of Labor Statistics, "College Enrollment and Work Activity of 2016 High School Graduates," BLS Economic News Release, April 27, 2017, https://www.bls .gov/news.release/hsgec.nr0.htm; Jolanta Juszkiewicz, "Trends in Community College Enrollment and Completion Data, 2015" (Washington, DC: American Association for Community Colleges, 2015); National Center for Education Statistics, "Undergraduate Retention and Graduation Rates," U.S. Department of Education, April 2017, https://nces.ed.gov/programs/coe/indicator_ctr.asp.

16. Richard Arum and Josipa Roksa, *Academically Adrift* (Chicago: University of Chicago Press, 2011).

17. This does not include the additional $89 billion from state, institutional, private, and employer grants. The largest items were spending on loans ($97.8 billion) and grants ($45.2 billion), with most of the latter going to Pell grants

($30.7 billion). Another $18 billion was devoted to tax subsidies. College Board, "Student Aid and Nonfederal Loans in 2015 Dollars over Time," College Board Trends in Higher Education, 2016, https://trends.collegeboard.org/student-aid/figures-tables/total-student-aid-and-nonfederal-loans-2015-dollars-over-time.

18. Further, "degree inflation" means that more job postings list a four-year degree as a requirement, though the occupation might not actually demand these credentials. One Harvard Business School report explains, "As more middle-skills jobs require mastery of one or more technologies, employers find it difficult to hire non-graduate talent with the requisite skills . . . Over time, employers defaulted to using college degrees as a proxy for a candidate's range and depth of skills." This has had repercussions on job seekers without these college credentials as well as on employers, who must pay substantially more for college graduates who are not necessarily any more productive than nongraduates. Joseph B. Fuller and Manjari Raman, "Dismissed by Degrees: How Degree Inflation Is Undermining U.S. Competitiveness and Hurting America's Middle Class," Accenture, Grads of Life, and Harvard Business School, October 2017, http://www.hbs.edu/managing-the-future-of-work/Documents/dismissed-by-degrees.pdf.

19. Stephanie Owen and Isabel Sawhill, "Should Everyone Go to College?" (Washington, DC: Brookings Institution, May 8, 2013), https://www.brookings.edu/research/should-everyone-go-to-college/.

20. I am indebted to the work of Robert Schwartz and Nancy Hoffman for many of these ideas. They note that nearly one-third of workers with two-year degrees outearn the average four-year degree holder. See Robert Schwartz and Nancy Hoffman, "High Quality Career and Technical Education," in *Education for Upward Mobility*, ed. Michael J. Petrilli (Lanham, MD: Rowman and Littlefield, 2016), chapter 7.

21. Robert G. Valletta, "Recent Flattening in the Higher Education Wage Premium: Polarization, Skill Downgrading, or Both?" NBER Working Paper no. 22935, December 2016, http://www.nber.org/papers/w22935.

22. Fuller et al., "Dismissed by Degrees."

23. Indeed, a 2017 report by Brookings and the National Center for the Middle Market found that 44 percent of executives in mid-sized firms say that "a lack of candidates with the right skills makes it difficult to recruit." Many of these companies lack the capacity to partner with educational and training organizations or offer internships and other within-firm training opportunities that might lead to advancement. Thomas A. Steward, Doug Farren, Marek Gootman, and Martha Ross, "Help Wanted: How Middle Market Companies Can Address Workforce Challenges to Find and Develop the Talent They Need to Grow," National Center for the Middle Market and Brookings Institution, August 2017, https://www.brookings.edu/research/brookings-ncmm-report/.

24. Petrilli, *Education for Upward Mobility*.

25. These earnings premiums were documented in comparison to control groups composed of students who demonstrated intention to earn a certificate or vocational degree in a given discipline but did not. Earnings were measured from five years prior to award date to seven years after the award. Ann Stevens, Michal Kurlaender, and Michel Grosz, "Career Technical Education and Labor Market Outcomes: Evidence from California Community Colleges," NBER Working Paper no. 21137, April 2015, http://www.nber.org/papers/w21137.

26. Larry Good and Ed Strong, "Reimagining Workforce Policy in the United States," in *Transforming U.S. Workforce Development Policies*, ed. Carl Van Horn, Tammy Edwards, and Todd Greene (Kalamazoo, MI: W. E. Upjohn Institute for Employment Research, 2015), 20.

27. In 2016, the Department of Labor (DOL) spent $90 million on apprenticeship grants, and there were over 505,000 individuals participating in the Registered Apprenticeship (RA) program. U.S. Department of Labor, "ApprenticeshipUSA," U.S. DOL Employment and Training Administration, 2016, https://doleta.gov /oa/data_statistics.cfm. Though the number of RAs grew in the final years of President Obama's administration (which made an explicit goal of expanding the nation's apprenticeship program), a very small fraction of workers benefit from on-the-job training experience in the United States, compared to other advanced nations. In 2015, RAs accounted for less than 0.2 percent of the workforce, compared to 3.7 percent of employed workers in Australia and Germany. Robert I. Lerman, "Are Employers Providing Enough Training? Theory, Evidence, and Policy Implications," prepared for National Academy of Sciences Symposium on the Supply Chain for Middle-Skill Jobs: Education, Training, and Certification Pathways, 2015, http://sites.nationalacademies.org/cs/groups/pgasite/documents /webpage/pga_168146.pdf. As Sarah Steinberg notes, if the United States had as many apprentices per capita as Germany, we would have seven million apprentices in this country. Sarah Ayres Steinberg, "5 Reasons Expanding Apprenticeships Will Benefit Millennials" (Washington, DC: Center for American Progress, December 2, 2013), https://www.americanprogress.org/issues/economy/news/2013 /12/02/79872/5-reasons-expanding-apprenticeships-will-benefit-millennials/.

28. A study of Canadian apprenticeships found that employers witness returns of $1.47 for every $1 spent on training. Canadian Apprenticeship Forum, "It Pays to Hire an Apprentice: Calculating the Return on Training Investment for Skilled Trades Employers in Canada" (Ottawa: Canadian Apprenticeship Forum—Forum canadien sur l'apprentissage [CAF-FCA], 2009).

29. Washington Workforce Training and Education Coordinating Board, "2012 Workforce Training Results—Apprenticeship" (Olympia, WA: Workforce Training and Education Coordinating Board, 2012).

30. John B. Horrigan, "Digital Readiness Gaps," Pew Research Center, September 20, 2016, http://www.pewinternet.org/files/2016/09/PI_2016.09.20_Digital-Readiness -Gaps_FINAL.pdf.

31. A certificate is similar to a degree awarded by an educational institution, though it is often more occupation specific and completed in a shorter period of time. It generally involves time spent in a classroom, and once it is awarded, it lasts a lifetime. Certifications and licenses, on the other hand, do not require classroom time and instead confer some indication of the mastery of a specific occupational skill. Licenses tend to be awarded by government agencies (think cosmetology or real-estate brokers), while certifications are often awarded by third parties. Both licenses and certifications must be renewed, but because occupational certifications are conferred by companies and other third parties, they might provide a better indication that the recipient has up-to-date competencies valued by employers. In general, it is important that employers specify the competencies or certifications they need. See Tamar Jacoby, "The Certificate Revolution," in *Education for Upward Mobility*, ed. Michael J. Petrilli (Lanham, MD: Rowman and Littlefield, 2016), chapter 3.

32. Jacoby, "Certificate Revolution," 55.

33. Anthony P. Carnevale, Stephen J. Rose, and Andrew R. Hanson, "Certificates: Gateway to Gainful Employment and College Degrees," Georgetown University Center on Education and the Workforce, June 2012, https://cew.georgetown.edu/wp-content/uploads/2014/11/Certificates.FullReport.061812.pdf.

34. Carnevale et al., "Career and Technical Education," 13.

35. Nancy Hoffman and Robert Schwartz, "Gold Standard: The Swiss Vocational Education and Training System" (Washington, DC: National Center on Education and the Economy, 2015), http://ncee.org/wp-content/uploads/2015/03/SWISSVETMarch11.pdf.

36. I am indebted to my colleague Martha Ross for sharing her expertise on the need for such collaboration and for intermediaries to play a role. For more details, see Steward et al., "Help Wanted."

37. Wage insurance protects against the economic losses that might accrue to displaced workers who must downshift to lower-paying jobs. Robert Litan argues that wage insurance payments be conditional on work and only last for two years from the initial date of unemployment, to encourage the displaced worker to aggressively search for a new job and accept a position even if it means a short-term pay cut. Such a system would also have the added benefit of exposing the worker to on-the-job training in a new occupation, rather than relying on a government-sponsored job training program. Robert Litan, "Wage Insurance: A Potentially Bipartisan Way to Help the Middle Class" (Washington, DC: Brookings Institution, February 24, 2015), https://www.brookings.edu/research/wage-insurance-a-potentially-bipartisan-way-to-help-the-middle-class/.

38. Stephen A. Wandner, "Wage Insurance as a Policy Option in the United States," Upjohn Institute Working Paper 16-250 (Kalamazoo, MI: W. E. Upjohn Institute for Employment Research, 2016), http://research.upjohn.org/cgi/viewcontent.cgi?article=1268&context=up_workingpapers.

39. Mark Muro and Joseph Parilla, "Maladjusted: It's Time to Reimagine Economic 'Adjustment' Programs" (Washington, DC: Brookings Institution, January 10, 2017), https://www.brookings.edu/blog/the-avenue/2017/01/10/maladjusted-its -time-to-reimagine-economic-adjustment-programs/.

40. Charles Dayton, Candace Hamilton Hester, and David Stern, "Profile of California Partnership Academies 2009–10," Career Academy Support Network, University of California, Berkeley, and California Department of Education, October 2011, http://www.cde.ca.gov/ci/gs/hs/documents/cpareport2010.pdf.

41. Stevens et al., "Career and Technical Education."

42. See Harry J. Holzer and Sandy Baum, *Making College Work* (Washington, DC: Brookings Institution, 2017); Thomas R. Bailey, Shanna Smith Jaggars, and Davis Jenkins, *Redesigning America's Community Colleges* (Cambridge, MA: Harvard University Press, 2015).

43. Researchers at Mathematica examined registered apprenticeships in ten different U.S. states and found that program participants had substantially higher earnings than nonparticipants (an average of nearly $100,000 over their careers). Further, the social benefits of registered apprenticeships outweighed the social costs by more than $49,000 over the career of an apprentice. Debbie Reed et al., "An Effectiveness Assessment and Cost-Benefit Analysis of Registered Apprenticeship in 10 States" (Oakland, CA: Mathematica Policy Research, 2012), https:// wdr.doleta.gov/research/fulltext_documents/etaop_2012_10.pdf.

44. Robert I. Lerman, "Can the United States Expand Apprenticeship? Lessons from Experience," IZA Policy Paper no. 46, 2012, https://www.econstor.eu/bitstream/10419 /91788/1/pp46.pdf.

45. Richard Hendra, David H. Greenberg, Gayle Hamilton, Ari Oppenheim, Alexandra Pennington, Kelsey Schaberg, and Betsy L. Tessler, "Encouraging Evidence on a Sector-Focused Advancement Strategy" (Oakland, CA: MDRC, June 2016), http:// www.mdrc.org/sites/default/files/WorkAdvance_2016_PreviewSummary.pdf.

46. It should be noted that some training programs are beginning to show promising results—Project QUEST, a comprehensive support program for individuals completing occupational training programs in San Antonio, Texas, recently participated in a randomized control trial that followed participants' outcomes for six years. The study revealed that the program produced positive, sustained impacts on wages, employment, and financial stability throughout the evaluation period. Mark Elliott and Anne Roder, "Escalating Gains: Project QUEST's Sectoral Strategy Pays Off" (New York: Economic Mobility Corporation, April 2017), http:// economicmobilitycorp.org/uploads/images/Escalating%20Gains_WEB.pdf.

47. P/PV's "Sectoral Employment Impact Study" found earnings and employment gains among participants in three different organizations across the country. Sheila Maguire, Joshua Freely, Carol Clymer, Maureen Conway, and Deena Schwartz, "Findings from the Sectoral Employment Impact Study" (New York: Public/Private Ventures, 2010), http://ppv.issuelab.org/resources/5101/5101.pdf.

48. Harry Holzer, "Higher Education and Workforce Policy" (Washington, DC: Brookings Institution, April 2015), https://www.brookings.edu/wp-content/uploads/2016/06/higher_ed_jobs_policy_holzer.pdf.

49. Richard V. Reeves and Isabel V. Sawhill, "Men's Lib!" *New York Times,* November 14, 2015, https://www.nytimes.com/2015/11/15/opinion/sunday/mens-lib.html.

50. Claire Cain Miller, "Why Men Don't Want the Jobs Done Mostly by Women," *New York Times,* January 4, 2017, https://www.nytimes.com/2017/01/04/upshot/why-men-dont-want-the-jobs-done-mostly-by-women.html?_r=0.

51. Reeves and Sawhill, "Men's Lib!"

52. Quoted in Miller, "Why Men Don't Want the Jobs."

53. Stevens et al., "Career Technical Education."

54. Reeves and Sawhill, "Men's Lib!"

55. Jena McGregor, "How Mark Zuckerberg's Paternity Leave Affects the Rest of Us," *Los Angeles Times,* December 6, 2015, http://www.latimes.com/business/la-fi-on-leadership-zuckerberg-20151206-story.html.

Chapter 7. Creating Jobs and Rewarding Work

1. Robert J. Gordon, *The Rise and Fall of American Growth* (Princeton, NJ: Princeton University Press, 2016).

2. Jared Bernstein, "The Reconnection Agenda: Reuniting Growth and Prosperity" (Washington, DC: Center on Budget and Policy Priorities, March 30, 2015), https://www.cbpp.org/research/full-employment/the-reconnection-agenda-reuniting-growth-and-prosperity; Jared Bernstein, "The Importance of Strong Labor Demand," in *Revitalizing Wage Growth* (Washington, DC: The Hamilton Project, 2018), 93–116.

3. Isabel Sawhill, Edward Rodrigue, and Nathan Joo, "One Third of a Nation: Strategies for Helping Working Families" (Washington, DC: Brookings Institution, May 2016), https://www.brookings.edu/wp-content/uploads/2016/07/one-third-of-a-nation.pdf.

4. See Jeffrey Sparshott, "Skilled Workers Are Scarce in Tight Labor Market," *Wall Street Journal,* February 2, 2017, https://www.wsj.com/articles/skilled-workers-are-scarce-in-tight-labor-market-1486047602.

5. Isabel Sawhill, "Inflation? Bring It On: Workers Could Actually Benefit," *New York Times,* March 9, 2018, https://www.nytimes.com/2018/03/09/opinion/inflation-unemployment-rate.html.

6. Jeff Spross, "You're Hired!" *Democracy,* no. 44 (Spring 2017), 50.

7. Neera Tanden, Carmel Martin, Marc Jarsulic, Brendan Duke, Ben Olinsky, Melissa Boteach, John Halpin, Ruy Teixeira, and Rob Griffin, "Toward a Marshall Plan for America: Rebuilding Our Towns, Cities, and the Middle Class" (Washington, DC: Center for American Progress, May 16, 2017), https://www.americanprogress.org/issues/economy/reports/2017/05/16/432499/toward-marshall-plan-america/.

8. *Encyclopaedia Britannica,* s.v. "Works Progress Administration," accessed August 4, 2017, https://www.britannica.com/topic/Works-Progress-Administration.

9. See Korin Davis and William A. Galston, "Setting Priorities, Meeting Needs: The Case for a National Infrastructure Bank" (Washington, DC: Brookings Institution, December 13, 2012), https://www.brookings.edu/research/setting-priorities-meeting-needs-the-case-for-a-national-infrastructure-bank/.

10. David Card and Alan Krueger, "Minimum Wages and Employment: A Case Study of the Fast-Food Industry in New Jersey and Pennsylvania," *American Economic Review* 84, no. 4 (1994): 772–793.

11. Hristos Doucouliagos and T. D. Stanley, "Publication Selection Bias in Minimum-Wage Research? A Meta-Regression Analysis," *British Journal of Industrial Relations* 47, no. 2 (June 2009): 205–470.

12. Congressional Budget Office, "The Effects of a Minimum-Wage Increase on Employment and Family Income" (Washington, DC: CBO, February 18, 2014), https://www.cbo.gov/publication/44995.

13. For additional review of these issues, see Isabel V. Sawhill and Quentin Karpilow, "A No-Cost Proposal to Reduce Poverty & Inequality" (Washington, DC: Brookings Institution, January 10, 2014), https://www.brookings.edu/research/a-no-cost-proposal-to-reduce-poverty-inequality/.

14. See Harry J. Holzer, "A $15-Hour Minimum Wage Could Harm America's Poorest Workers" (Washington, DC: Brookings Institution, July 30, 2015), https://www.brookings.edu/opinions/a-15-hour-minimum-wage-could-harm-americas-poorest-workers/; Lizzie O'Leary, Paulina Velasco, and Jana Kasperkevic, "Tired of Waiting for Congress, Majority of U.S. States Have Raised the Minimum Wage," *Marketplace*, June 30, 2017, https://www.marketplace.org/2017/06/30/economy/tired-waiting-congress-majority-us-states-have-raised-their-minimum-wage.

15. Ekaterina Jardim, Mark C. Long, Robert Plotnick, Emma van Inwegen, Jacob Vigdor, and Hilary Wething, "Minimum Wage Increases, Wages, and Low-Wage Employment: Evidence from Seattle," NBER Working Paper no. 23532, June 2017, http://www.nber.org/papers/w23532. Specifically, they found that the higher minimum "reduced hours worked in low-wage jobs by around 9 percent," and reduced the number of low-wage jobs (those paying less than $19 an hour) by 6.8 percent. They found that the higher hourly income did not offset the income lost from working fewer hours.

16. Michael Reich, Sylvia Allegretto, and Anna Godoey, "Seattle's Minimum Wage Experience 2015–16," Center on Wage and Employment Dynamics Policy Brief (Berkeley, CA: Institute for Research on Labor and Employment, June 2017), http://irle.berkeley.edu/files/2017/Seattles-Minimum-Wage-Experiences-2015-16.pdf.

17. Gene Falk and Margot L. Crandall, "The Earned Income Tax Credit: An Overview" (Washington, DC: Congressional Research Service, January 19, 2016), https://fas.org/sgp/crs/misc/R43805.pdf.

18. Center on Budget and Policy Priorities, "Policy Basics: The Earned Income Tax Credit" (Washington, DC: CBPP, October 21, 2016), https://www.cbpp.org/research/federal-tax/policy-basics-the-earned-income-tax-credit.

19. Sawhill and Karpilow, "No-Cost Proposal."

20. "Release: Sen. Sherrod Brown and Rep. Ro Khanna Introduce Legislation to Raise the Wages of Working Families," Congressman Ro Khanna Press Release, September 13, 2017, https://khanna.house.gov/media/press-releases/release-sen-sherrod-brown-and-rep-ro-khanna-introduce-landmark-legislation.

21. Tax Policy Center, "T17-0202," Tax Policy Center Model Estimates, Distribution Tables by Percentile, August 23, 2017, http://www.taxpolicycenter.org/model-estimates/earned-income-tax-credit-eitc-expansion-options-march-2017/t17-0202-increase-earned.

22. Tax Policy Center, "T17-0024," Tax Policy Center Model Estimates, Revenue Tables, May 5, 2017, http://www.taxpolicycenter.org/model-estimates/earned-income-tax-credit-eitc-expansion-options-march-2017/options-expand-earned.

23. Neil Irwin, "What Would It Take to Replace the Pay Working-Class Americans Have Lost?" *New York Times,* December 9, 2016, https://www.nytimes.com/2016/12/09/upshot/what-would-it-take-to-replace-the-pay-working-class-americans-have-lost.html.

24. Elaine Maag, "Investing in Work by Reforming the Earned Income Tax Credit" (Washington, DC: Tax Policy Center, May 20, 2015), http://www.taxpolicycenter.org/sites/default/files/alfresco/publication-pdfs/2000232-investing-in-work-by-reforming-the-eitc.pdf; Adam Thomas and Isabel V. Sawhill, "A Tax Proposal for Working Families" (Washington, DC: Brookings Institution, January 5, 2001), https://www.brookings.edu/research/a-tax-proposal-for-working-families-with-children/.

25. See Sawhill and Karpilow, "No-Cost Proposal."

26. According to the Survey of Consumer Finances, 24 percent of income accrued to the top 1 percent, compared to 39 percent of wealth in 2016. Jesse Bricker et al., "Changes in U.S. Family Finances from 2013 to 2016: Evidence from the Survey of Consumer Finances," *Federal Reserve Bulletin* 103, no. 3 (September 2017), https://www.federalreserve.gov/publications/files/scf17.pdf.

27. Accenture, "The 'Greater' Wealth Transfer," 2015, https://www.accenture.com/us-en/insight-capitalizing-intergenerational-shift-wealth-capital-markets-summary.

28. The House version of the GOP's Tax Cuts and Jobs Act would have doubled the level of the estate tax exemption and repealed it after six years. The final version of the act did not eliminate the tax, though it did double the exemption.

29. Joint Committee on Taxation, "History, Present Law, and Analysis of the Federal Wealth Transfer Tax System" (Washington, DC: JCT, March 16, 2015), https://www.jct.gov/publications.html?func=startdown&id=4744.

30. Tax Policy Center, "Who Pays the Estate Tax," in Tax Policy Center's *Briefing Book* (Washington, DC: TPC, 2016), http://www.taxpolicycenter.org/briefing-book/who-pays-estate-tax.

31. Frank Newport, "Americans React to Presidential Candidates' Tax Proposals," *Gallup,* March 17, 2016, http://news.gallup.com/poll/190067/americans-react-presidential-candidates-tax-proposals.aspx.

32. Marcus D. Rosenbaum, Mollyann Brodie, Robert J. Blendon, and Stephen R. Pelletier, "Tax Uncertainty: A Divided America's Unformed View of the Federal Tax System" (Washington, DC: Brookings Institution, June 1, 2003), https://www.brookings.edu/articles/tax-uncertainty-a-divided-americas-unformed-view-of-the-federal-tax-system/.

33. Robert B. Avery, Daniel Grodzicki, and Kevin B. Moore, "Estate vs. Capital Gains Taxation: An Evaluation of Prospective Policies for Taxing Wealth at the Time of Death," Finance and Economics Discussion Series (Washington, DC: Federal Reserve Board, April 1, 2013), https://www.federalreserve.gov/pubs/feds/2013/201328/201328pap.pdf.

34. Lily L. Batcheler, "Reform Options for the Estate Tax System: Targeting Unearned Income," Testimony before the U.S. Senate Committee on Finance, May 7, 2010, https://papers.ssrn.com/sol3/papers.cfm?abstract_id=1601652.

35. Jane G. Gravelle and Steven Maguire, "Estate and Gift Taxes: Economic Issues" (Washington, DC: Congressional Research Service, January 19, 2006), https://admin.naepc.org/journal/issue02c.pdf.

36. Douglas Holtz-Eakin, David Joulfaian, and Harvey S. Rosen provide empirical evidence that the receipt of large inheritances actually decreases the incentive to work. Their results indicate that a single person receiving an inheritance of about $150,000 is four times more likely to leave the labor force than an individual receiving an inheritance below $25,000. Douglas Holtz-Eakin, David Joulfaian, and Harvey S. Rosen, "The Carnegie Conjecture: Some Empirical Evidence," *Quarterly Journal of Economics* 108, no. 2 (1993): 413–435.

37. Office of Management and Budget, Tables 2.1 and 2.5 in "Historical Tables," https://www.whitehouse.gov/omb/budget/Historicals.

38. Darien B. Jacobson, Brian G. Raub, and Barry W. Johnson, "The Estate Tax: Ninety Years and Counting," *Statistics of Income Bulletin* 120 (2007): 118–128.

39. Franklin D. Roosevelt, "Message to Congress on Tax Revision," June 19, 1935, available at http://www.presidency.ucsb.edu/ws/?pid=15088.

40. Lynda Laughlin, "Who's Minding the Kids? Child Care Arrangements: Spring 2011" (Washington, DC: U.S. Census Bureau, April 2013), https://www.census.gov/prod/2013pubs/p70-135.pdf

41. James P. Ziliak, "Proposal 10: Supporting Low-Income Workers through Refundable Child-Care Credits," in *Policies to Address Poverty in America*, ed. Melissa S. Kearney and Benjamin H. Harris (Washington, DC: Hamilton Project, June 2014), http://www.hamiltonproject.org/assets/legacy/files/downloads_and_links/child_care_credit_ziliak.pdf.

42. Tax Policy Center, "How Does the Tax System Subsidize Child Care Expenses?" in *Briefing Book* (Washington, DC: Tax Policy Center), http://www.taxpolicycenter.org/briefing-book/how-does-tax-system-subsidize-child-care-expenses.

43. Ziliak, "Proposal 10."

44. Tax Policy Center, "How Does the Tax System Subsidize?"

45. Elaine Maag, "What Would a Refundable Child Care Credit Mean?" TaxVox: Individual Taxes (Washington, DC: Tax Policy Center, May 4, 2017), http://www.taxpolicycenter.org/taxvox/what-would-refundable-child-care-credit-mean.

46. "The PACE Act of 2017," Representative Kevin Yoder and Representative Stephanie Murphy, Bill Summary, https://stephaniemurphy.house.gov/uploadedfiles/pace_act_one_pager.pdf.

47. The Lee-Rubio tax reform plan offered in 2015 would have increased the child tax credit by $2,500 per child. It would be partially refundable, but because it would not be phased out at higher incomes, it would largely benefit higher-income families with children who currently receive little or no child tax credit. Elaine Maag, "Reforming the Child Tax Credit: How Different Proposals Change Who Benefits" (Washington, DC: Urban Institute, December 2015), http://www.taxpolicycenter.org/sites/default/files/alfresco/publication-pdfs/2000540-Reforming-the-Child-Tax-Credit-How-Different-Proposals-Change-Who-Benefits.pdf.

Chapter 8. A Bigger Role for the Private Sector

1. In May 2017, the government was responsible for 22.3 million jobs, while there were 123.9 million private-sector employees. Bureau of Labor Statistics, "Employment, Hours, and Earnings from the Current Employment Statistics Survey," Series ID CES0500000001 and CES9000000001.

2. Gallup, "Confidence in Institutions," n.d., http://www.gallup.com/poll/1597/confidence-institutions.aspx.

3. Author's analysis of Bureau of Labor Statistics, Series IDs COMPRNFB and OPHNFB, retrieved from the Federal Research Bank of St. Louis (FRED).

4. Lawrence Mishel and Jessica Schieder, "CEOs Make 276 Times More than Typical Workers," Economic Policy Institute Economic Snapshot, August 3, 2016, http://www.epi.org/publication/ceos-make-276-times-more-than-typical-workers/.

5. Facundo Alvaredo, Anthony B. Atkinson, Thomas Piketty, and Emmanuel Saez, "The Top 1 Percent in an International and Historical Perspective," *Journal of Economic Perspectives* 27, no. 3 (Summer 2013): 3–20.

6. Alfred Marshall, *Principles of Economics* (London: Macmillan and Co., 1920), book 3, chapter 5, para. 5, available from http://www.econlib.org/library/Marshall/marP1.html.

7. John R. Graham, Campbell R. Harvey, and Shiva Rajgopal, "The Economic Implications of Corporate Financial Reporting," *Journal of Accounting and Economics* 40, no. 1–3 (2005): 3–73.

8. German Gutierrez and Thomas Philippon, "Investmentless Growth: An Empirical Investigation," *Brookings Papers on Economic Activity,* September 2017, https://www.brookings.edu/bpea-articles/investment-less-growth-an-empirical-investigation/.

9. See, for example, Andrew Haldane and Richard Davies, "The Short Long," presented at the 29th SUERF Colloquium, Brussels, May 11, 2011; James M. Poterba and Lawrence H. Summers, "A CEO Survey of U.S. Companies' Time Horizons and Hurdle Rates," *Sloan Management Review* 37, no. 1 (1995): 43–53.

10. Dominic Barton, James Manyika, Timothy Koller, Robert Palter, Jonathan God-sall, and Joshua Zoffer, "Measuring the Economic Impact of Short-Termism," McKinsey Global Institute, February 2017, http://www.mckinsey.com/global-themes /long-term-capitalism/where-companies-with-a-long-term-view-outperform -their-peers.

11. The report authors developed a five-factor "Corporate Horizon Index" to catego-rize companies as "long term" or "short term." These five factors were invest-ments (the ratio of capital expenditures to depreciation), earnings quality (accruals as a share of revenue), margin growth (the difference between earnings growth and revenue growth), earnings growth (the difference between earnings-per-share growth and true earnings growth), and quarterly targeting (incidence of beating or missing earnings-per-share targets by less than two cents).

12. Barton et al., "Measuring the Economic Impact of Short-Termism," 2.

13. Ibid., 7, exhibit 4.

14. William A. Galston and Elaine C. Kamarck, "More Builders and Fewer Traders: A Growth Strategy for the American Economy" (Washington, DC: Brookings Insti-tution, June 2015), 1, https://www.brookings.edu/wp-content/uploads/2016/06 /CEPMGlastonKarmarck4.pdf.

15. Quoted in Alana Semuels, "How to Stop Short-Term Thinking at America's Companies," *Atlantic*, December 30, 2016, https://www.theatlantic.com/business /archive/2016/12/short-term-thinking/511874/.

16. Dominic Barton, "Capitalism for the Long Term," *Harvard Business Review*, March 2011, https://hbr.org/2011/03/capitalism-for-the-long-term.

17. Robert B. Reich, *Saving Capitalism* (New York: Vintage Books, 2016), 127.

18. Bureau of Labor Statistics, "Union Affiliation Data from the Current Population Survey," Series ID LUU0204906600.

19. Steven Pearlstein, "Businesses' Focus on Maximizing Shareholder Value Has Numerous Costs," *Washington Post*, September 6, 2013, https://www.washingtonpost .com/business/economy/businesses-focus-on-maximizing-shareholder-value-has -numerous-costs/2013/09/05/bcdc664e-045f-11e3-a07f-49ddc7417125_story .html?utm_term=.d9381597e745.

20. Lynn A. Stout, "The Shareholder Value Myth," *Cornell Law Faculty Publications*, no. 771 (April 19, 2013): 4, http://scholarship.law.cornell.edu/cgi/viewcontent .cgi?article=2311&context=facpub.

21. Based on conversation with Steven Pearlstein, September 16, 2017.

22. Daniel M. G. Raff and Lawrence H. Summers, "Did Henry Ford Pay Efficiency Wages?" *Journal of Labor Economics* 5, no. 4 (October 1987): S57–S86.

23. Raff and Summers also consider the possibility that higher wages enabled Ford to attract a more skilled labor force. Although there were long queues for these better-paying jobs, they reject the hypothesis that greater worker selection ex-plains the large improvements in productivity.

24. Jason Furman and Peter Orszag, "A Firm-Level Perspective on the Role of Rents in the Rise in Inequality," Presentation at Columbia University, New York, October 16,

2015; Council of Economic Advisers, "Labor Market Monopsony: Trends, Consequences, and Policy Responses" (Washington, DC: Executive Office of the President, October 2016), https://obamawhitehouse.archives.gov/sites/default/files/page/files/20161025_monopsony_labor_mrkt_cea.pdf.

25. Dan Andres, Chiara Criscuolo, and Peter N. Gal, "Frontier Firms, Technology Diffusion and Public Policy: Micro Evidence from OECD Countries," OECD, 2015, https://www.oecd.org/eco/growth/Frontier-Firms-Technology-Diffusion-and-Public-Policy-Micro-Evidence-from-OECD-Countries.pdf.

26. Market concentration across most industries increased between 1997 and 2007. Concentration is measured by looking at the proportion of all revenues flowing to the top firms in an industry, often the top four or the top eight firms. When a relatively small number of firms dominates an industry, they gain market power that can limit competition and create rents. Eliminating or reducing such rents can improve efficiency and produce a more equitable distribution of rewards. Council of Economic Advisers, "Economic Report of the President" (Washington, DC: Executive Office of the President, February 2016), https://obamawhitehouse.archives.gov/sites/default/files/docs/ERP_2016_Book_Complete%20JA.pdf. Also, see Luigi Zingales, "Towards a Political Theory of the Firm," *Journal of Economic Perspectives* 31, no. 3 (Summer 2017): 113–130.

27. David Autor, David Dorn, Lawrence F. Katz, Christina Patterson, and John Van Reenan, "The Fall of the Labor Share and the Rise of Superstar Firms," NBER Working Paper no. 23396, May 2017, http://www.nber.org/papers/w23396.

28. Joseph R. Blasi, Richard B. Freeman, and Douglas L. Kruse, *The Citizen's Share: Reducing Inequality in the 21st Century* (New Haven, CT: Yale University Press, 2013).

29. Brent Snavely, "Ford Takes a $2 Billion Charge Due to Pensions, Benefits," *USA Today*, January 22, 2017, https://www.usatoday.com/story/money/cars/2017/01/22/ford-takes-2-billion-charge-due-pensions-benefits/96918140/.

30. Andrea Ahles, "Southwest Airlines to Pay $620 Million in Profit-Sharing to Employees," *Star-Telegram*, February 11, 2016, http://www.star-telegram.com/news/business/aviation/sky-talk-blog/article59739921.html.

31. National Center for Employee Ownership, "Data Show Widespread Employee Ownership in U.S.," NCEO, accessed January 4, 2018, from https://www.nceo.org/articles/widespread-employee-ownership-us.

32. National Bureau of Economic Research Shared Capitalism Project, "Table 2: Size of Financial Stakes in Shared Capitalism Programs," National Center for Employee Ownership, https://www.nceo.org/assets/pdf/articles/GSS-2014-data.pdf.

33. Christopher Tkaczyk, "My Five Days of 'Bleeding Green,'" *Fortune*, March 3, 2016, http://fortune.com/publix-best-companies/.

34. National Bureau of Economic Research Shared Capitalism Project, "Table 1: Participation in Shared Capitalism, 2002–2014," National Center for Employee Ownership, https://www.nceo.org/assets/pdf/articles/GSS-2014-data.pdf.

35. Blasi, Freeman, and Kruse, *Citizen's Share*, 171.

36. Ibid.

37. Steven F. Freeman, "Effects of ESOP Adoption and Employee Ownership: Thirty Years of Research and Experience," University of Pennsylvania Organizational Dynamics Working Paper 07-01, January 4, 2007, https://repository.upenn.edu /cgi/viewcontent.cgi?referer=https://www.google.com/&httpsredir=1&article =1001&context=od_working_papers.

38. Blasi, Freeman, and Kruse, *Citizen's Share*, 194.

39. John Case, "The Life-Changing Magic of Turning Employees into Shareholders," *Atlantic*, September 8, 2016, http://www.theatlantic.com/business/archive/2016 /09/life-changing-magic-of-turning-employees-into-shareholders/498485/.

40. Blasi, Freeman, and Kruse, *Citizen's Share*.

41. See National Center for Employee Ownership, "ESOPs and Preferred-Status Certification" (Oakland, CA: NCEO, May 24, 2017), http://www.nceo.org/assets/pdf /EO_Preferred-Status.pdf.

42. Joseph R. Blasi, Richard B. Freeman, and Douglas L. Kruse, "Capitalism for the Rest of Us," *New York Times*, July 17, 2015, http://www.nytimes.com/2015/07/18/opinion /capitalism-for-the-rest-of-us.html. For an overview of how the law came into existence, see Allan Sloan, "The Executive Pay Cap That Backfired," *ProPublica*, February 12, 2016, https://www.propublica.org/article/the-executive-pay-cap-that-backfired.

43. A report by the National Center for the Middle Market shows that, while most midsized firms "understand that talent planning is an important strategic concern," fewer than half implement strategies to address this concern. National Center for the Middle Market, "Mastering Talent Planning: A Framework for Success" (Columbus, OH: National Center for the Middle Market, 2016), http://www .middlemarketcenter.org/Media/Documents/talent-succession-planning-talent -review-human-resources-planning-performance-management_NCMM_Talent _Planning_Flagship_FINAL_web.pdf.

44. Thomas Friedman, *Thank You for Being Late* (New York: Farrar, Straus, and Giroux, 2016).

45. Aaron Pressman, "Can AT&T Retrain 100,000 People?" in *Fortune*'s "100 Best Companies to Work For," *Fortune*, March 15, 2017, http://fortune.com/att-hr -retrain-employees-jobs-best-companies/.

46. John Donovan and Cathy Benko, "AT&T's Talent Overhaul," *Harvard Business Review*, October 2016, https://hbr.org/2016/10/atts-talent-overhaul.

47. Friedman, *Thank You for Being Late*, 215.

48. Pressman, "Can AT&T Retrain 100,000 People?"

49. Friedman, *Thank You for Being Late*, 218.

50. Robert I. Lerman, "Are Employers Providing Enough Training? Theory, Evidence, and Policy Implications," Prepared for National Academy of Sciences Symposium on the Supply Chain for Middle-Skill Jobs: Education, Training, and Certification Pathways, 2015, http://sites.nationalacademies.org/cs/groups/pgasite/documents /webpage/pga_168146.pdf.

51. As Peter Cappelli notes, some of this decline might be attributable to the decline in lifetime employment and reduced job tenure, exacerbating the spillover effect

in which firms cannot recoup the costs of their training investments. Peter H. Cappelli, "Skill Gaps, Skill Shortages and Skill Mismatches: Evidence and Arguments for the United States," *ILR Review* 68, no. 2 (2015): 251–290.

52. These two forms are identified through the Occupational Information Network (O*NET), a database of education and training requirements for different occupations funded by the U.S. Department of Labor. Anthony P. Carnevale, Tamara Jayasundera, and Andrew R. Hanson, "Career and Technical Education: Five Ways That Pay Along the Way to the B.A.," Georgetown University Center on Education and the Workforce, September 2012, https://www.insidehighered .com/sites/default/server_files/files/CTE_FiveWays_FullReport_Embargoed .pdf.

53. Carnevale et al., "Career and Technical Education." Also, access to training varies by industry. The Association for Talent Development found that, among participating organizations, health care and pharmaceutical organizations spent an average of nearly three times that of manufacturing organizations on training and development per employee. Laurie Miller, "2014 State of the Industry Report: Spending on Employee Training Remains a Priority," Association for Talent Development, November 8, 2014, https://www.td.org/Publications/Magazines/TD /TD-Archive/2014/11/2014-State-of-the-Industry-Report-Spending-on-Employee -Training-Remains-a-Priority.

54. It suggested that 93 percent of firms with fifty or more employees and 72 percent of firms with twenty or more employees provided formal training in 1994. Lerman, "Are Employers Providing Enough Training?"

55. Employees tend to report a lower incidence of training than their employers. A study by Accenture in 2011 found that only 21 percent of U.S. employees received any employer-provided training in the last five years, while a survey of employers indicated that 40 percent of employers offered some type of training. Lerman, "Are Employers Providing Enough Training?"

56. Council of Economic Advisers, "Economic Report of the President" (Washington, DC: Executive Office of the President, February 2015), https://obamawhitehouse .archives.gov/sites/default/files/docs/cea_2015_erp.pdf.

57. As Facundo Sepúlvedah notes, studies of employer-sponsored training in European firms consistently find positive effects of training on labor productivity. Other research shows that employer-based training can increase a worker's wages by 3 to 11 percent, with formal training yielding higher returns than informal training. Research on the returns to training in Canada showed that employer-sponsored coursework resulted in a 5 to 7 percent return to male wages and a 7 to 9 percent return for women, with the returns only significant for lower-skilled workers. Facundo Sepúlvedah, "Training and Productivity: Evidence for US Manufacturing Industries," *Oxford Economic Papers* 62, no. 3 (July 2010): 504–528; Carnevale et al., "Career and Technical Education"; Wen Ci, Jose Galdo, Marcel Voia, and Christopher Worswick, "Wage Returns to Mid-Career Investments in Job Training through Employer-Supported Course Enrollment: Evidence for

Canada," Institute for the Study of Labor (IZA), IZA discussion paper no. 9007, April 2015, http://ftp.iza.org/dp9007.pdf.

58. The funding that does exist is primarily available through the Workforce Investment Act and the Trade Adjustment Assistance Program, whose budgets have decreased as a share of the federal budget since 1979. According to Kevin Hollenbeck at the Upjohn Institute, state subsidies for incumbent worker training amounted to between $500 and $800 million, or 1 percent of total private sector training costs (estimated at $50 to $60 billion per year) in 2006. See Kevin Hollenbeck, "Is There a Role for Public Support of Incumbent Worker On-the-Job Training?" Upjohn Institute Policy Paper 2008-001 (Kalamazoo, MI: W. E. Upjohn Institute for Employment Research, 2008); Carnevale et al., "Career and Technical Education"; Kelly S. Mikelson and Demetra Smith Nightingale, "Estimating Public and Private Expenditures on Occupational Training in the United States," prepared for U.S. Department of Labor Employment and Training Administration, December 2004, https://wdr.doleta.gov/research/FullText_Documents/Estimating%20Public%20and%20Private%20Expenditures%20on%20Occupational%20Training%20in%20the%20United%20States.pdf.

59. Kevin Potter and Jackie Hakimian, "New Employee-Training Credits and Incentives Opportunities in New York," Deloitte, January 2016, https://www2.deloitte.com/content/dam/Deloitte/us/Documents/Tax/us-tax-mts-new-employee-training-credits-and-incentives-opportunities-in-new-york.pdf.

60. The study found that primary sector jobs were created or retained at a public cost of less than $9,000 per worker, and the program yielded rates of return of 38.9 percent to the state, 5.4 percent to the worker, and 16.6 percent to the firms. Hollenbeck, "Is There a Role for Public Support?"

61. Alastair Fitzpayne and Ethan Pollak, "Worker Training Tax Credit: Promoting Employer Investments in the Workforce," Aspen Institute Future of Work Initiative, May 2017, https://assets.aspeninstitute.org/content/uploads/2017/05/Worker-Training-Tax-Credit.pdf.

Chapter 9. Updating Social Insurance

1. Daniel S. Hamermesh and Elena Stancanelli, "Long Workweeks and Strange Hours," *ILR Review* 68, no. 5 (October 2015): 1007–1018. Also, see chapter 4 for a comparison of France and the United States.

2. Martin Feldstein makes a strong argument for a system of private accounts to insure against unemployment, poor health, and retirement costs. He notes that some other countries have mixed systems (of private and social provision). The advantages of private accounts are that they encourage personal responsibility and reduce moral hazard. The disadvantage is that they do less to provide a floor of benefits for all and thus usually must be supplemented with means-tested forms of assistance. They do not foster social solidarity, and may not be

politically acceptable in a nation that already has adopted a pay-as-you-go social insurance system. For example, President George W. Bush's effort to create private accounts to replace Social Security failed. In the end, Feldstein recognizes the need to balance social and personal responsibility. Martin Feldstein, "Rethinking Social Insurance," *American Economic Review* 95, no. 1 (March 2005): 1–24.

3. For nice overviews of social insurance, and why it is needed, see Feldstein, "Rethinking Social Insurance"; Michael J. Graetz and Jerry L. Mashaw, "True Security: Rethinking American Social Insurance," *Milken Institute Review* (Fourth Quarter, 1999); Patricia Owens, "An Overview of Social Security Disability Insurance," in *SSDI Solutions: Ideas to Strengthen the Social Security Disability Insurance Program*, McCrery-Pomeroy SSDI Solutions Initiative (West Conshohocken, PA: Infinity Publishing, 2015), chapter 2.

4. Aesop, *Aesop's Fables*, trans. V. S. Vernon Jones, illus. Arthur Rackham, introduction and notes by D. L. Ashliman (New York: Barnes & Noble, 2003), 146.

5. In 2015, life expectancy at age 65 was 19.4 years. Centers for Disease Control and Prevention, "Health, United States, 2016" (Washington, DC: U.S. Department of Health and Human Services, 2016), table 15.

6. C. Eugene Steuerle, "Social Security Must Be Fair for Everyone, Not Just Retirees," *Washington Post*, October 6, 2016, https://www.washingtonpost.com/news /in-theory/wp/2016/10/06/social-security-needs-to-be-fair-for-everyone-not-just -retirees/?utm_term=.386aa5b95bef.

7. Mark Aguiar and Erik Hurst found that leisure increased by 6–8 hours per week for men and 4–8 hours per week for women between 1965 and 2003, corresponding to an additional 7–9 weeks of vacation per year, under the assumption of a 40-hour workweek. Mark Aguiar and Erik Hurst, "Measuring Trends in Leisure: The Allocation of Time over Five Decades," *Quarterly Journal of Economics* 122, no. 3 (2007): 969–1006.

8. This is a slight improvement from previous years. When the Federal Reserve first began asking this question in 2013, 50 percent of respondents indicated that they were ill-prepared for this size of an expense. Board of Governors of the Federal Reserve System, "Report on the Economic Well-Being of U.S. Households in 2016" (Washington, DC: Federal Reserve Board, May 2017), https://www .federalreserve.gov/publications/files/2016-report-economic-well-being-us -households-201705.pdf.

9. John P. Robinson, "Happiness Means Being Just Rushed Enough," *Scientific American*, February 19, 2013, https://www.scientificamerican.com/article/happiness -means-being-just-rushed-enough/.

10. James Gleick, *Faster: The Acceleration of Just about Everything* (New York: Vintage Books, 2000), 280.

11. "Why Is Everyone So Busy?" *Economist*, December 20, 2014, https://www .economist.com/news/christmas-specials/21636612-time-poverty-problem -partly-perception-and-partly-distribution-why.

12. Elizabeth Arias, Melonie Heron, Jiaquan Xu, "United States Life Tables, 2014," *National Vital Statistics Reports* 66, no. 4 (2017): table 21.

13. Ibid.

14. Michael Chernew, David M. Cutler, Kaushik Ghosh, and Mary Beth Landrum, "Understanding the Improvement in Disability Free Life Expectancy in the U.S. Elderly Population," NBER Working Paper no. 22306, June 2016, http://scholar .harvard.edu/files/cutler/files/w22306.pdf.

15. Barry P. Bosworth, Gary Burtless, and Kan Zhang, "Later Retirement, Inequality in Old Age, and the Growing Gap in Longevity between Rich and Poor" (Washington, DC: Brookings Institution, January 2016), https://www.brookings.edu/wp -content/uploads/2016/02/bosworthburtlesszhang_retirementinequalitylongev ityfullpaper.pdf.

16. The average retirement age for men was nearly sixty-four in 2013, an increase of about two years since the mid-1990s. The average female retirement age has been rising for the past half-century, but this largely reflects the increasing work-force participation of women over this period. Alicia H. Munnell, "The Average Retirement Age—An Update," Center for Retirement Research at Boston College, no. 15-4 (March 2015).

17. Social Security Administration, "Retirement Planner: Full Retirement Age," accessed August 14, 2017, from https://www.ssa.gov/planners/retire/retirechart .html.

18. Barry P. Bosworth, Gary Burtless, and Kan Zhang, "What Growing Life Expectancy Gaps Mean for the Promise of Social Security" (Washington, DC: Brookings Institution, February 12, 2016), https://www.brookings.edu/research/what-growing -life-expectancy-gaps-mean-for-the-promise-of-social-security/.

19. Auerbach et al. assess the effects of these growing life expectancy gaps on the receipt of different major entitlement programs. They find that even when programs that disproportionately serve lower-income individuals are included (i.e., disability insurance and Medicaid), the "net lifetime benefits are becoming significantly less progressive over time because of the disproportionate life expectancy gains among higher-income adults." Alan J. Auerbach, Kerwin K. Charles, Courtney C. Coile, William Gale, Dana Goldman, Ronald Lee, Charles M. Lucas, Peter R. Orszag, Louise M. Sheiner, Bryan Tysinger, David N. Weil, Justin Wolfers, and Rebeca Wong, "How the Growing Gap in Life Expectancy May Affect Retirement Benefits and Reforms," NBER Working Paper no. 23329, April 2017, 29, http://www.nber.org/papers/w23329.

20. Pew Research Center, "The Rise in Dual Income Households," Pew, June 18, 2015, http://www.pewresearch.org/ft_dual-income-households-1960-2012-2/.

21. Wendy Wang, Kim Parker, and Paul Taylor, "Breadwinner Moms," Pew Research Center, May 29, 2013, http://www.pewsocialtrends.org/2013/05/29/breadwinner -moms/.

22. AEI-Brookings Working Group on Paid Family Leave, "Paid Family and Medical Leave: An Issue Whose Time Has Come," AEI and the Brookings Institution,

May 2017, https://www.brookings.edu/wp-content/uploads/2017/06/es_20170606
_paidfamilyleave.pdf.

23. Heather Boushey, *Finding Time* (Cambridge, MA: Harvard University Press, 2016).

24. Ibid, 5.

25. Ibid., 58–59.

26. Women's increased participation in the economy contributed 11 percent of the growth of GDP between 1979 and 2012, according to Eileen Appelbaum, Heather Boushey, and John Schmitt. This is the equivalent of $1.7 trillion in 2012. Eileen Appelbaum, Heather Boushey, and John Schmitt, "The Economic Importance of Women's Rising Hours of Work," Center for American Progress and the Center for Economic and Policy Research, April 2014, https://www.americanprogress .org/wp-content/uploads/2014/04/WomensRisingWorkv2.pdf.

27. See Eleanor Krause and Isabel V. Sawhill, "What We Know and Don't Know about Declining Labor Force Participation: A Review" (Washington, DC: Brookings Institution, May 2017), https://www.brookings.edu/wp-content/uploads/2017 /05/ccf_20170517_declining_labor_force_participation_sawhill1.pdf.

28. To be sure, as noted above, women are working less at home, and if we combine hours of work at home with hours of work in the market, they may be working less. But consider the following: first, hours of work at home is a much more subjective and difficult to measure activity than work in the market. Second, work (at home) undoubtedly expands to fill the time available, and there is simply less time available for it now than in the past. Third, in one's own home, one has considerable choice and autonomy about what work to do. These points are in no way meant to deny the fact that families are smaller or that household appliances, prepared foods, and other time-saving innovations have played a role in reducing the burden of work in the home. It is simply to suggest a bit of skepticism about whether adults, working parents in particular, have more leisure than in the past.

29. Boushey, *Finding Time*, 68.

30. U.S. Census Bureau, "Historical Living Arrangements of Children," Table CH-1: Living Arrangements of Children under 18 Years Old: 1960 to Present, revised April 3, 2017, https://www.census.gov/data/tables/time-series/demo/families /children.html.

31. The redistribution occurs not at a single point in time but over the life cycle of payment and benefit distribution. The payroll taxes used to fund the system are regressive, but the benefits are progressive, with lower-wage workers receiving more than their higher-wage counterparts.

32. Bosworth, Burtless, and Zhang, "Later Retirement."

33. Individuals may choose to retire earlier or later than the normal retirement age, but their benefits are then adjusted, so that expected lifetime benefits are the same. By delaying retirement to age seventy, for example, annual benefits are increased by 8 percent a year thereafter for those born in 1943 or later. Social

Security Administration, "Retirement Planner: Delayed Retirement Credits," accessed August 14, 2017, https://www.ssa.gov/planners/retire/delayret.html.

34. Figures are for those born in 1960 or later. Anne Alstott, *A New Deal for Old Age* (Cambridge, MA: Harvard University Press, 2016), 98–99.

35. Ibid., 4–5.

36. See Eugene Steuerle, *Dead Men Ruling* (New York: Century Foundation Press, 2014).

37. The SSDI program has been growing rapidly, in part because of an aging population, in part because the program was liberalized in 1984, and in part because of changes in the economy that make it difficult for people to find work during their disability-prone years. See David H. Autor and Mark G. Duggan, "The Growth in the Social Security Disability Rolls: A Fiscal Crisis Unfolding," *Journal of Economic Perspectives* 20, no. 3 (Summer 2006): 71–96.

38. Patricia P. Martin and David A. Weaver, "Social Security: A Program and Policy History," *Social Security Bulletin* 66, no. 1 (2005), https://www.ssa.gov/policy/docs/ssb/v66n1/v66n1p1.html.

39. Congressional Budget Office, "An Update to the Budget and Economic Outlook: 2017 to 2027" (Washington, DC: CBO, June 2017), https://www.cbo.gov/system/files/115th-congress-2017-2018/reports/52801-june2017outlook.pdf.

40. Social Security, including both OASI and DI (together known as OASDI) is funded via a 12.4 percent payroll tax levied equally on employers and employees up to a maximum of $118,500 in 2016. The disability insurance portion is 1.8 percentage points of the total (0.9 percent on both employees and employers). The Medicare tax is levied at a rate of 2.9 percent of wages, and there is no wage cap. High-earning filers pay a higher rate on top earnings. Employers pay a federal unemployment tax of 0.6 percent on the first $7,000 of a worker's wages, up to a cap of $42 per year. States also levy an unemployment payroll tax to fund this benefit, though the rate and wage base differ by state. Center on Budget and Policy Priorities, "Policy Basics: Federal Payroll Taxes" (Washington, DC: CBPP, updated March 23, 2016), https://www.cbpp.org/research/federal-tax/policy-basics-federal-payroll-taxes.

41. See Feldstein, "Rethinking Social Insurance."

42. President Roosevelt introduced the idea of social insurance, rather than welfare assistance, to America. He conceived a basic form of what is now Social Security—a work-related contributory scheme to protect against economic insecurity of the elderly. Social Security Administration, "Historical Background and Development of Social Security," accessed August 14, 2017, https://www.ssa.gov/history/briefhistory3.html.

43. Author's analysis of Bureau of Economic Analysis, "Table 1.1.3: Real Gross Domestic Product, Quantity Indexes," National Data, U.S. Department of Commerce, last revised on July 28, 2017.

44. For a more fleshed out proposal that illustrates what I have in mind, see Debra Whitman, Marc Freedman, and Jim Emerman, "Social Security Lifelong Learning Benefits" (Washington, DC: AARP, 2017).

45. Bureau of Labor Statistics, "Table 32: Leave Benefits: Access, Civilian Workers, March 2016," data from the National Compensation Survey, https://www.bls.gov /ncs/ebs/benefits/2016/ownership/civilian/table32a.pdf.

46. The Council of Economic Advisers found that programs to promote access to both paid and unpaid leave can improve employers' long-term productivity through enhanced worker recruitment, retention, and motivation. Council of Economic Advisers, "The Economics of Paid and Unpaid Leave" (Washington, DC: Executive Office of the President, June 2014), https://obamawhitehouse .archives.gov/sites/default/files/docs/leave_report_final.pdf.

47. Ernst and Young, "Viewpoints on Paid Family and Medical Leave: Findings from a Survey of US Employers and Employees," Ernst and Young, March 2017, http://www.ey.com/Publication/vwLUAssets/EY-viewpoints-on-paid-family-and -medical-leave/$FILE/EY-viewpoints-on-paid-family-and-medical-leave.pdf.

48. Francine D. Blau and Lawrence M. Kahn, "Female Labor Supply: Why Is the United States Falling Behind?" *American Economic Review* 103, no. 3 (May 2013): 251–256.

49. Berit Brandth and Elin Kvande, "Flexible Work and Flexible Fathers," *Work, Employment, and Society* 15, no. 2 (June 2001): 251–267; Lenna Nepomnyaschy and Jane Waldfogel, "Paternity Leave and Fathers' Involvement with Their Young Children: Evidence from the American Ecls-B," *Journal of Community, Work, and Family* 10, no. 4 (November 7, 2007): 427–453.

50. Pedro Carneiro, Katrine V. Loken, and Kjell G. Salvanes, "A Flying Start? Maternity Leave Benefits and Long-Run Outcomes of Children," *Journal of Political Economy* 123, no. 2 (April 2015): 365–412; Christopher J. Ruhm, "Parental Leave and Child Health," *Journal of Health Economics* 19, no. 6 (November 2000): 931–960; Michael Baker and Kevin Milligan, "Maternal Employment, Breastfeeding, and Health: Evidence from Maternity Leave Mandates," *Journal of Health Economics* 27 (2008): 871–887.

51. Juliana Menasce Horowitz, Kim Parker, Nikki Graf, and Gretchen Livingston, "Americans Widely Support Paid Family and Medical Leave, But Differ over Specific Policies," Pew Research Center, March 23, 2017, http://www.pewsocialtrends .org/2017/03/23/americans-widely-support-paid-family-and-medical-leave-but -differ-over-specific-policies/.

52. Two proposals are worth mentioning. On the left, the FAMILY Act, sponsored by Representative Rosa DeLauro (D-CT) and Senator Kirsten Gillibrand (D-NY) calls for a new trust fund administered by the SSA with its own dedicated source of revenue. The fund would be financed by a new 0.2 percent payroll tax on both employees and employers. The revenue would be used to finance up to twelve weeks of family and medical leave (for the same reasons specified under the Family and Medical Leave Act [FMLA]) to any employee who currently qualifies for disability insurance under SSA. Workers on leave would receive 66 percent of their previous earnings, up to $4,000/month. On the Republican side of the aisle, the Strong Families Act, introduced by Senator Deb Fisher (R-NE) would

offer firms a nonrefundable 25 percent tax credit on wages paid to employees while they are on family or medical leave. The credit would be capped at $3,000. It would be available to firms offering at least two weeks of leave (as defined in the FMLA) at a 100 percent replacement rate. Rather than provide a universal benefit funded through social insurance, this proposal attempts to incentivize employers to offer their own paid leave policies to their employees.

53. AEI-Brookings Working Group on Paid Family Leave, "Paid Family and Medical Leave."

54. Since 2010, the Social Security program has operated on negative cash flow. Unless the payroll tax is increased, benefits reformulated, or the cap on taxable wage income increased, the old-age and survivors' fund will be depleted around 2035, and the disability insurance fund will be depleted even sooner. See Drew DeSilver, "5 Facts about Social Security," Pew Research Center Fact Tank, August 18, 2015, http://www.pewresearch.org/fact-tank/2015/08/18/5-facts-about -social-security/.

55. Two of the most notable efforts to analyze and recommend reforms that would improve trust fund solvency are the Domenici-Rivlin Debt Reduction Task Force, convened by the Bipartisan Policy Center, and the Simpson-Bowles Deficit Reduction Plan. Both plans consisted of a variety of measures that would reduce the federal deficit, including reforms to Social Security funding mechanisms and benefit allocation. Both suggested raising the cap on payroll taxes, adjusting benefits, and either raising the retirement age or adjusting the benefit formula for increases in longevity, among many other reforms. Senator Pete Domenici and Dr. Alice Rivlin, "Domenici-Rivlin Debt Reduction Task Force Plan 2.0" (Washington, DC: Bipartisan Policy Center, 2010), https://bipartisanpolicy.org/wp-content /uploads/sites/default/files/D-R%20Plan%202.0%20FINAL.pdf; National Commission on Fiscal Responsibility and Reform, "The Moment of Truth" (Washington, DC: White House, December 2010), http://momentoftruthproject.org/sites /default/files/TheMomentofTruth12_1_2010.pdf.

56. As Melissa Favreault and Eugene Steuerle note, the spousal benefit has received criticism for a variety of reasons—the system is rooted in an outdated model of the typical American family in which there is only one breadwinner and a stay-at-home mother; benefits are not rooted in the spouse's need, but rather in one's marital history and lifetime earnings; it might exacerbate existing inequalities by granting disproportionate benefits to those more likely to marry (higher-earners and whites). Favreault and Steuerle model three reforms to the existing system, including earnings sharing, replacing most of the spouse benefit with a minimum, and full spouse replacement with caregiver credits. Each reform was found to modestly reduce poverty. Melissa M. Favreault and C. Eugene Steuerle, "Social Security Spouse and Survivor Benefits for the Modern Family," Center for Retirement Research at Boston College Working Paper 2007-07, February 2007, http://crr.bc.edu/working-papers/social-security-spouse-and-survivor-benefits -for-the-modern-family/.

57. See chapter 6 in Commission on Retirement Security and Personal Savings, "Report of the Commission on Retirement Security and Personal Savings" (Washington, DC: Bipartisan Policy Center, June 2016), http://bipartisanpolicy.org/wp-content/uploads/2016/06/BPC-Retirement-Security-Report.pdf.

58. Office of the Chief Actuary, "Proposed Provision: E1.1. Increase the Payroll Tax Rate (Currently 12.4 Percent) to 15.4 Percent in 2018 and Later," Social Security Administration, July 13, 2017, https://www.ssa.gov/oact/solvency/provisions/charts/chart_run189.pdf.

59. For example, the inflation-adjusted income of the median family headed by an older American increased 64 percent between 1979 and 2016, compared to 9 percent for those ages thirty-five to forty-four. Gary Burtless, "The *Washington Post* Paints a False Picture of Elderly Americans," *Real Clear Markets,* October 11, 2017, http://www.realclearmarkets.com/articles/2017/10/11/the_washington_post_paints_a_false_picture_of_elderly_americans_102913.html.

60. Social Security and Medicare Boards of Trustees, "A Summary of the 2017 Annual Reports" (Washington, DC: Social Security Administration, 2017), https://www.ssa.gov/oact/trsum/.

61. Senators Lindsey Graham, Rand Paul, and Mike Lee introduced legislation in 2011 that would increase the full retirement age to seventy by 2032 and then index it to longevity thereafter. Representative Reid J. Ripple introduced the "Save Our Social Security Act of 2016," in July 2016, which would increase the normal retirement age by two months per year between 2022 and 2034 and then index it to longevity thereafter. "Graham, Paul, and Lee Introduce Plan for Social Security Reform," Lindsey Graham Press Release, April 13, 2011, https://www.lgraham.senate.gov/public/index.cfm/press-releases?ID=505ED429-802A-23AD-4985-C1E83E514E0D; "S.O.S. Act of 2016," H.R. 5747, 114th Congress, 2016; see also Martin Feldstein, "Balancing Lost Tax Revenue the Reagan Way," *Wall Street Journal,* April 26, 2017, https://www.wsj.com/articles/balancing-lost-tax-revenue-the-reagan-way-1493245888.

62. Gary Burtless, "Should Congress Raise the Full Retirement Age to 70?" (Washington, DC: Brookings Institution, June 2, 2016), https://www.brookings.edu/articles/should-congress-raise-the-full-retirement-age-to-70/.

63. In her book *A New Deal for Old Age: Toward a Progressive Retirement,* Anne L. Alstott argues that our current benchmark of sixty-five reflects only late middle age for many higher-income individuals, while many low-wage workers, particularly those in physically demanding jobs, are unlikely to stay in the workforce until sixty-five and tend to die sooner. Alstott's proposal would enable these lower-wage workers to claim retirement benefits early with a smaller penalty than that posed under the current system, while higher-wage workers would face a larger penalty. Further, this reformed system would enable those who do not wish to permanently withdraw from the workforce to slowly cut back their hours, switch to a less-demanding position, or take a new, lower-paid job. It would offer half-benefits between seventy-three and seventy-six that would not affect full benefits payable at age seventy-six.

64. See Alicia H. Munnell, "Phased Retirement Is Not the Path to Retirement Security," Research Foundation of CFA Institute 4, 2009, http://www.cfapubs.org /doi/abs/10.2470/rf.v2009.n4.8.

65. On unemployment insurance, see Raj Chetty, "Why Do Unemployment Benefits Raise Unemployment Durations? Moral Hazard vs. Liquidity," NBER Working Paper no. 11760, November 2005, http://www.nber.org/papers/w11760; Marcus Hagedorn, Fatih Karahan, Iourii Manovskii, and Kurt Mitman, "Unemployment Benefits and Unemployment in the Great Recession: The Role of Macro Effects," NBER Working Paper no. 19499, October 2013, http://www.nber.org/papers /w19499. On disability insurance, see Scott Winship, "How to Fix Disability Insurance," *National Affairs*, no. 23 (Spring 2015); Council of Economic Advisers, "The Long-Term Decline in Prime-Age Male Labor Force Participation" (Washington, DC: Executive Office of the President, June 2016), https://obamawhitehouse .archives.gov/sites/default/files/page/files/20160620_cea_primeage_male_lfp .pdf; Alan B. Krueger, "Where Have All the Workers Gone?" Princeton University, October 2016. On Social Security, the CBO reported in 1990 that "studies disagree on the magnitude of the effect," but "a number of studies, however, concluded that each dollar of Social Security wealth . . . reduces private wealth by between zero and 50 cents." The article includes the caveat that these results are highly uncertain. Congressional Budget Office, "Social Security and Private Saving: A Review of the Empirical Evidence," CBO Memorandum (Washington, DC: CBO, July 1998).

66. Research on New Jersey employers' experiences with the state's paid leave program revealed no instances in which the employers were aware of abuse. Evidence from California indicates that fears about abuse and negative effects on productivity and profitability prior to the implementation of the paid family leave law were largely unfounded, and, in fact, many employers reported cost savings resulting from the law. Sharon Lerner and Eileen Appelbaum, "Business as Usual: New Jersey Employers' Experience with Family Leave Insurance" (Washington, DC: Center for Economic and Policy Research, 2014), http://cepr.net/publica tions/reports/business-as-usual-new-jersey-employers-experiences-with-family -leave-insurance; Ruth Milkman and Eileen Appelbaum, *Unfinished Business: Paid Family Leave in California and the Future of U.S. Work-Family Policy* (Ithaca, NY: Cornell University Press, 2013).

67. Referencing evidence from an earlier analysis, David Autor notes that "a substantial share of the growth in the SSDI system following the 1984 reforms reflects the program's increasing role as a de facto safety net for individuals whose primary barrier to employment is limited labor market opportunities rather than debilitating health conditions." David H. Autor, "The Unsustainable Rise of the Disability Rolls in the United States: Causes, Consequences, and Policy Options," NBER Working Paper no. 17697, December 2011, http://www.nber.org/papers/w17697, 13–14. Scott Winship similarly suggests that the portion of SSDI beneficiaries qualifying on the basis of "vocational factors" (demographic and work-related factors)

has increased substantially over recent decades. Each year since 2003, he reports that half of new beneficiaries are eligible based on these vocational factors in addition to qualifying medical conditions. However, he says that this increase is largely unrelated to labor market conditions. Winship, "How to Fix Disability Insurance."

Chapter 10. Conclusion

1. William Golding, *Lord of the Flies* (London: Faber and Faber, 1954).
2. E. J. Dionne, Thomas Mann, and Norman Ornstein, *One Nation after Trump* (New York: St. Martin's Press, 2017), chapter 10.